About Island Press

Island Press is the only nonprofit organization in the United States whose principal purpose is the publication of books on environmental issues and natural resource management. We provide solutions-oriented information to professionals, public officials, business and community leaders, and concerned citizens who are shaping responses to environmental problems.

In 2001, Island Press celebrates its seventeenth anniversary as the leading provider of timely and practical books that take a multidisciplinary approach to critical environmental concerns. Our growing list of titles reflects our commitment to bringing the best of an expanding body of literature to the environmental community throughout North America and the world.

Support for Island Press is provided by The Bullitt Foundation, The Mary Flagler Cary Charitable Trust, The Nathan Cummings Foundation, Geraldine R. Dodge Foundation, Doris Duke Charitable Foundation, The Charles Engelhard Foundation, The Ford Foundation, The George Gund Foundation, The Vira I. Heinz Endowment, The William and Flora Hewlett Foundation, W. Alton Jones Foundation, The John D. and Catherine T. MacArthur Foundation, The Andrew W. Mellon Foundation, The Charles Stewart Mott Foundation, The Curtis and Edith Munson Foundation, National Fish and Wildlife Foundation, The New-Land Foundation, Oak Foundation, The Overbrook Foundation, The David and Lucile Packard Foundation, The Pew Charitable Trusts, Rockefeller Brothers Fund, The Winslow Foundation, and other generous donors.

Plundered Promise

Plundered Promise

Capitalism, Politics, and the Fate of the Federal Lands

Richard W. Behan

ISLAND PRESS
Washington ♦ Covelo ♦ London

Copyright © 2001 by Richard W. Behan

All rights reserved under International and Pan-American Copyright Conventions. No part of this book may be reproduced in any form or by any means without permission in writing from the publisher: Island Press, 1718 Connecticut Avenue, N.W., Suite 300, Washington, DC 20009.

ISLAND PRESS is a trademark of The Center for Resource Economics.

Photo cover image copyright © Steve Holmer, 1999, Willamette National Forest, Oregon

Library of Congress Cataloging-in-Publication Data

Behan, Richard W.
    Plundered promise : capitalism, politics, and the fate of the federal lands / Richard W. Behan.
        p. cm.
Includes bibliographical references and index.
    ISBN 1-55963-848-6 — ISBN 1-55963-849-4
    1. Public lands—United States—Management—History. 2. Corporations—United States—History. 3. Capitalism—United States—History. I. Title.
    HD216 .B44 2001
    333.1'0973—dc21
                                                                00-012997

British Library Cataloguing in Publication Data available.

Printed on recycled, acid-free paper

Manufactured in the United States of America
10 9 8 7 6 5 4 3 2 1

To the memory of

ARNOLD W. BOLLE
A gentle man, a powerful force,
and both a helper and a hero

and to

HELEN SWAN BOLLE
Heroic helper

Contents

Preface

This book will call seriously into question the past two centuries of federal land use. Preeminently, the lands have been attractive as factors of production that could be reduced readily to private possession, or as a public source of private goods and services that could be reduced readily to cash. To express this history in terms less polite but no less accurate, the federal lands have been plundered.

The plunder was conscious and deliberate, because the U.S. Constitution was written to promote the welfare of the private individual, not that of the public at large. For perhaps seven generations the policy of plunder was no worse than neutral in its impact on the general welfare, but today the impact is demonstrably and significantly negative. Consequently, the book will argue for a distinct shift in focus—if only because the privatization of productive land and the liquidation of commodity values are both now nearly complete, after two hundred years of ingenious, energetic, and sustained effort.

The public lands in future years should be devoted instead to the production or enrichment of public services—those features of land held in common that cannot be privatized and need not be liquidated to be of great value to society at large. So dedicated, the federal lands can be a focal point for a rejuvenated public life in the United States, providing a badly needed sense of community and shared destiny. Such is the promise of the federal lands.

The book also will call seriously into question the institutional mechanisms, both economic and political, that continue to drive the liquidation of the nation's heritage of public resource assets. Those mechanisms served us tolerably well for most of two centuries, too, but by the end of the second, American capitalism had become corrupted, and American politics had become predatory. Both institutions have overshot, and American society at large, to its substantial distress, has been drawn into their service.

The institutional engine driving the overshoot is the modern corporation, an abstraction of human imagination almost unknown two centuries ago. Chartered by various political bodies—the British Parliament, in the case of such early corporations as the British East India Company, and state governments in the United States since then—corporations initially served the public interest virtually by definition. They were strictly limited as to purpose and lifespan; their stockholders were subject to personal liability; and their charters could be revoked, and often were, for violating the interests of society at large.

Today, corporations have all but escaped social control, many becoming transnational behemoths with allegiance to no nation, and certainly to none of the states in the United States. Growing larger without limit through mergers and acquisitions, they are institutions that have no precedent in human history. With the creation of the World Trade Organization to consolidate and exercise their power, they are coming perilously close to displacing the political nation-state as the dominant influence in human affairs. Under the guise of "nontariff barriers to free trade" they can and do challenge and override environmental, consumer safety, and labor laws enacted by democratically elected domestic governments. They threaten the preeminence of national identities in that process. To say they threaten to disintegrate cultures is scarcely an overstatement. (Not a few brand names are recognized everywhere in the world.)

For two reasons, the culture of the American people is particularly vulnerable to disintegration. First is the rich and rewarding background of diversity the "melting pot" displays: Most of us are immigrants who undertook American citizenship with differing cultural heritages, and tolerance and unity remain as difficult challenges. Far more significant is the disintegrating impact of the U.S. Constitution, which was written deliberately to prevent our coming together. It has succeeded brilliantly. In the pages to follow we will see why and how—and that there may be another means of sustaining a viable and rewarding sense of community.

Throughout human history, *land*—seen as "home" or "place"— has been unfailingly capable of binding people together. The sense of community is particularly acute when land is held in common, a circumstance starkly exhibited by tribal cultures occupying land communally, without the necessity for rights of private ownership. Ours is not such a culture, but, even so, we do have a landmass that is held in common, and its dimensions are extraordinary.

If the federal lands were concentrated in the center of the country, they would cover almost exactly and entirely the states of Wisconsin, Michigan, Illinois, Ohio, Indiana, Kentucky, Tennessee, Alabama, Minnesota, Iowa, Missouri, Arkansas, North and South Dakota, Nebraska, Kansas, and Oklahoma. Shifted slightly to the left, the federal lands would fill the entire Central Time Zone, with a bit left over.

If only to counteract the disintegrating effects of the U.S. Constitution, it might be wise and certainly quite pleasant to reinforce our sense of national community. The federal lands, held in common, exhibit great promise for doing so, but not without serious alterations in both federal land policy and the social processes by which it is made.

That is not a modest set of complaints.

It is perhaps audacious for a single writer to enter such comprehensive criticism. It is perhaps more audacious still for a single writer to suggest comprehensive improvements. No writer, however, is in fact a single writer, and both the criticisms and the suggestions to follow depend heavily on many others. Those others will be identified in the citations, but I want to express collectively my gratitude here, and to make a traditional, thoroughly justified claim that the errors in this book, and its shortcomings, are unequivocally my own.

I feel some compulsion to document my gratitude as well to some grand teachers and talented colleagues, and many others who shaped this volume.

I am obliged, deeply and in random order, to Miss Reese and Miss Jackson, John Potzger, Arnie and Helen Bolle, Hugh Raup,

Ernie Gould, Hank Vaux, Bob Wambach, Fritz Mosher, Al McQuillan, Debra Salazar, Perry Hagenstein, Marion Clawson, Clarence Glacken, Dennis Dykstra, John Baden, Helen Ingram, Stew Pickford, Bob Nelson, Gregg Cawley, Hanna Cortner, Roger Clark, Bill Weiland, Albert Lepawsky, Chris Leman, Julie Gorte, Bob Lee, Gordon Browder, Bruce Babbitt, Lee Nye, John Ostheimer, Michael Frome, Paul Weingart, Tom Bonnicksen, Kurt Russo, Ronnie Dugger, Bill Banzhaf, Dave Garrett, Larry Phillips, John Freemuth, Ben Twight, Chuck Minor, Jerry Franklin, Gordon Bradley, Dennis LeMaster, John Clark, Thom Alcoze, Paul Hirt, Pete Hanson, Brent Wood, Ted Schlapfer, Gisela McCormick, Bill Horswill, Dave Walker, Sally Fairfax, John Krutilla, Joe Cox, Tom Nimlos, Ross Gorte, Mert Richards, Barbara Dean, John Sisk, Carl Reidel, Les Pengelly, Jerry and Jane Weller, Cynthia Miller, Mike Porter, Tom and Polly McCarthy, Dick Berry, Al Sample, Andy Holland, Steve Schulman, Bill Terry, Tom Payne, Wally Covington, Bern Shanks, Scott Wallinger, Bill Ferrell, Hester Turner, Todd Baldwin, Bob Chadwick, Adela Backiel, Bill Holmes, Dick Shannon, Mary Elizabeth Braun, Butch Larson, Chuck DeRidder, Doris Aitken, Dick Alston, Pete Steen, Bill Shands, Erv Zube, Charles Wilkinson, Gail Achterman, Herb Winer, Susan Flader, Grace Herndon, Henry Carey, Dale Goble, Daniel Kemmis, Randal O'Toole, Judy Austin, Susan Buck, Jack Dieterich, Jim Kennedy, John Leshy, John Vohs, Lynn Day, Neil Paulson, Paul Bofinger, Bud Moore— and of course to my resident and loving critic, Ann, and my family, upstream and down.

Chapter One

The Overture,
in Theory and Practice

A Swatch of the Planet, a Parade of People

The existence of the federal lands today is a legacy of European traditions and institutions of land tenure. These lands were once the "crown lands" of various European sovereignties, and that status was achieved by fiat. "Crowns" of various sorts—English, French, Dutch, Portuguese, Spanish—made a habit, a few brief centuries ago, of claiming various lands around the globe to be their own. One or another explorer was rowed to one or another beach, there to raise one or another flag and proclaim, "This is ours." It is one of history's greatest injustices that such flimsy and arbitrary claims have been sustained.

After the Revolutionary War, the crown lands in the United States became the "original public domain," and from that the status of "federal lands" was derived. This is accurate history, but not complete, because it ignores the prior occupancy of the land by American Indians.

Initially by indifference and eventually by force, Native Americans and their land institutions were overridden and displaced, in a pattern characteristic of European imperialism in the New World. Only near the end of the twentieth century did serious scholarship begin to grasp the genocidal magnitude of European incursion into the Americas. From Columbus forward, it is likely that a hundred million humans met premature and premeditated death at the hands of the Europeans, from the Conquistadors to the slaughter of Amazonian Indians that continues to this day.[1]

We have national parks, national forests, federal grazing districts, national wildlife refuges, national monuments, and national recreation areas today because the lands were taken in violence. In the history of these lands, there is no greater social injustice, and there are lots of others, as we shall see. None is less capable of just redress.

As the fate and the future of federal lands continue to unfold, we must continue to address the fact of this override and forcible displacement. It is a hugely complex issue, and the situation can only be improved, not "resolved" in any definitive way. Indeed, the efforts to resolve the issue—various laws to "settle" the "claims" of Native Americans—have always worked to their disadvantage, if not their devastation. This much can be said about such regrettable history: We cannot ignore it, and we must not forget it. Chapter 6 will touch on the issue again.

Plundered Promise

The federal lands constitute a public asset of astonishing extent. They include some 80 million acres in national parks and monuments; 90 million acres in national wildlife refuges; 192 million acres in national forests and grasslands; 270 million acres of lands overseen by the Bureau of Land Management; and another 41 million acres in military reservations and other lesser categories.[2]

---

1. See David E. Stannard, *American Holocaust: Columbus and the Conquest of the New World* (New York: Oxford University Press, 1992); and Ward Churchill, *A Little Matter of Genocide: Holocaust and Denial in the Americas, 1492 to the Present* (San Francisco: City Lights Books, 1997).

2. See John B. Loomis, *Integrated Public Lands Management: Principles and Applications to National Forests, Parks, Wildlife Refuges, and BLM Lands* (New York: Columbia University Press, 1993), p. 19.

In total, 673 million acres are held in common. That is nearly one third of the total land area of all fifty states, some 2.5 acres of federal land for every fortunate citizen in the country.[3]

If the national parks were combined into one piece of land, it could hold Alabama, Louisiana, and Maine within its boundaries. The wildlife refuges so aggregated could contain New York, North Carolina, and Pennsylvania. The national forests could accommodate California and Oregon, with enough space left over for Mississippi. We could fit Texas, Utah, and Idaho into the BLM lands, and the miscellaneous categories of federal land would nearly fill up Missouri.

Few nations on the planet enjoy such an immense landscape as common property. Six hundred and seventy-three million acres amounts to 1.05 million square miles. If you wanted that much land in western Europe, you would have to buy Spain, France, Italy, Switzerland, Germany, Belgium, the Netherlands, Denmark, Sweden, England, Ireland, and about a fourth of Poland.

A public asset of this magnitude should be of great public benefit, at least equal to the direct and indirect costs of maintaining and holding the property. The direct costs amount to slightly more than $4 billion per year—the annual total expenditures of the four primary federal land management agencies. The indirect or "holding" costs are measured by the best alternative use of the asset. If the lands were sold, say for $200 per acre, and if the proceeds were invested at 6 percent, a rough estimate of holding costs would be another $8 billion or so per year. Do the American people derive $12 billion worth of annual benefits?

Aside from the recreational use of the lands, and the satisfaction of maintaining wildlife populations in the national refuges, public benefits are difficult to find. Public benefits of $12 billion per year cannot be imagined.

The reason for this is starkly simple: We have deliberately chosen to dedicate the federal lands not to public purposes but to the production of private wealth.

The 673 million acres are only the residue of the public

---

3. Assuming a U.S. population of about 270 million. For an up-to-the-minute estimate, see the Web site of the U.S. Census Bureau: http://www.census.gov/cgi-bin/popclock.

estate. Some 816 million acres of the original inventory were given or sold to private individuals, land speculators, homesteaders, railroad corporations, and veterans of the Revolutionary War. Another 329 million were granted to the states. For the first century of the nation's history, the idea of holding land as common property was antithetical, both to the intent of the U.S. Constitution of empowering citizens to pursue their own welfare, and to the opportunities and possibilities of emerging capitalism.

Only after displacing the Native Americans could there be federal lands at all.[4] And only after shifting two thirds of those lands to private ownership did we decide to designate national parks, forests, and wildlife refuges, beginning late in the nineteenth century; the BLM lands were not granted permanent status as public land until 1976.

In spite of public ownership, however, the production of private wealth has continued without challenge or even serious question. Through sales, leases, permits, licenses, contracts, concessions, and other devices, public land minerals, timber, forage, wildlife, recreation opportunities, and water resources continue to be transferred to private use, enjoyment, and financial gain.

The idea of seeking public benefits from our public asset simply never took hold.

Yet nowhere in public policy was it allowed that the lands should be abused in producing private wealth. They were to be used conservatively, typically by imposing in statute the biological "sustained yield" limits on renewable resource use, and similar conservative constraints on nonrenewable resource extraction.[5] Furthermore, resource management professions were put in place to assure such benign administration.

Neither policy nor professional management was sufficient. Commodity values in minerals, timber, water, forage, and wildlife were claimed by private and typically corporate interests, and liquidated. The transfer of public wealth into private hands was

---

4. For an intelligent treatment of this sad issue, see Jerry Mander, *In the Absence of the Sacred: The Failure of Technology and the Survival of the Indian Nations* (San Francisco: Sierra Club Books, 1991).

5. A notable exception was the Mining Law of 1872, which imposed no conditions of any sort on the extraction of hardrock minerals. Professor Dale Goble furnished this observation.

incalculable, but nowhere and seldom was sustainability the least de facto concern. The landscapes left behind were damaged accordingly, and so were many localized communities.

The liquidation was not unanswered. The great waves of "conservation" a century ago, and lately of "environmentalism," stood in opposition and were responsible for regulatory legislation. It was probably naive to suppose that biological limits on economic incomes could be imposed and sustained by political actions, but the development of the federal lands was not done in a sustainable manner. The lands were simply stripped of their resource values.[6]

Today, the use of the federal lands to produce private wealth has become counterproductive. As we will see, the contribution of most commodity production to the nation's well-being, on a net basis, is negative, and utilizing social assets to reduce social welfare is not good public policy.

Most Americans, probably, are unaware of the shared good fortune in their collective ownership of 673 million acres. This is tragic because of what we might have prevented. Had all Americans—not just the small minorities of corporate beneficiaries and their environmental critics—known what was taking place on the federal lands the widespread social and biophysical damages might have been prevented. A prospective triumph, however, is yet possible.

Because of the peculiarities in the U.S. Constitution, to be detailed later, there is no national and enduring res publica, a "public thing" to bind Americans together in a tangible sense of community.[7] (A good example of a res publica is the British monarchy, for which the British people share much pride and affection.) The federal lands, even the most damaged ones, hold great promise as an enduring res publica for the American people.

---

6. Such has been the pattern everywhere and always, apparently. See Donald Ludwig, Ray Hilborn, and Carl Walters, "Uncertainty, Resource Exploitation, and Conservation: Lessons from History," in *Science* 260 (April 2, 1993): 35–36. "Wealth or the prospect of wealth generates political and social power that is used to promote unlimited exploitation of resources," the authors state. No culture has been able to leave money on the table.

7. The term res publica and the general thrust of the argument here—that land can and should serve as a tangible basis for a sense of community—are taken from an elegant volume, *Community and the Politics of Place*, by Daniel Kemmis (Norman: University of Oklahoma Press, 1990). We will encounter more of Kemmis's book in later chapters.

These lands constitute one third of our national habitation. If they were seen by all as lands held truly in common, producing public values instead of private wealth, a sense of national community might be forged around them. What public values might result if we no longer used the federal lands for mining, logging, grazing, and water impoundments? Made aware of the promise of the federal lands, American people could answer that question with specificity and enthusiasm.

The barriers to realizing this promise, and the root causes of our overuse of the federal lands, lie in the nature of what our economic and political institutions have become. They have become the agents of plunder.

Corrupted Capitalism and Predatory Politics

At the turn of the millennium, our two great institutions of social discourse—the economic and political systems—can no longer be characterized in the terms and imagery of conventional thought.

The term *free market capitalism* bespeaks an economic institution in service to society. It summons images of independent consumers making free choices in the marketplace, and of independent entrepreneurs risking their assets in rigorous competition for the consumers' favor, without which they would not survive. There is great appeal in such images, placing maximum reliance as they do on individual initiative and freedom of choice.

If freedom of choice is truly characteristic and omnipresent, why is the number of our citizens consigned to poverty systematically increasing? Are more and more people freely choosing poor nutrition, inadequate housing, shoddy education, and to forgo health care altogether?

As we will see later in the book, ten percent of American families are designated by the Department of Agriculture as "food deficient," and one-sixth of American citizens have no systematic access to health care. Millions of Americans have no homes at all, and inadequate public education is the subject of more political rhetoric and less substantive attention than any other issue of national concern.

Has capitalism been transformed into an aggressive, corrupted institution that serves less and less to fulfill the material needs of societies at large, and more and more simply to enrich inanimate corporations, their managers and stockholders, and the vultures of corporate finance?

The argument here is that capitalism has triumphed over the society it originally served: It has drawn that society into its service, instead. The engine of triumph has been the corporation, originally given viability in the United States by state charter and now capable of becoming an immortal and transnational juggernaut accountable to no one.[8] The difference between free-market capitalism and corporate capitalism is not trivial, and it will be explored in a coming chapter.

Majoritarian democracy might be a good term to describe the view that Americans hold about their political system. It too rests on the freedom of the individual, this time to participate through open elections in the process of constructing public policy. Majoritarian democracy summons images of the U.S. president and the Congress listening intently to their constituents and fashioning public policy in the interests of the American people—or at least a majority of them. In this conventional view, democracy is another institution in service to society at large and subject to that society's will. Society's power in the marketplace, to destroy one producer by favoring its competition, is matched by society's power in politics, to turn the rascals out.

How is it, then, so many rascals survive to make governing a lifelong career, terminated only by voluntary retirement? Do we base our votes in fact on our representatives' positions on the various issues? Could it be that elections are not determined by policy debates but are won instead by the most heavily financed prosecution of a negative television campaign?[9]

---

8. A number of recent books document and specify the malignant growth, the invulnerability, and the social havoc wrought by transnational corporations. See William Greider, *One World Ready or Not: The Manic Logic of Global Capitalism* (New York: Simon and Schuster, 1997); David Korten, *When Corporations Rule the World* (West Hartford and San Francisco: Kumerian Press and Berrett-Koehler, 1996); Jerry Mander and Edward Goldsmith, eds., *The Case Against the Global Economy* (San Francisco: Sierra Club Books, 1996); Kevin Danaher, ed., *Corporations Are Gonna Get Your Mama: Globalization and the Downsizing of the American Dream* (Monroe, MA: Common Courage Press, 1996); Joshua Karliner, *The Corporate Planet: Ecology and Politics in the Age of Globalization* (San Francisco: Sierra Club Books, 1997); and John Cavanagh and Richard Barnet, *Global Dreams: Imperial Corporations and the New World Order*, reprint edition (New York: Touchstone Books, 1995).

9. The transition to an uglier practice of politics has been explained as a failure of the great political ideologies, conservatism and liberalism. It is an intriguing and telling argument. See E. J. Dionne, Jr., *Why Americans Hate Politics* (New York: Simon and Schuster, 1991).

Much public policy is clearly not in the interests of society at large—or even of a majority. We spend more on "corporate welfare" than on programs of social welfare. In 1993, almost half the 4 million corporations in the United States paid no federal income tax at all. Among those that do pay, taxes on corporate income fell from 28 percent of federal income tax collected in 1956 to 11 percent in 1996.[10]

Do we see, through the mechanism of the political action committee, the domination of American politics by American corporate interests? A number of contemporary books argue that point persuasively.[11] The argument made here is that American politics has become predatory, not in the sense that politicians wage vicious campaigns against their opponents, or that interest groups attack each other, but in the sense that corporate interests have evolved ever more refined means of preying upon the wealth and assets of the public at large. To serve their own ends, corporate interests have co-opted the political system, and once again we see an institution turned against the society it once served. The facts and extent of this co-optation will be detailed in chapter 5.

The careful reader will have noticed a structural element common to the current forms of both capitalism and politics in America. It is the modern corporation. Capitalism could not have become corrupted, nor could our politics have become predatory, without the immortality and the unlimited growth potential of the corporation, and without its peculiar, mindless, relentless drive for markets, profit, power, growth, and lately for political dominance.

---

10. Cited in Charles Lewis, *The Buying of the Congress* (New York: Avon Books, 1998), p. 240.

11. See Donald Bartlett and James Steele, *America: Who Stole the Dream?* (Kansas City: Andrews and McMeel, 1996); Daniel Hellinger and Dennis R. Judd, *The Democratic Facade* (Pacific Grove, CA: Brooks/Cole, 1991); Kevin Phillips, *Arrogant Capital: Washington, Wall Street, and the Frustration of American Politics* (Boston: Little, Brown, 1994); William Greider, *Who Will Tell the People? The Betrayal of American Democracy* (New York: Simon and Schuster, 1992); Sam Smith, *Sam Smith's Great American Political Repair Manual: How to Rebuild our Country so the Politics Aren't Broken and Politicians Aren't Fixed* (New York: W. W. Norton, 1997); Charles Lewis, *The Buying of the President* (New York: Avon Books, 1996); Charles Lewis, *The Buying of the Congress* (New York: Avon Books, 1998); and Charles Lewis, *The Buying of the President 2000* (New York: Avon Books, 2000).

As long as corporations reflected the personalities of their founders—say, Henry Ford, Andrew Carnegie, or John D. Rockefeller—they could exhibit some human attributes, some emotions, even a sense of social responsibility. But as the management of corporations became professionalized and wholly separated from ownership, the corporation itself could shed any such human frailties, to concentrate on short-term cash flow or "stockholder value" as uncompromised objectives. The corporation was no longer the creature of its founder; subsequent managers had to become creatures of the corporation.

The corporate genie has left the bottle. Impersonal corporations first encouraged and eventually created a self-destructive consumer society. Today, the most powerful corporations rampage through the economy externalizing every possible cost, dismissing workers by the thousands and exporting their jobs to slave labor, child labor, or sweatshop labor; laying waste to ecosystems anywhere in the world to acquire raw materials: paper-shifting profits to lowest-tax jurisdictions; and finally turning capitalism into corruption. They dominate the mass media, indoctrinating society with a system of corporate values; they have overturned a century of regulatory policy; they have legalized corporate participation in electoral campaigning; and finally they have turned politics into predation. The structure of the corporation, once clearly in service to society, has become a threatening menace.

The Federal Lands Today: Biophysical Decline and Social Injustice

The federal lands have become a balkanized mosaic of single-use landscapes: grazing here, logging there, a water impoundment downstream, a designated wilderness area or national park nestled in between. And the lands are in dismal condition—timberlands are overcut, rangelands are overgrazed, fisheries are depleted, rivers are overdammed, parks are overused, and subsidized mining ravages landscapes. These are biophysical problems. Political acrimony, legal gridlock, management paralysis, and serious externalized costs characterize the federal lands as well. These are social problems.

The biophysical problems of the federal lands are not permanent, and they may not be terribly serious. We have hit these lands hard, but we have hit them quickly—the damage has been done prominently in the last three or four decades and almost totally in the last ten. The biophysical restoration of the land is a matter of modest investment over a moderate planning horizon, but the existing institutional structures are indifferent.

The political conflict over the lands is now more bitterly prosecuted, arguably, than at any time in our nation's history. Organized and powerful voices accuse the land management agencies of dereliction, pointing to the overcut forests, over-dammed rivers, overgrazed rangelands, overused parks. But powerful economic, prominently corporate voices—and powerful bureaucratic ones—dissent, and mount counterattacks.

Decision making for the federal lands has become strongly centralized, and more and more frequently it is the Congress that engineers compromises between the contestants and enshrines the deals in statute. A rising number of increasingly complex laws is constructed by a diminished number of participants, all of whom now are full-time and permanent residents of Washington, D.C. Large professionalized and bureaucratized corporate lobbies and industrial trade associations tilt with large professionalized and bureaucratized environmental groups, their conflicts brokered by large professionalized staffs of the relevant congressional committees. The complex laws are then administered by the large professionalized and bureaucratized land management agencies.

Few citizens across the country know much or care much about this circumstance, described wryly by a critic as the "Potomocentric" management of the federal lands. Many seem unaware or unconcerned that democratic participation in determining the fate of the federal lands for them has been centralized and usurped.

To assert that there is no consensus on the purposes of the federal lands is to illuminate the obvious. Not so apparent are the social costs of all the disagreement, and of several decades of detailed legislation that has resulted from it.

Consider the productive resources devoted to maintaining the "public lands subgovernment." The several thousands of lobbyists, specialists, professionals, staffers, and executives in environmental organizations, industry trade associations, land management agencies, and congressional committees who fashion the public land laws are neither badly educated nor poorly compensated. The net benefits of their efforts to society at large, however, are less and less conspicuous. Laws are enacted, but the biophysical condition of the public land assets does not improve, and the satisfaction of any of the contestants is no more than fleeting.

Consider the productive resources devoted to maintaining administrative and legal propriety in the land management agencies. Are they approaching a stasis of procedural paralysis, in which the preparation of detailed land management plans, environmental impact statements, records of decisions, and other legal documentation is displacing meaningful, on-the-ground investment in protection, management, and facilities? According to the Grace Commission, the U.S. Forest Service spent $200 million per year—10 percent of its annual budget—preparing roughly 150 land management plans mandated by the National Forest Management Act of 1976. Completed after about fifteen years of effort, virtually all of the plans were formally appealed, and many were litigated. The Forest Service spent an additional $150 million per year processing the appeals and lawsuits.[12] During that time, the levels of timber cutting—the largest single influence on both the biophysical and the social consequences of federal forest management—first rose by multiples in the 1980s and then fell by multiples in the 1990s, utterly independent of the costly and detailed plans. The drivers were, respectively, budgets and lawsuits.

The situation in the national forest system is symptomatic of the federal lands in general. Extremely valuable because of its increasing scarcity, public capital is misallocated; capable people engage in zero-sum games; and managerial talent is absorbed in a growing paper chase. But the biophysical condition of the federal lands continues to decline, and so does the general public benefit derived from those lands.

----

12. See *Resource Hotline,* a newsletter formerly published by the American Forestry Association, Vol. 7, No. 18, December 17, 1991. Forest Service Chief Dale Robertson, testifying before the Senate Energy Committee's Subcommittee on Public Lands, National Parks, and Forests, said his agency was spending as much as $150 million a year to cope with its appeals workload. At the start of FY 1986, before the forest plans were completed, the agency was confronted with 163 appeals of administrative decisions. At the start of FY 1992, the number had grown to 1,453.

There is a social counterpart to the biophysical decline. Because of the diminished productivity of the federal lands, economic insecurity and tax-base erosion have become commonplace. Communities and families of hard-working people in the primary resource vocations—logging, ranching, mining, milling— have been victimized, heavily impacted, and impoverished. Also impoverished were the features of the federal lands that have nothing to do with commerce: natural beauty, biological diversity, wildlife habitat, carbon sinking, recreational values—the public services that contribute to the well-being of all Americans.

Suffering at once, then, are the lands, the people who work the lands, and the general public values that might otherwise be derived from them. The major winners, described in the popular press and the literature, have been the resource-extracting corporations.[13]

The transfer of public wealth to private hands was easily rationalized when public resources benefited Jefferson's "hardy yeoman." But some yeomen proved hardier than others: taking corporate form, they became immortal. The Northern Pacific Railroad of the nineteenth century was granted millions of acres of federal forest and mineral lands in the Northwest. It begat the Burlington Northern Corporation in the twentieth century, which spun off Burlington Resources Limited Partnership, which sold its timberlands to Plum Creek Timber Company; and Plum Creek's savaging, in the 1980s, of both the forests and the people in Montana was described in book form.[14] But the beneficiaries

---

13. The literature here is large and robust. See, for a few examples, Donald Worster, *Rivers of Empire* (New York: Oxford University Press, 1992); Charles Wilkinson, *Crossing the Next Meridian* (Washington, DC: Island Press, 1992); Patricia Limerick, *The Legacy of Conquest* (New York: W. W. Norton, 1987); Bernard Shanks, *This Land Is Your Land: The Struggle to Save America's Public Lands* (San Francisco: Sierra Club Books, 1984); Grace Herndon, *Cut and Run: Saying Goodbye to the Last Great Forests in the West* (Telluride, CO: Western Eye Press, 1991); Richard Manning, *The Last Stand: Logging, Journalism, and the Case for Humility* (Salt Lake City: Peregrine Smith Books, 1991); Marc Reisner, *Cadillac Desert* (New York: Penguin Books, 1986); Alston Chase, *Playing God in Yellowstone* (New York: Harcourt, Brace, Jovanovich, 1987); and Michael Frome, *Regreening the National Parks* (Tucson: the University of Arizona Press, 1992).

14. See Manning, *The Last Stand*.

of liquidating the wealth on public land extend beyond the bottom lines of immortal corporations.

The secondary resource vocations in the public lands community have prospered: the executives, directors, managers, and technicians of the large resource-extracting corporations; the professional cadres of the federal land management agencies; the professional environmental and corporate lobbyists; the professional staffs of the relevant congressional committees; and the professional politicians who chair those committees. Economic insecurity is not a chronic reality in these vocations.

Is there anomaly or inequity here? Not according to several orthodox arguments. As corporate executives are quick to assert, the American corporation is an agent of society, simply and benignly responding to signals from a system of free markets to provide American people with the goods and services they want and need. It is subject to social control through the mechanism of marketplace competition. All this is manifested in popular thought as well; many are persuaded that we have a system of "free-market capitalism." And, as national political figures, congressional staffs, and federal bureaucrats are quick to assert, the federal government is also an agent of society, simply and benignly responding to representative democracy to provide the American people with the public services they want and need. The government is subject to social control, through the electoral process. Again there is a parallel in conventional thought; many are persuaded that they live in a majoritarian democracy of personal freedom.

Orthodoxy has it, in summary, that the corporation and the federal government are subject to social control and their actions are undertaken primarily to benefit society at large.

Reality has it otherwise. Land and people are degraded, public wealth is captured and liquidated, and the responsible agents thrive. What has happened? The answer is complex and many-faceted. It has to do with institutions, with the way institutions define a society's resource base, with the profound abundance of the U.S. resource base today, and with the capacity of economic and political institutions to "overshoot"—to escape from their service to society. The following section will introduce these themes, which will be elaborated upon further as the book unfolds.

Institutions, Natural Resources, and the Concept of Institutional Overshoot

The Notion of "Institutions"

Whenever the phrase "That's just how things are done" is invoked, the speaker is referring to an *institution*. In a typical case, an exasperated parent could be enforcing the institution of daily bathing, but any socially evolved, socially adopted, and eventually regularized procedure, practice, or technique can be considered an institution. From specialized labor to monogamous marriage to mass production, institutions condition and are conditioned by social discourse and interaction.

Societies are often identified and defined by the institutions they construct, develop, maintain, and modify. The "basket weavers" of southwestern antiquity and "western democracies" are examples.

The Linkage Between Institutions and "Natural Resources"

Less well understood is the notion that "natural resources" are identified and defined by institutions, too. Petroleum was not a natural resource to Alaskan Eskimos in isolated, roadless villages until their culture was influenced by Euro-Americans who taught them the use of snowmobiles. Nor was petroleum a major resource to those Euro-Americans until they worked out the desirability and the technique of internal combustion engines.

"Resources are not," wrote Erich Zimmerman, a genius geographer with a penchant for the piquant. "They become."[15]

Zimmerman noted the equivalence of social and "natural" determinants of those substances and services that come to be known as "resources." Absent the institutions, the resource remains "neutral stuff," to use Zimmerman's elegant term.

---

15. E. W. Zimmerman, *World Resources and Industries* (rev. ed.) (New York: Harper and Brothers, 1951). Zimmerman's introductory essay about the nature of "resources" underlies the treatment here. He published it first in 1939, and it has had far more influence in the disciplines of geography and sociology than in the technical curricula of professional resource management. Certainly, the idea of a resource "becoming" as a result of cultural appraisal has escaped the popular imagery of contemporary environmentalism.

With the development of differential distilling, kerosene displaced whale oil for residential, commercial, and community lighting. That propelled petroleum into the category of resource, and relegated whale oil, in large measure, to the category of neutral stuff. Gasoline was a dangerous and annoying by-product in embarrassing surplus, to be burned off as waste—until internal combustion engines were fashioned and the institution of automotive transport established, at which time petroleum's status as resource was magnified and assured.[16]

Endowing a particular substance that is found in the biophysical environment with a set of particular social institutions transforms neutral stuff into the category of resource. Cast in the arcane notation of academe, the concept becomes:

$R = f(S,U,T)$, where

R = resource

S = spontaneously occurring substance (or service)

U = socially perceived and institutionalized utility

T = institutionalized technical capability

Or, in words: A resource is a function of some spontaneously occurring substance or service, its perceived and agreed-upon utility, and the institutionalized technical knowledge with which to realize the potential utility.[17]

Resources seen in this way take on some surprising properties, including their collective abundance, and rationalize a novel set of

---

16. See Daniel Yergin, *The Prize: The Epic Quest for Oil, Money, and Power* (New York: Simon and Schuster, 1991). Yergin's work is itself epic, lending empirical support to Zimmerman's thinking, and to the notion of institutional overshoot as well. He depicts, with extraordinary scholarship, governments recruited into the service of oil companies. History, however, was unkind to Yergin. His chronology ends just as the Gulf War began. That was the most unequivocal example of military might brought to the defense of corporate capitalism since federal troops broke up the Pullman strike.

17. Some will complain that this view is anthropocentric, but clearly it is not exclusionary of other species of sentient beings. Moose and mice, geese and grizzly bears make similar appraisals of their environments, and see utility in some—but not all—of the elements therein. The technologies of mice and grizzly bears may seem primitive, but consider a spider's.

solutions to the environmental problems of contemporary concern. Chapters to follow will inquire further. For now, we need only keep in mind that public land resources are as dynamic, fluid, fleeting, and as subject to profound change as the human institutions that establish their significance.

The Origin and Development of Economic and Political Institutions

The creation and continual adaptation of institutions might be viewed as humanity's primal preoccupation throughout the millennia.

Early in human time the institutions attending bodily and family-group survival must have been awkward and demanding, at least by contemporary standards.

Each family unit provided itself with everything it needed, relying on an institution we could call *generalized subsistence*.[18] With only his hands and hind legs, the male "hunted" as best he could, we suppose most successfully in the linear pursuit of either dim-witted or sedentary animals. The female with only her hands and hind legs "gathered" as best she could, concentrating, we also suppose, on nuts and berries close to the ground and unprotected by discouraging thorns. Neutral stuff abounded, in the form of large and meaty but dangerous and swift animals, and in the fruits of tall trees. Though our ancestors' perception of the utility in these potential resources was probably quite real, their institutional means to exploit them—their technologies—were not adequate.

But say a neighboring woman was possessed of extraordinary agility and a disregard for heights. She was able, because of her unusually long legs and sense of balance, to climb trees; because

---

18. There is much room here for intertemporal and/or moralizing mischief about relative qualities of living standards. Convention has it that generalized subsistence provides survival, but also much discomfort. Indeed, Thomas Hobbes wrote in *Leviathan* about the American Indians of the 1500s as follows: "And the life of man was solitary, poore, nasty, brutish, and short." That imagery supported the notion of a New World of "wilderness" populated only by "savages," and hence rationalized the genocidal occupation by northern Europeans, but sustaining it in retrospect requires an overtly racist declaration of superiority. We know now that Hobbes was simply wrong. There is evidence that subsistence cultures, both existing and prehistoric ones, enjoy and enjoyed an abundance of both resources and leisure. See Marshall Sahlins, *Stone Age Economics,* as described in detail and cited in Mander, *In the Absence of the Sacred.* See also John Goudy, *Limited Wants, Unlimited Means: A Reader on Hunter-Gatherer Economics and the Environment* (Washington, DC: Island Press, 1998).

she enjoyed the novel view from the treetops, she was willing. Specialized labor was imminent. She would pick the arboreal fruit and exchange some of her product for the nuts and berries gathered by her more traditional companions. Clearly apparent here is the corollary appearance of bartered exchange—another institution. And resources were becoming.

The neighboring male was equally innovative. Noting the frequency of failure in linear pursuit of animals, he persuaded a dozen of his counterparts to adopt a new technique. They managed to surround and quickly slay a wooly mammoth, and realized an exponential increase in per-capita production. More resources had become.

Generalized subsistence was being displaced by more productive institutions of specialized labor, bartered exchange, and cooperative hunting. Different procedures and practices were being socially evolved and socially adopted, and eventually they would become regularized. The new institutions made possible a substantial increase in per-capita consumption. If life is difficult and brief, a state of underconsumption is widespread; rising per-capita consumption is a good measure of an improving standard of living.

It could also be said that the prehistoric "economy" was "developing." If the primal task of any economy is the provisioning of its participants, we see here the creation and adoption of improved economic institutions. Other economic institutions lay far in the future—the organizing of markets for various goods and services, the monetizing of the system, the separation of management and labor, the corporate form of enterprise, and the crapshoot trading of foreign exchange derivatives are some examples—but the process had begun.

There eventually appeared some specialized laborers whose task it was to study the institutions of provisioning, and they would be called *economists*. In isolating and describing the varieties of economic organization, they would insist that any economic order must address three inescapable fundamental questions: what to produce, how much to produce, and who gets it? Furthermore, any economic order must adhere to some basic canons. First, the economy must realize as much production as possible from its given stock of physical, capital, and human resources: It must be efficient in production. And second, the goods and services produced must be consumed by society at large in a fair and just manner: The economic order must be equitable in the distribution of its output.

No grouping larger than a family was necessary to practice generalized subsistence, but the increased productivity of the new set of institutions—cooperative specialized labor in particular—carried with it an acute need for social organization and the maintenance of community. Far larger groups of people than small family units would need to be identified, organized, stabilized, and maintained. For that, our progenitors had to fashion another set of institutions. They had to make and enforce the rules of individual and collective conduct that would bind large groups of people into stable communities capable of sustained and productive interaction.

That is not a bad description of "politics." Prime ministers, presidents, privy councils, parliaments, and *Robert's Rules* did not spring fully formed from the minds of our antecedents. All that lay far in the future, too, and another category of specialized laborers called *political scientists* would appear to chronicle and characterize it. They would think and write about varieties of political organization, much as the economists would do about provisioning schemes. Any political order, the political scientists would insist, must be just.

"Economics" and "politics" have become separate entities altogether arbitrarily, and that separation is maintained most vigorously in the departments of each on various university campuses. Indeed, "political economy" was a respected topic for study well into the present century. The fissuring was unfortunate. For purposes of clarity if not convention, however, let us approach the two sets of institutions for the most part singularly and separately.

Consider, for example, the concept of "economic development." On it rests the difference between "underdeveloped" and "developed" economies, often encountered in the parlance of the World Bank. On it can rest as well the category of the *overdeveloped* economy—a term never so encountered.

An underdeveloped economy is one, it could be said, in which the institutions are insufficient to provide all the participants with a sustainable and dignified standard of living. Per-capita underconsumption is prevalent.

An underdeveloped political system is more difficult to specify. If economic underdevelopment imposes an inadequate level of per-capita consumption, perhaps political underdevelopment imposes an inadequate level of human and civil rights. Or if political institutions are unable to provide a reliably stable community, to foster an interactive and interdependent economy, that could be described also as political underdevelopment. Or it might be said more generally that an underdeveloped political system is not accepted by a sufficient number of citizens to provide the security of informed consent.

Developed economies and political systems are more easily conceptualized. Per-capita consumption is sufficient for a sustainable and dignified standard of living, and the adequacy of human and civil rights is guaranteed. The knowledgeable agreement of the polity stabilizes the system.

The Concept of Institutional Overshoot

As the construction, maintenance, and development of institutions continues, both economies and political systems can and do become *over*developed. This could be called *institutional overshoot,* and the condition exists in the United States today.

Societies have created, maintained, and modified institutions to serve themselves, to achieve what they have defined and redefined over the millennia as a better life. Institutions have always been the servants of society, but when institutional overshoot occurs, the roles are reversed. Society is drawn into the service of its institutions.

THE OVERDEVELOPED ECONOMY

The overdeveloped economy is characterized by a generalized state of hyperconsumption.[19] The productive capacity of the system has become more than equal, far more than equal, to the task of providing a decent standard of living. Huge expenditures must

---

19. The use of "overdeveloped" here is by no means novel. Leopold Kohr authored *The Overdeveloped Nations: The Diseconomies of Scale* in 1977, and his thinking on the matter was carried forward to a wider, certainly a more popular audience, by his student E.F. Schumacher. The latter's most well-known book, probably, was *Small Is Beautiful.* Schumacher's thoughts, and Kohr's legacy, live on in the E. F. Schumacher Society of Great Barrington, Massachusetts, and similar groups in the U.K. and Germany. Schumacher Societies are being established as well in the Netherlands and in Japan. The U.K. and U.S. groups maintain sites on the World Wide Web at http://www.oneworld.org/schumachersoc/ and http://members.aol.com/efssociety/index.html, respectively.

now be made, therefore, in the most compelling communication technologies, orchestrated by the most creative minds in society, to stimulate even higher levels of consumption—"hyperconsumption" by definition.

Consumption no longer drives production in the overdeveloped economy: It becomes production driven, and the sustainability and dignity of the way people live are placed in jeopardy. Hyperconsumption diminishes standards of living.

One pertinent example, reflecting our concern about the federal lands, is our society's hyperconsumption of high-fat, low-fiber red meat, toward the production of which we allocate hundreds of millions of public acres and hundreds of millions of public dollars.

An economist would say we are consuming hamburgers and steaks in the range of negative marginal returns: Our consumption levels do not enhance, but absolutely detract from personal and public health. The nutritional votes on that issue have been tallied: Obesity has become a nationwide epidemic,[20] and some 70 percent of deaths in the United States are related to "the overconsumption of beef and other foods high in cholesterol and saturated fat."[21]

Diminished personal and public health is a direct social cost, and it is not trivial. Neither are the environmental damages of overgrazing, feedlot pollution, and the solid wastes of fast-food packaging, which also constitute direct social costs.

Enormous benefits are bestowed on the producers, processors, and vendors of red meat, virtually all corporate and large. Corporate holders of federal grazing leases, corn growers and feedlot operators, the transnational corporations transforming rain forests into cattle factories and shipping to the United States, the meat-packing industry, and the fast-food franchisers are a few of the institutional agents that no longer serve, but are served by, society at large.

---

20. See "Let Them Eat Fat," by Greg Critser, *Harper's* 300, 1798 (March 2000).

21. From a "briefing kit" prepared by Beyond Beef, 1130 17th Street NW, Washington, DC, 20036, and available on the Internet at http://www.mcspotlight.org/media/reports.

Similar cases can be made for the consumption levels of cellulose and energy—two more commodities commonly produced on the federal lands and characterized by large corporate operations. Paper and paper products constitute the largest proportion of solid waste clogging the nation's landfills: We spend $325 million annually to dispose of 4 million tons of junk mail, half never opened.[22] And one of the major consequences of our hyperconsumption of fossil fuels is a planet that is gradually assuming the atmosphere of a greenhouse.

Taken altogether, the hyperconsumption induced by the persuasion of corporate producers and sellers does great damage in both social and environmental dimensions.[23]

There are unconscionable exceptions to the general case of hyperconsumption. Malnutrition, substandard housing, inadequate education, and inaccessible health care all flourish in our overdeveloped economy, and they do so to a greater extent today than a generation ago. Our ability to assure a just and equitable distribution of the economy's output, and to assure thereby a sustainable and dignified standard of living for all members of our society, has regressed.

At one time, the progressive income tax was a thoughtful and effective political means of redistributing wealth, and therefore of seeking an equitable distribution of consumption. But in the first term of Ronald Reagan's presidency, with the passage of the 1981 Economic Recovery Tax Act, the progressivity of the federal income tax was effectively eliminated. To maintain our convenient dichotomy, however, that should be considered more accurately a political problem than an economic problem.

THE OVERDEVELOPED POLITICAL SYSTEM
In the overdeveloped political system, personal freedom has been transformed into individual license. Citizens were empowered to

---

22. See the Web site of the Consumer Research Institute, Inc., of Ithaca, New York: http://www.stopjunk.com/environment.html.

23. An excellent description of generalized hyperconsumption is contained in Alan Thein Durning, *How Much Is Enough? The Consumer Society and the Future of the Earth* (New York: W. W. Norton for Worldwatch Institute, 1992).

pursue their own well being by the Constitution, but empowerment is excessive when some citizens prosper by plundering the
wealth of society at large. Corporate citizens do so routinely by
exercising the politics of predation.

But corporate citizens are not alone. Certainly, they have their
hired guns in the nation's capital—well-connected partners in the
Washington law firms—but they also have many accomplices.
Elected officials prosper from corporate financing of expensive
election campaigns, and the "unelected government" enjoys levels of job security and career permanence unprecedented in the
history of public service. Examples and details will appear in
chapter 5.

The unelected government is composed of "subgovernments,"
or "power clusters," or "iron triangles," each devoted to a particular and specialized segment of public policy, such as education,
health, defense, commerce, and banking and finance, etc. The federal lands triangle encompasses the land management and
resource agencies at one corner, the relevant congressional committees and their staffs at another, and the affected industry and
environmental lobbying groups at a third.

Iron triangles operate independently, almost completely isolated from each other, but the personnel in each of them display
four common features. They are intimately acquainted with one
another, typically on a first-name basis. They are highly mobile
within the triangle (but rarely between triangles), moving from
one corner to another often and easily. They are all professionals
whose career permanence is virtually absolute. And none of them
has faced or will face an election: All are appointed or hired. These
are the "policy professionals," and few leave Washington, D.C.,
involuntarily. Later chapters will detail their activities.

In an overdeveloped political system, governance is a self-inter-
ested and self-sustaining industry, and because of its professionalized and permanent fragmentation, it is dysfunctional and counterproductive. The purpose and intent of political structures, as
we have seen, is to stabilize communities so they can enjoy the
benefits of complex and coordinated behavior. The overdeveloped
political system threatens to destabilize the national community in
the United States, however, as it continues to magnify the mal-
distribution of both income and wealth. Enriching the rich by

impoverishing the non-rich is not a politically sustainable course of action, as history demonstrates with clarity, frequency, and ease.

The political consequences of enriching the rich can be postponed, however.

The consequences can be shifted to the future: if those who are impoverished are not yet born, the present can remain temporarily tranquil. Corporate capitalism and iron triangles continue to prey on society at large, but since 1980 they have also preyed massively on society to come. Not before in the nation's history has so much wealth been transferred to the rich, and not before has so large a burden been imposed on the unborn.

In the twelve years of the Reagan and Bush presidencies, the financial obligation of society to come—that is to say, the national debt—more than quadrupled. In 1980 the debt stood at $909.1 billion. Twelve years later it had risen to slightly more than $4 trillion.[24] We borrowed three times more money from future taxpayers in those twelve years than we did during the administrations of all the previous American presidents combined. By the end of the Clinton administation, the debt was pushing $6 trillion, having risen another 50 percent. We have spent much of this borrowed money on programs of "corporate welfare," while redistributive social programs were cut to the bone.

There is perhaps no better example of the way corporations prey on the public purse than the savings and loan debacle of the late 1980s. That plunder of public assets was unprecedented in financial magnitude, and the episode has no equal in history for systematic political hypocrisy and deceit.

In 1980 the iron triangle for banking and finance constructed a new law. Congress passed it, and President Ronald Reagan signed it, a law that raised from $40,000 to $100,000 the amount of assets in a single S&L account that is covered by federal insurance. Furthermore, the account was insured, not the depositor. Citibank distributed brochures explaining the virtues of multiple accounts, with which a single depositor could arrange federal

---

24. See the Web site of the U.S. Treasury, relative to the public debt: http://www.publicdebt.treas.gov/opd/opdhisto.html.

insurance for $1.4 million of personal assets. The effect of the law was to shift the load of loan risk from the S&Ls directly to the federal government.[25]

Then, at the behest of Jake Garn of Utah in the Senate and Rhode Island's Fernand St. Germain in the House, Congress deregulated the savings and loan industry in 1982. President Reagan concurred once again, and signed the legislation. Free to do anything they pleased, and from any consequential risk, the S&Ls expanded their portfolios into adventures far riskier and more lucrative than traditional residential mortgages: hotels, casinos, resorts, office buildings, shopping malls, and junk bonds. The Wall Street firm of Merrill Lynch, Pierce, Fenner, and Smith quickly saw the profit potential in brokering the certificates of deposit of local S&Ls on the national market, and did so briskly. (Merrill Lynch's CEO, Donald Regan, had left Wall Street to serve as chief of staff in the Reagan White House.)

No longer were S&Ls the folksy institutions where local people placed their savings to finance the construction of their neighbors' homes. Merrill Lynch's success in nationalizing the markets for CDs transformed the entire industry into an uncontrolled, coast-to-coast, high-flying frenzy of speculation, greed, fraud, and predictable disaster. A savings and loan in Peoria, Illinois, could sell its CDs in San Francisco at a double-digit interest rate and then loan out the funds at a higher rate still for a casino or shopping mall. The money poured in, the shaky loans multiplied, and the house of cards grew skyward. It had to end, and it did, with hundreds of S&Ls declaring bankruptcy. It was time for the federal government to repay the depositors, but the Federal Savings and Loan Insurance agency had only a fraction of the necessary funds.

According to the General Accounting Office at the time, settling the S&L accounts would cost at least $325 billion. It would have to be provided directly by the U.S. taxpayers, one way or another, sooner or later.

---

25. See James Ring Adams, *The Big Fix: Inside the S&L Scandal* (New York: John Wiley, 1991).

The magnitude of the disaster became clear just prior to the 1988 presidential election. The Democrats and the Republicans conferred and agreed that neither party would make it a campaign issue. Neither did. With the enthusiastic consent of both Republicans and Democrats once more, Congress then disguised the payments to obscure the pain. Had taxes been raised to generate the $325 billion, the impact on society at large would have been immediate, conspicuous, and stark, and so would the culpability of the responsible political figures. Instead, the Treasury was directed to sell forty-year bonds to finance the repayments. Adding forty years of interest payments would more than quadruple the obligation of the taxpayers, but taxes could remain constant, and the magnitude of the disaster would be concealed.

Factoring in the finance charges raised the total cost of the S&L scandal to $1.5 trillion, equivalent to more than one-quarter of the entire existing national debt. Until the year 2029 we will spend on average $37.5 billion per year for the bailout.

The real pain of the S&L payoff is measured in opportunity costs—in what we might otherwise do with our tax dollars. The list of critical public problems crying for attention and investment—including the restoration of our abused and damaged federal lands—is long and serious. But $37.5 billion per year will yield exactly zero public benefits; we will spend $1.5 trillion for nothing.

Senators John Glenn, Alan Cranston, Donald Riegle, John McCain, and Dennis DeConcini were reprimanded by the Senate Ethics Committee for their complicity in the scandal.[26] Charles Keating and a few other S&L executives served prison time. No other penalties were assessed the corporate predators and their accomplices in the banking and finance triangle.

The corporate plunder of public assets displayed in the savings and loan episode was neither isolated nor unusual. The federal lands have suffered as well.

---

26. In the late 1990s Senator Glenn flew once more into space, again a national hero. Senator McCain became a presidential candidate.

A Case Study: The Liquidation of Montana's Forests

Much of the discussion thus far has been abstract, or it has dealt with issues at some distance from the federal lands. Much of the discussion to follow in chapter 2 will lead us into further abstractions. At this stage, a concrete example of overshooting institutions might well be in order. The plunder of Montana's forests was indicative, not unique.

Land Tenure and Resources Becoming

In order to stimulate the settlement of the public domain, the federal government in the 1800s took steps to develop the nation's transportation infrastructure—canals in the East, wagon roads in the Midwest, and railroads in the high plains and transmountain West.

To encourage construction of the transcontinental routes, the government first granted a railroad—the Northern Pacific Company, for example—a strip of land on which to locate the railbed, typically two hundred feet wide, more or less from Chicago to the West Coast. Then, to collateralize the borrowing of construction capital, alternate square miles of federal land on each side of the right of way were granted to the company as well, in a checkerboard pattern.[27] Across the territory of Montana, the ownership-checkerboard for the Northern Pacific was eighty miles wide, which amounted to forty square miles of public land for each mile of track built.

In all, the Northern Pacific grant came to 47 million acres, close to one-third the size of the national forest system today. (Most of the granted lands in the Cascade Mountains in Washington later became part of the forest land base of the Weyerhaeuser empire.) Fourteen million acres were in Montana—15 percent of the state, or 21,875 square miles, roughly the combined area of Vermont, New Hampshire, and Connecticut. Montana is a big state.

---

27. Often the bonds were bought by the U.S. Treasury and, to the credit of the land-grant railroads, virtually all the public debt was repaid with interest. Not so the private debt: The private financing of the transcontinental roads was saturated with deception, fraud, waste, and corruption.

For decades, the minimum price for federal lands had been pegged at $1.25 per acre. The granting of alternate square miles of land to the railroad builders halved the public's ownership— but Congress saw fit, in the publicly owned part, to double the minimum price to $2.50 per acre. With rail access, the lands were no doubt worth twice as much, so the nation built its transcontinental roads at a net public cost of zero. That is clever public policy.

The Northern Pacific competed furiously with James Hill, building the Great Northern, to see who would reach the West Coast first. The NP won that contest, and competition between the two roads continued for most of a century. Then they saw the virtues of corporate consolidation and, together absorbing the Burlington Road as well, they formed the Burlington Northern Railroad—demonstrating the immortality and unconstrained growth that characterize the modern corporation.[28]

Later the Burlington Northern would spin off the Plum Creek Timber Company, a homey enterprise that came to be known as "the Darth Vader of the industry."[29] We will visit Plum Creek Timber Company soon.

East of the Continental Divide in Montana, much of the railroad land appeared to the Northern Pacific to be nearly valueless. It did not appear valueless to the Texas cattlemen, who saw in those sweeping grasslands a prime place to summer-fatten their herds of longhorns. Nor did it appear valueless to sheep raisers, who saw the same grass but a different utility. Cattle and sheep grazing took hold, as two appraisals of the biophysical environment were made.

These were the appraisals of an immigrant culture, however. Another appraisal had been made centuries earlier by Native Americans, but their technology relied on bison, not cattle or sheep, to capture the potential value in the grasslands.

Then the invading culture perceived great utility in "buffalo robes." With access provided by the railroads, the bison were

---

28. In the late 1990s the company acquired yet another former competitor and became the Northern Pacific Santa Fe Railroad. Early in the twenty-first century it sought a merger with the Canadian National Railway.

29. Quoted in Manning, *The Last Stand*, p. 33.

slaughtered nearly to extinction, and the Native Americans' resource essentially disappeared. So did the Native Americans from much of eastern Montana.

Once property rights were established by the fiat of the railroad land grants, and once the grassland resource was redefined by the domestic livestock industry, the institutions were in place to form the large ranches dominating eastern Montana today.

Other institutions arose to define other resources. The U.S. Mining Law of May 10, 1872, declared that "all the valuable mineral deposits in lands belonging to the United States . . . are hereby declared to be free and open to exploration and purchase . . . by citizens of the United States."[30]

Such citizens as the Amalgamated Copper Company, Incorporated, made good use of that law in Montana.[31] Financed by National City Bank of New York (later Citicorp) and owned by the Standard Oil Company (part of which became the Exxon Corporation), Amalgamated Copper played a colorful role in Montana's history.[32] Eventually sold, Amalgamated became the Anaconda Copper Mining Company, which dominated the economic and political affairs of the state. It owned the newspapers across Montana, and it virtually owned the state legislature. Montana wore "the copper collar" well into the mid-1900s.

To supply its hardrock mines with heavy mining timbers, Anaconda (ACM) acquired 680,000 acres of timberland, mostly from the Northern Pacific, and built a huge sawmill at Bonner, Montana. As far as anyone knew, the mining timbers would always be necessary, so a "sustained yield" policy guided timber cutting on the ACM lands.

In the early 1950s a trainload of logs trundled to the sawmill every week or so, and a trainload of mining timbers crawled away. A quarter century later, trainloads of logs thundered toward the

---

30. The U.S. Mining Law of May 10, 1872 (Ch. 152, 17 Stat.91; 30 U.S.C. 22, 28, 28b), Sec. 1.

31. The history of copper mining in Montana, and much else, is described in K. Ross Toole, *Montana: An Uncommon Land* (Norman: University of Oklahoma Press, 1959).

32. Citicorp and Exxon, we will see, are still major beneficiaries today of what is known as "corporate welfare."

mill every day, and trainloads of plywood, dimension lumber, and pulp chips raced away. Timber cutting had obviously skyrocketed: Had the conservative, sustained-yield policy been broached?

The policy had become irrelevant to the Anaconda Company, and so had the 680,000 acres of forestland. The company had switched to open-pit technology, and mining timbers had lost their utility.[33] To Anaconda's managers, the timberlands had become neutral stuff. The forest land and the mill might as well be sold off.

Liquidating the Industrial Forests

Meanwhile, in the rootless milieu of corporate America, Champion Paper Company and U.S. Plywood merged to form the Champion International Corporation, and it was on a tear of acquisitions. In 1972 it bought the Anaconda sawmill, including the 680,000 acres of Anaconda's forestland for $110 each.[34] Then it bought the Hoerner-Waldorf pulp mill; it bought the Intermountain Lumber Company; it bought the St. Regis Lumber Company with its 200,000 acres of forest near Libby, Montana. Then Champion International built, at the Bonner site, the largest plywood mill on earth.

This expansion was typical of the great consolidation in the forest products industry in the 1970s and 1980s. Dozens of small local sawmills, plywood mills, logging companies, and pulp mills were absorbed by national or international corporations. In a parallel development, the array of state and regional trade associations were absorbed into national groups and aggregated: Eventually, a single National Forest Products Association appeared to argue the industry's case in the nation's capital.

American capitalism and American politics were tipping into their overshoot modes, with dire consequences for the federal lands. The private lands of the timber companies would fare no better.

Plum Creek Timber Company was on a tear as well. Originally

---

33. Open-pit technology also transformed neutral stuff into copper ore, as far lower grades were rendered economic to operate.

34. See "Accelerated Cutting on Private Industrial Timberlands," by Dr. Alan G. McQuillan, in the *Missoula Independent,* November 7, 1991.

a sleepy little outfit near Kalispell, Montana, it had been bought by the Burlington Northern, and vested with what was left of the Northern Pacific land grant. The residue was not trivial. Even after the huge transfers of land to Weyerhaeuser, even after the disposal of grazing lands east of the Continental Divide, even after setting up Anaconda in the mine prop business, Plum Creek remains the second largest holder of timberland in the entire Northwest. (The first is Weyerhaeuser.)

Then Plum Creek became a corporate giant, buying up its share of local wood-processing mills. Headquartered in Seattle, Plum Creek plugged into overshooting capitalism. (Plum Creek is not, in fact, a corporation; it was organized first as a limited partnership, and hence paid no federal income tax whatsoever. It has since become a real estate investment trust and still doesn't.)

Champion International's corporate headquarters in Stamford, Connecticut, are a long way from Montana. From that distance, the trees in the timber inventory appeared not as a forest, a biophysical organism of rich and immense complexity, but simply as an "asset." The mills appeared only as assets, too, with utterly no connection to the economic security of the hardworking men and women who ran them, or to their communities.

The forest products industry, to use author Kevin Phillips's term, was "financialized." Both Champion and Plum Creek undertook programs of "accelerated harvest" on their forestlands. They chose to manage their capital assets for maximum immediate financial return, and that meant cutting their forests as quickly as markets for the products would allow.

The very cheapest way to log the steep timbered slopes of western Montana is to clear-cut them and then to drag the logs straight downhill with bulldozers, their blades dropped into the soil to act as brakes. Champion adopted this technique exclusively, and the ecological damage was incalculable. To the bean counters in Stamford, that damage was an "externality." Only the numbers in their ledgers had any significance: The distinction between abstract assets and concrete forests—and real people—was invisible.

In eighteen years, Champion stripped the old-growth timber from its 880,000 acres, shipped off the products, and reinvested its liquidated assets in a white-paper pulp mill in Michigan. And then, in 1990, Champion International put up for sale its entire Montana complex of mills and forestland.

Plum Creek's accelerated harvest was not far behind Champion's, but the company did a better technical job of logging. And Plum Creek did not sell out and leave; it bought Champion's 880,000 acres of land.[35] The Stimson Lumber Company of Portland, Oregon, bought Champion's solid-wood mills at Bonner and Libby; Stone Container bought the pulp mill, and Champion International was gone.

Liquidating the National Forests

The logging of national forestland was not as ecologically severe as what Champion did, but the rate of cutting was finally unsustainable—in spite of federal laws to the contrary.

The ten national forests in Montana total about 18 million acres. After World War II all were expected to contribute to the rapidly increasing flow of timber products. That was not always the case. Montana's national forests were established mostly in the first decade of the twentieth century, and for about five decades thereafter they were touched only lightly.

During that time a profession of forest management was developed. Professional forestry was palpably idealistic, and there was only a vague, intangible boundary between the profession and the federal agency.[36] The mission of both was twofold: to protect the forest from exploitive overuse by the timber industry, and to prevent it from burning up. The foresters' success in the latter even-

---

35. One must be careful, however, about applauding Plum Creek's "conversion" too loudly or certainly too soon. In 1995, the company signed a "landmark agreement" with the U.S. Fish and Wildlife Service concerning the management of grizzly bear habitat on Plum Creek lands in the Swan Range of northwestern Montana. The following year, the company announced plans to sell off 150,000 acres of prime grizzly habitat for rural subdivisions. Plum Creek's savagery may differ in degree from Champion's, but not in kind. (See Jeffrey St. Clair, "Bottom Lines," in *Wild Forest Review,* January/February 1996.)

36. The classic description of this situation is in Herbert Kaufman, *The Forest Ranger: A Study in Administrative Behavior* (Baltimore: Johns Hopkins Press for Resources for the Future, 1960). Kaufman describes the western forestry schools as virtual seminaries for preparing Forest Service professionals; how the faculties were staffed by retired agency people or masters of forestry from Yale—the school endowed with Gifford Pinchot family money; and how the Forest Service reinforced the idealism and fidelity to both profession and agency, once the young forestry graduates had entered into professional employment.

tually proved embarrassing and misguided. Decades of near-total fire suppression interrupted the natural combustion of the annual accumulation of dead leaves, needles, twigs, brush, grass, and old trees. As knowledge slowly grew of the essential sanitation role of natural fire, so did the "fuel loads." By the time of such conflagrations as those in Yellowstone National Park in 1988, it was apparent that fire would somehow have to be reintroduced into forestland management.

The other challenges to the survival of the forest were private enterprise and the profit motive. The timber industry, the early professional foresters assumed, would forever lodge greater demands for timber than could be tolerated, and only the rationing scheme of sustained yield stood in the way. Annual cutting could never be allowed to exceed annual growth.

The small local sawmills in Montana needed timber only to satisfy local markets. The foresters made small, well-thought-out timber sales to accommodate them, and nowhere was the sustained-yield limit approached. But in the Douglas fir country of the Pacific Northwest, large forest products corporations were cutting their own lands heavily to meet the needs of national markets—for both lumber and plywood, and for paper products as well. Bound by no sustained-yield constraint, their inventories of timber dwindled accordingly.

As World War II ended, the federal timber supplies took on growing significance. National demand for housing, pent up during the war, washed upstream from the building contractors to the lumber brokers to the sawmills and into the forests of Montana.

No one has explained what happened better than Paul Hirt, in a book with a provocative and accurate title: *A Conspiracy of Optimism: Management of the National Forests since World War Two*.[37] And no one has explained why it happened better than David Clary, in *Timber and the Forest Service*.[38] Professional forestry originated in pre-industrial Germany. Neither the stratified

37. Paul W. Hirt, *A Conspiracy of Optimism: Management of the National Forests Since World War Two* (Lincoln: University of Nebraska Press, 1994).

38. David A. Clary, *Timber and the Forest Service* (Lawrence: University of Kansas Press, 1986).

culture there, nor the political economy of mercantilism, nor the existing technology was subject to visible change; institutional stasis prevailed. Wood products were crucial to economic prosperity and national security, and there were no likely substitutes. The early foresters' sustained-yield scheme assured a perpetual supply of such products, and they saw their calling justifiably as a mission of great import.

Clary portrays the messianic enthusiasm of the U.S. Forest Service for timber production as driven by the same imagery. Assuring society of a perpetual supply of timber was a secular mission. The contemporary reality in the United States, however, is not institutional stasis, but rapid development and finally overdevelopment. For every use of wood there are many technical substitutes, all clamoring for market share, and the strategic social value of wood products has greatly diminished. For many years the professionals in the agency failed to see this, and carried on energetically with their mission.

They discovered, moreover, that the sustained-yield constraint could be made to give ground. Periodic growth rates could be stimulated by adding capital to the forest in the form of the "management practices"—planting, thinning, fertilization, and fire suppression. If growth limited harvest, and if growth could be expanded, then harvesting could expand, too. The heavy application of capital came to be known as "intensive forestry," and the conspiracy of optimism was born.

One form of intensive forestry came to overshadow all the others. On millions of acres of unroaded national forestland, billions of board feet of old-growth timber were spatially and economically inaccessible. This was a colossal opportunity: Build the access roads, and cutting rates could skyrocket. Formerly inaccessible timber could be added to the base inventory, and the sustained-yield policy could remain in force. The federal foresters took to road building with boundless vigor—and the forest products industry, the equally optimistic co-conspirator, saw to it that the necessary capital flowed freely. It did so with unexpected generosity, because the capital came from public, not corporate, sources. Lobbying vigorously, the industry drove the Forest Service budget for road building ever and dramatically higher.

"Allowable cuts" escalated as a consequence. Increased cutting could be tolerated biologically, but the public financing of the access roads was an enormous direct subsidy to the forest products industry. The other means of elevating the sustained-yield constraint—through capital intensive management practices—continued apace.

Intensive management in Montana achieved a plateau in the Bitterroot National Forest in the 1960s. Clear-cutting the old growth, terracing the mountainsides to accumulate the moisture from snowfall, and subsequent mechanical planting of nursery-grown seedlings were the most expensive investments in subsequent crops of timber in the state's history.

All the other contemporary forest resources—wildlife habitat, forage for domestic grazing, watershed protection, and natural beauty—were sacrificed for the production, a century hence, of commercial timber.

A political controversy erupted and played out, the details of which we will take up in a later chapter. It could have been resolved equitably and amiably. The local ranchers and the local loggers were neighbors, all enjoyed hunting and fishing, and none was immune to the natural beauty of the Bitterroot Valley. Some sort of selective cutting could have kept the local sawmills supplied, retained the other resource values, and rendered the terracing and the planting unnecessary. But overdeveloped institutions prevailed.

We will see how the controversy played out instead, into the hands of the centralized policy professionals in Washington, D.C. Their answer was a statutory fix. The National Forest Management Act mandated a new system of national forest planning, but the plans would have not the slightest effect on intensive management, or on the liquidation and privatization of the timber values in Montana's national forests. Both continued without interruption. Forest Service budgets for road building and timber sale preparation continued to grow.

Eventually, the illusion of sustained yield was dropped altogether. Not by the professional managers in the Forest Service, and not by the forest plans, but by Congress. No laws were repealed or amended, but a beguiling change in terminology took place. For years the term *allowable cut* had been used to limit annual cutting to no more than annual growth—the essence of sustained yield. The new term was *allowable sale quantity*, or ASQ. ASQs were established not in technical measurements of forest

growth, nor in the forest planning process, but in the language of
Forest Service budgets. They were not limits on cutting but higher
targets intended to increase production.

Hirt explains:

> In the mid-1980s, Congress . . . imposed timber harvest
> targets on the Forest Service. Two powerful congressmen
> from the timber state of Oregon, Republican Senator
> Mark Hatfield and Democratic Representative Les
> AuCoin, succeeded in attaching amendments to . . .
> appropriations bills—directing the Forest Service to
> increase the harvest levels . . . *above the already high targets
> set by the Reagan administration.* [Italics in the original.] By
> legislative amendment, the two congressmen boosted tim-
> ber harvests in the Pacific Northwest 10–30 percent
> between 1986 and 1989.[39]

Murmurs of discontent among the field foresters escalated to
outright dissent, in the form of an organization called the Forest
Service Employees for Environmental Ethics. It was popular initially among younger, lower-level professionals in the agency, but
by 1989 the forest supervisors at a national meeting were telling
Forest Service Chief Dale Robertson that the ASQ's were "unre-
alistically high."[40] Even a former agency head, retired chief R.
Max Peterson, whose term of office had spanned the Reagan
years, was willing to say in public, "Anybody—on the back of an
envelope—could have figured out that the rate of harvest cannot
be sustained."[41]

By the 1980s public assets were defenseless against a determined attack. No law, no agency, no dedicated public land manager, no professional standards, no tradition, no policy, and no
precedent could or would stand in the way of the corporate acquisition of public wealth.

---

39. Hirt, *A Conspiracy of Optimism*, p. 272.

40. The conference was held in Tucson, Arizona, and the printed record was
known as the *Sunbird Proceedings*. The supervisors documented their concerns in a section called "Feedback to the Chief."

41. Quoted in Perri Knize, "The Mismanagement of the National Forests," in
Atlantic Monthly, October, 1991, p. 107.

In Montana the forest supervisors felt pressures from Washington that were threefold and relentless. First, their forest plans, written with knowledge of local forest conditions by their interdisciplinary teams, were sent back to them from Washington to have higher cutting levels justified.[42] The second pressure was budgetary. A succession of budget directors repeatedly slashed the Forest Service requests for funding of amenity resources, such as forest recreation, watershed protection, and wildlife habitat needs. Left intact or increased were the requests for road construction and timber sale preparation. The third pressure was the most direct. The budget bias was reflected in actual appropriations, and with those appropriations came Senator Hatfield's ASQs. He pegged them at the highest level he could, given existing political realities and his own current budget of personal favors and obligations.[43]

Cutting national forest timber in excess of its sustained-yield capacity was patently illegal, but Congress scarcely paused. Steven Lewis Yaffee explains:

> The economic interests and political leaders in the Northwest wanted a high level of timber supplied from federal lands, the Congressional delegation carried these interests into the budgeting process, and the Appropriations process funded a large timber sale program year after year, *regardless of whether the magnitude of the program conflicted with other law, such as that contained in the National Forest Management Act or the Endangered Species Act.*[44] [Emphasis added.]

Thus the "accelerated harvest" of Champion International and Plum Creek forestlands, done with some pretense but no inten-

---

42. The Washington official who did this was the assistant secretary of agriculture, Mr. John Crowell. Mr. Crowell came to the Reagan administration from the Louisiana-Pacific Corporation, the largest single purchaser of national forest timber.

43. Vincent DeWitt, an attorney in the Office of General Counsel, U.S. Department of Agriculture, described Senator Hatfield's procedure in a personal discussion with the author.

44. Steven Lewis Yaffee, *The Wisdom of the Spotted Owl: Policy Lessons for a New Century,* (Washington, DC: Island Press, 1994), p. 242.

tion of sustainability, was replicated on Montana's national forests. There it was called "meeting the ASQ." Both terms were euphemisms. Earlier in history the practice was called "cut out and get out."

The forest supervisors continued their dissent. They told Regional Forester John Mumma in Missoula that they could not meet the timber targets and still meet the statutory requirements for environmental quality. Mumma chose to support his supervisors. He directed them to meet environmental quality standards first, even if that meant leaving the ASQs unmet.

Mumma's action cost him his job. Offered an immediate transfer to Washington, he chose instead to retire. Forest Service Chief Dale Robertson explained that the offer was a "routine transfer" and referred to "poor performance ratings."[45] (Mumma had a file full of agency awards for superior performance.) Assistant Secretary of Agriculture John Beuter endorsed Robertson's explanation, and according to one published account so did "the Flat Earth Society and several prominent citizens of Mars."[46]

After 1990, the harvest of timber in Montana plummeted, on both industrial and national forestlands. There simply wasn't much left to cut.

Corrupted capitalism and predatory politics triumphed in Montana, and the greatest beneficiary was not the people of Montana, not the people of the northwest region, not the people of the United States, not even any real, tangible people possessed of bones and blood. Instead, the prime beneficiary was a pure abstraction, a corporation known as Champion International, which converted its assets to cash and fled. For most of a quarter century the bulk of the national forest timber was processed in Champion International mills too, so the company privatized, liquidated, and fled with the public wealth of Montana's national forests as well.

---

45. Robertson explained the Mumma "reassignment" in a press release issued September 24, 1991.

46. See R.W. Behan, "The Trashing of the Forests in the Northern Rocky Mountains and What to Do Next," in *Wild Forest Review* 1, 3–4 (February–April 1994). Quoting one's own work is no doubt immodest, but the official explanation of Mumma's ouster was an offense to anyone's good sense.

Society at large paid the direct costs of intensive management activities and invested millions of dollars in access roads. It is left with the social costs of damaged watersheds, degraded wildlife habitat, angry scars on Montana's once fabled natural beauty, and a depressed economy. Society served its corporate institutions with distinct generosity.

Generalizing from Montana's Case

Montana is only a sample. There are national forests in most of the other states of the nation, and federal lands administered by other agencies. The trashing of public values has been ubiquitous, and so has the imposition of social costs—frequently, pervasively, to benefit the disembodied, the abstract, the corporate. Society has been inducted into the service of its institutions and into the service of wealth.

It might be gratifying or comforting to posit a conspiracy here, but society's induction into the service of its institutions happened without design, without malice, without sinister intent. Institutions gain momentum, and that is probably enough to explain the overshoot mode we suffer.

It is important to understand that all our institutions had simple and benign human origins, as people sought better ways. Everyone alive today has a heritage of enthusiastic participation in the construction and maintenance of the institutions that have inducted us.

Richard Manning understands and appreciates this, in applauding his logger grandfathers, both of whom savaged a respectable number of trees in their times. Manning, a reporter for the *Daily Missoulian,* wrote a book about the trashing of Montana's forests entitled *Last Stand: Logging, Journalism, and the Case for Humility.* He describes our sharing of history, our commonality of responsibility, and he draws the correct conclusion. Let us listen to him, as he traces the human history of forest exploitation, describing the deforestation of China, more than a thousand years ago; then India, the Middle East, Greece, Rome, Spain, France, and England:

> The great forests of Europe were gone by the time my people left England for Maine, and now the white pines of Maine are gone, as they are in the upper Midwest. Now I

stand here in the Northwest among the pine and fir that are falling all around me. Mostly I see them stacked on trucks headed for the mills that punctuate every drainage in the Pacific Northwest: Washington, Oregon, North Idaho, western Montana, British Columbia, northern California, and Alaska. Now the line [of deforestation] cannot move west, hemmed by the Pacific Ocean, and beyond, hemmed by the deforested deserts of Asia, where the soil has been so damaged that the Chinese fir no longer will grow. There our linear logic becomes circular. The line of forests does not stretch infinitely off into space, but arcs straight back to our beginnings. At the beginnings of this great circle, we meet ourselves.

My grandfathers are dead now, disappeared. Their marks on me are hidden deep in psyche and gene, so I can hide and deny my legacy of logging, my complicity. Most of us can, standing as we do a generation or two or a state or two removed from the people who sweat and saw. Living as we do among white plastered walls that hide the web of lumber studs within. Our houses lie hidden behind a band of maple trees, imported and planted to conjure the peace of a gone forest. Now, though, as we catch clear sight of the ocean to our west, it appears that this conjuring of the ghost forests will soon be all that remains. Soon we will be reduced to accepting a row of planted trees as substitutes for the web of mystery we call a forest. We struck this bargain in pursuit of wealth, but if we follow through, it shall become the ultimate measure of our poverty. Given this prospect, it seems time to cease denying our legacy and future, to face the consequences of what we and our grandparents have done.[47]

The consequences of what we have done are visible in the landscapes and communities of Montana, and elsewhere in the federal lands domain. They are also apparent in the overshoot of our economic and political institutions.

Richard Manning lost his job because his book offended the Champion International Corporation. Champion was a large advertiser in the *Daily Missoulian*, and the paper was owned by

---

47. Manning, *The Last Stand*, pp. 16–17.

another out-of-state corporation, Lee Enterprises of Davenport, Iowa.

Lee Enterprises is not a media giant on the order of Disney or Time-Warner. In terms of savaging its labor force, however, and tilting the revenue stream hugely toward top management, Lee Enterprises yields nothing.

In desperation over inadequate salaries, two competent reporters at the *Missoulian* finally quit their jobs in the mid-1990s. Patricia Sullivan's salary was $32,136 and Ron Selden's, after ten years on the job, was $25,480. The CEO of Lee Enterprises, Richard Gottleib, was paid in 1995 more than $1,460,000, plus stock options.[48] His predecessor, Lloyd Schermer, was paid $4,570,402 in 1990 and $6,261,374 in 1991, nearly two hundred times the salary of Ms. Sullivan.[49]

The disregard shown by Lee and Champion for the welfare of the people they employed cannot be divorced from their treatment of the local communities and the natural resources from which they profited. Far from unusual, this was indicative of the state of affairs throughout Montana.

Now What?

There was no conspiracy, only institutions escaping their servitude to society, as consequences of what we and our grandparents have done. Manning insists that we face those consequences, and he suggests that we accept responsibility for the future as well as the past. In the vernacular and in short, he says, "OK. That's where we've been. Here's where we are. Now what?"

A case for humility is starkly apparent. We need to reconstitute our economic and political institutions so that real people become once again the primal beneficiaries, not the disembodied, the corporate. What can one author have to say that is even marginally important? If that question does not induce humility, then there is, Richard Manning, no case to be made.

One productive strategy is to exploit the work of others. For

---

48. See *Treasure State Review: A Montana Periodical of Journalism and Justice* 14 (Winter–Spring 1996). Published by Wood Fire Ashes Press, Big Fork, Montana.

49. Ibid.

the larger questions of institutional reform, Kevin Phillips, William Greider, Herman Daly, and John Cobb will be relied upon. Some original comment about the damaged federal lands will be offered in subsequent pages, but two contemporary writers, Daniel Kemmis and Steven Yaffee, will be enlisted in that effort as well.

Conclusion

If social injustices and biophysical decline of the federal lands are functions of economic and political overshoot, we need to understand the earlier stages in the development of those economic and political systems.

The chapters to follow will characterize, beginning two centuries ago, four stages in the evolution of American economic and political institutions and the federal lands policies and uses that emerged from them. There will be a few forays into abstractions and theory that will arc out some distance from the federal lands. These transits will be palatable, hopefully, and if our lands are not always in sight, they will always be in mind.

Chapter Two

The Foundations of License: The Economics and Politics of Freedom, 1788–1891

Cultures, Resources, and One Hundred Years

As every schoolchild learns, America is the Home of the Free and a Land of Opportunity; we have always exulted in the prospect of individual growth, development, success, and prosperity. Free-market capitalism permits this, and the U.S. Constitution promotes it.

This chapter will argue that free-market capitalism was closely approximated in 1788, and that the Constitution, ratified that year, was a political parallel: Both systems sought to assure the general welfare by encouraging the pursuit of private gain.

The Constitution provided a limited government of paternalistic aristocrats who quickly invoked Jefferson's dictum: that government is best which governs least.[1] There was no need to "reg-

---

1. The phrase is widely attributed to Jefferson but has never been found, apparently, in his writings. It is attributed less frequently to Thomas Paine and appears explicitly in Thoreau's *Civil Disobedience*.

ulate" the economy of free-market capitalism. Society reliably depended almost exclusively on a system of free markets to optimize simultaneously the welfare of the individual and the welfare of society at large. But the economics and politics of freedom by some malign momentum became the economics and politics of license, and the liberty to pursue individual well-being became eventually a rationale for the corporate plunder of public assets.

To understand what the federal lands would be called upon to do in the nation's first century, we will look at the nature of the resource base in the late 1700s, and consider as well the peculiar status of the American "wilderness."

The pursuit of private gain meant the pursuit of a rising standard of living. That would be achieved by elevating the rates of per-capita consumption, and that would depend on the adequacy of the resource base to support it. The scarcity or abundance of resources was defined physically by the absolute quantity of the substances involved—the S factor in the functional notation of resources. Scarcity or abundance was also defined institutionally by social perceptions of utility—the U factor—and by the T factor of technology. The construction of iron ships, for example, was beyond the technical reach of the great New England yards, so shipbuilding resources—oak and pine—were accordingly, and relatively, scarce. The great iron ore deposits in what would become Minnesota remained neutral stuff.

Petroleum, aluminum, and uranium were also neutral stuff. Benjamin Franklin tinkered with a kite, a key, and disaster, but the generation and transmission of electricity lay far in the future too, and so therefore did a particular utility of copper. The neutrality of these kinds of stuff was occasioned by the absence of T factors.

Other elements of the biophysical environment lacked social perceptions of value or utility. The grizzly bear comes to mind, and the whooping crane, and the wolf, and "endangered species" of any variety. Just so "old-growth forests," "biodiversity," and "Wilderness." These things were appreciated not in the least by the citizens of the late 1700s, and hence remained neutral stuff.

The "howling wilderness" was the object of exploration, subjugation, occupation, and exploitation, and the word *wilderness* was used explicitly, often with the chilling adjective. Spelling it with a capital *W,* however, denotes the wilderness *resource,* the undeveloped land appreciated by present-day citizens primarily for its provision of experiential or psychic pleasure.[2] As described by historian Roderick Nash, "by the middle decades of the nineteenth century wilderness was recognized as a cultural and moral resource."[3] In Zimmerman's terminology, Wilderness was not, but it became.

In the history of the wilderness resource, however, there is a grave error of fact. It is enshrined with great clarity in the statutory definition of wilderness:

> A wilderness, in contrast with those areas where man and his own works dominate the landscape, is hereby recognized as an area where the earth and its community of life are untrammeled by man, where man himself is a visitor who does not remain.[4]

There has been no land like that in North America for the past eighteen thousand years, since the land bridge from Siberia provided ingress to the continent. "Man and his own works" were omnipresent when Europeans arrived in 1492. Some 100 million people—one-fifth of the world's population—were already living in North and South America.[5] Eighteen million of them occupied what would become the continental United States. Their cultures had developed over not centuries but millennia: patterns of land use and occupancy; a network of coast-to-coast transport and commerce; villages, towns, and cities—for cities there were; and their governments.[6] Cahokia, in what is

---

2. The transition of wilderness from fearsome to attractive is chronicled in Roderick Nash, *Wilderness and the American Mind* (New Haven: Yale University Press, 1967).

3. Ibid., p. 67.

4. The Wilderness Act, P.L. 88-577, Sec. 2 (c).

5. See Ronald Wright, *Stolen Continents: The "New World" through Indian Eyes* (Boston: Houghton Mifflin, 1992), p. 4.

6. See Francis Jennings, *The Founders of America: How Indians Discovered the Land, Pioneered in It, and Created Great Classical Civilizations; How They Were Plunged into a Dark Age by Invasion and Conquest; and How They Are Now Reviving* (New York: W. W. Norton, 1993). An earlier work, to which Jennings owes much but fails to acknowledge, is Patricia Nelson Limerick, *The Legacy of Conquest: The Unbroken Past of the American West* (New York: W. W. Norton, 1987).

today southern Illinois, was a city of forty thousand people, the contemporary equal of London or Paris.[7] And the federated government of the Iroquois Nations served as a model for the U.S. Constitution.[8]

All this could be said to have "dominated the landscape." The American "wilderness" was not "tamed" or "settled" by European immigrants. Settled already for thousands of years, it was invaded and conquered by the force of European and finally American arms.[9]

If resources result from cultural appraisals, differing cultures will depend on differing resource bases, even when they appraise the same biophysical environment. The European appraisals were conditioned by differing technologies—the wheel, domesticated-animal energy, metallurgy, and gunpowder among them—and by differing institutions—property rights, the priority of accumulating personal wealth, racism, Christianity, and indifference to the maintenance of community, embodied as we will see in the U.S. Constitution. If conquest, occupation, and the seizure of wealth were the objectives, the European technologies and institutions were patently superior to those of the Native Americans, as history, even contorted history, has proven.

By contemporary standards the "U" variables and the "T" variables were primitive in colonial times. Wants and needs were simple and basic, unmanipulated by mass-media advertising. Proprietary producers could only respond to such autonomous preferences, as free-market theory asserts: They did not influence the consumers. The technologies were almost exclusively mechanical in nature. Products were fashioned from raw materials with cutting tools and fastening devices. Manufacturing was small in scale, calling for capital investment well within the limits of indi-

---

7. Wright, *Stolen Continents*, p. 91.

8. For an excellent account of the influence on the U.S. Constitution of the Great Binding Law of the Iroquois, see Jerry Mander, *In the Absence of the Sacred: The Failure of Technology and the Survival of the Indian Nations* (San Francisco: Sierra Club Books, 1991), especially chapter 13, "The Gift of Democracy." Among the Founding Fathers who applauded the Iroquois's success with federation were James Madison, Benjamin Franklin, William Livingston, John Adams, and Thomas Jefferson.

9. A detailed account of the waves of European invasion is contained in Churchill, *A Little Matter of Genocide.*

vidual savings and credit. Transportation, other than walking, consisted of saddle animals, wagons, barges, and wooden ships at sea. Sources of energy included water power, coal, wood, and in the plantation economy the energy of human slaves. Whale oil and candles provided lighting.

The resource base of the Constitutional Americans, however, was vastly more abundant than that of the Native Americans, due to the differing U and T variables. It could support a larger population at much higher levels of per-capita consumption, and it soon did.

Comparing the resource base of the Constitutional Americans to our resource base two centuries later shows the earlier case to be one of relative scarcity. Contemporary Us and Ts have transposed great quantities of neutral stuff into prized resources that literally did not exist in the late 1700s.

Comparing the resource base of the Constitutional Americans to that of the Native Americans and comparing the resource base of the 1790s to that of the twenty-first century illuminates important distinctions between cultures and between time periods. Relative scarcities or abundances are important, since they determine the range of social options in making land-use decisions. Furthermore, such comparisons force a frame of mind—nimble and fluid—that is appropriate for thinking about resources as biosocial constructs, as we will need to do in later chapters.

Another comparison is often of great immediacy: How does the existing resource base measure up to the existing demands lodged against it? As the 1700s drew to a close, the limits of the resource base were probably quite visible. Rising levels of per-capita consumption and a rapidly increasing population pressed relentlessly on the relevant substances.

A rational response to this sort of scarcity is to add physical quantities to the resource base—to occupy and develop more land, exploit more forest resources, turn out more cattle to graze, etc. This was pursued enthusiastically and without interruption for nearly a century, and it called for a policy of making public land private.

The new federal government found itself possessed of "crown" lands, coincidentally with a strong aversion to anything resembling a crown. First, the states turned over their colonial land claims—some 237 million acres—to the federal government, and then Mr. Jefferson bought another 560 million acres from France. This was a huge amount of land in the wrong kind of ownership—public ownership, a fact that did violence to the strategic underpinnings of the new government and the existing economic system. For both institutions, the welfare of the individual was paramount. For free-market capitalism to assure individual prosperity, the land must be in private hands. For the political system to achieve that, nothing could stand in the way—certainly not unfettered democracy which might empower a "tyrannical" majority capable of asserting its prerogative over individual interests. The policy consequence of all this was a century-long program of transferring federal land to private ownership and consequent exploitation.

An episodic departure from the policy of privatizing the federal lands occurred in 1872. Congress decreed perpetual public ownership for the northwest corner of what would become Wyoming and called it Yellowstone National Park, but that wasn't meant to challenge the privatization rationale. The idea that private interests might jeopardize a broader public interest was not explicitly recognized in federal lands policy until 1891. We will take up the details of the Forest Reserve Act in Chapter 3, but 1891 can be seen, accurately if arbitrarily, as the conclusion of the period in which the foundations of license were laid.

Building the Foundations of License

This section will describe in some detail, to provide the bases for later comparisons, the institutions of free-market capitalism and constitutional government at the time of ratification. "Free-market capitalism" was a proximate reality, but "majoritarian democracy" was unknown, deliberately precluded so that aristocratic paternalism might flourish.

The citizens of the United States in the 1780s were facing the task of establishing a basis of institutions. They needed to provision themselves—to assure efficient production from their stock of physical, capital, and human resources, and to assure an equitable scheme of consumption. For that they would need one set of institutions. And in order to maintain their professed unity they would need a parallel set of institutions: a just system of constructing and enforcing the rules for individual and joint behavior.

The Founding Fathers insisted on subjecting a new political system to deliberate design but left the economic system unchallenged, to develop autonomously, randomly, possibly capriciously. It might well have been that they were happy, even prospering within the set of extant economic institutions and were reluctant to tamper. Thus, they would design a political system to reinforce their prosperity. One historian some twelve decades into the future would make that argument—which we will encounter in due course.

Or it might have been thought at the time, as it is by some economists today, that a free-market system is a divine creation, and that the responsible deity would retain the oversight for its nurture.

Free-Market Capitalism: A Reasonably Accurate Description of Economic Affairs in the Late 1700s

A good approximation of free-market capitalism was evident at the time of the Revolution. That it no longer exists will be demonstrated shortly, but first a datum is necessary. We need to understand something of its history if we want to comprehend its overshoot.

It is tempting to suggest that the Founding Fathers had read a volume called *An Inquiry into the Nature and Causes of the Wealth of Nations* by a sometimes professor of moral philosophy at the University of Glasgow, Dr. Adam Smith, who had the book published in 1776. It is tempting to posit further that they accepted its argument, could see no reason to challenge the clarity of its analysis, agreed that it portrayed an accurate representation of economic affairs in the new United States, and as a result turned their attention forthwith and singularly to the design of the Constitution. They would have done so because Dr. Smith described the workings of an economy that achieved everything an ideal economic system should achieve. It arranged productive resources in a way that guaranteed efficient production. It rewarded the owners of the various resources—physical, capital, and human resources—in a way that guaranteed equitable consumption. Thus, the basic canons of economic structure were fulfilled.

The social optima of efficient production and equitable consumption resulted automatically, Dr. Smith wrote, "as if by an invisible hand," when individuals were allowed to strike the best bargains they could in a system of *free markets*. The markets attended initially to the allocation of productive resources and thereafter to the distribution of the goods and services that had been produced. What those markets needed most was massive inattention, so as not to interfere with or distort their functioning. They needed to be left alone. The French term was *laissez-faire,* and Dr. Smith's book provided an unprecedented exposition.

The irresistible appeal of free-market economics springs from the concept of "consumer sovereignty." The consumer is king, and the values in the hearts and minds of all consumers constitute the origin of every economic signal or stimulus. Initially in "consumer goods markets" those values are expressed by what consumers offer to pay, and producers are everywhere and forever subservient.

Keep in mind, if this sounds awkward, quaint, or flawed, that it is a paraphrase of the free-market system described by Dr. Smith and elaborated by his successors, not an expression of reality today.

Let us set a scene in the late 1700s. As a sovereign consumer, you have in your heart and mind an utterly unmanipulated, wholly autonomous feeling of need, say with respect to a pair of shoes. You imagine a pair of black calfskin shoes with pewter buckles. On Saturday, all the many cobblers of your town display their wares in the village square. The "producers" have brought with them two products: the black calfskins (fortunately) and a brown pigskin model with bone buckles. Other citizens with similar senses of need arrive, too. These "consumers" are likewise endowed with sovereign primacy in the marketplace, and there are a lot of them, too. The "market for consumer goods," in this case for shoes, is open for business.

Consumers interact with producers, inquiring and bargaining about prices. No one is compelled to buy. No one is compelled to sell. Few if any transactions take place initially as a result, but a great deal of information is flowing: The consumers are discovering which cobbler is asking the lowest price, and the cobblers are learning the money-measured intensity of esteem expressed by consumers for black calfskin shoes with pewter buckles. Brown pigskins are simply "not selling."[10]

---

10. Note the facilitation of the market process by the clever invention of "money." The "common medium of exchange" did two things. One was universally important: It eliminated the difficult comparative evaluations in bartered transactions. The other was hugely unfortunate: It allowed the study of economics to be quantified.

As the process continues, buyers adjust their bid-prices and sellers their asked-prices according to the information they are gaining. When everyone is fully informed, the "market clearing price" has been established. It will tend to be close to the lowest of the initially asked-prices, painfully below the next-lowest, and impossibly below the highest. Notice the superiority of the consumers' position: The price of shoes has been set according to their evaluations, and the producers must yield. Such is the nature of consumer sovereignty.

Transactions take place at the market-clearing price until all the black calfskin shoes with pewter buckles have exchanged hands. The consumers take their shoes home, and the producers take home their gross revenues—and their lessons.

What have the cobblers learned? They have learned "what to produce" and "how much," two fundamental questions in any economic system. Consumers expressed their preference for black calfskin, so the cobblers know to produce more of them, accordingly, and to terminate the brown pigskin line.

When the consumers are sovereign, the economy will always produce what they want, and as much or as little as they want. The appeal of Dr. Smith's market system cannot be denied, but there are more virtues still.

Recall the fortunate producer whose initial asked-price was very close to the market-clearing price. He could undersell his fellow craftsmen only if his production costs were lower. That was possible only if he was more efficient in the use of resources, to yield more shoes for a given level of labor and raw materials. His competitors, not so clever or careful, would eventually have to exit the cobbling business. The competition of the marketplace, exploited by the sovereign consumer, thus fulfills the first canon of economic organization: Efficiency in production is achieved automatically.

The other canon requires the economy's aggregate output to be distributed fairly among society at large. Relying again on the sovereign consumer's pursuit of self-interest, this too is assured in free-market capitalism. To see how, we will need to inquire further into some of the details of our example.

Suppose the successful cobbler, John, has two sons, Steadfast and Carefree, who work with him in the shop. The sons are named appropriately, since the first is a serious and clever lad with dexterous hands who makes four pairs of shoes each day. His brother, a freer spirit, spends his evenings in various sorts of exhausting revelry, and hence appears at his cobbler's bench with neither a clear head nor such dexterous hands. With these marginal handicaps, he constructs only two pairs of shoes daily. John is a loving and forgiving father, but he follows the convention of the day and pays on a piecework basis. Because Steadfast adds twice as much to society's aggregate output, his wage-income is thus twice that of Carefree's. That means Steadfast can buy twice as much as Carefree in the consumer goods markets.. Their subsequent consumption is by no means equal, but it is by all means fair.

Put another way, the value of Steadfast to society is double that of his lighthearted, heavy-headed sibling. Shouldn't someone who is more valuable to society at large have the right to claim more of its output?

The amount and kind of individual consumption in a free-market system is determined by our value to society, as that is measured in the "producer goods markets." In these markets, we have either labor or raw materials to sell to producers, or capital to loan, or some combination. Our total income is thus established and in every case—witness Steadfast and Carefree—it will reflect our value to society at large. Our incomes will be different, and the subsequent levels of consumption made possible will be, too, but that is supremely equitable.

An economic system that decides what to produce and how much, that produces efficiently, that assures a fair distribution of goods and services, and that does all this spontaneously, relying only on the self-interest of the participants bargaining in both sets of markets, is an ingenious system indeed. Channeling the unabashed pursuit of private gain to achieve the public good is a truly amazing feat of institutional innovation.

Adam Smith explained free-market capitalism with critical thinking and carefully wrought language. In his entire text there is not a single display of analytical geometry, not a single differential equation, not a single calculation. (In the appendix there does appear a calculation of the duties accruing to the trade in salted herring.) He simply used words to argue that the institution of mercantilism had overshot, prescribing free markets instead.

Because they engage infrequently in critical thinking and even more rarely in carefully wrought language, few contemporary economists seem aware or concerned that capitalism is over-shooting now. As the modern discipline of economics became wholly quantified, it was transformed into an exercise in applied mathematics and propelled into general irrelevance. It addresses no longer the behavior of people and societies in their tasks of provisioning, but only the sterile behavior of numbers.[11]

Quantitative economics and its applied derivative, "management science," have contributed, subtly perhaps, but directly to the overshoot of capitalism. They are taught both vigorously and rigorously in schools of business administration and have succeeded in elevating pure numbers to a position of preeminence in the management of modern enterprise. The derisive term *bean counting* is fully warranted; see, for example, those we encountered at Champion International who saw forests and employees merely as assets.

In the late 1700s only verbal economics was available, and the operative elements of Adam Smith's free-market system were in place and working in the United States. The economic system

---

11. Similar criticism appears in the literature of economics. Leopold Kohr, an economist himself with impressive credentials, had this to say: "Since aggregates could be more easily grasped on a statistical basis, *political economy,* with its reliance on deductive reasoning, was abandoned in favour partly of *statistical economy,* with its dependence on quantitative checking, but primarily in favor of *mathematical economy,* with its surrealistic love of symbols and diagrams. Though this transformation of the science, which began in footnotes and ended by supplanting the text, was hailed as a great advance, happening at the very time when further development seemed to have become impossible, mathematical economy did essentially nothing but obscure rather than illuminate the subject. It expressed in a difficult patois what previous theorists had formulated in elegant prose. [Cf. Adam Smith.] It is to conceptual economics what bricklaying is to architecture. Not a single new concept can be said to have arisen as a result of the mathematical approach, not the marginal analysis, not the multiplier, not the propensity to consume, not the quantity theory of money, nor the various equilibrium concepts. They all sprang from the realm of philosophical speculation for which the mathematical economists provided not the spark but either proof or illustration. The spark was provided by the speculators, the dreamers, or, as Keynes called them, 'academic scribblers.' This is true even of such mathematically gifted economists as Cournot, Walras, Jevons, or Pareto whose philosophical perception was often greatly sharpened by the additional talent, but not created by it." See Leopold Kohr, *The Overdeveloped Nations: The DisEconomies of Scale* (New York: Schocken Books, 1977), pp. 163–164.

had by no means overshot. It was an institution in the service of society.

The Founding Fathers, therefore, were unable to see any compelling problems in the economic system. Difficulties of efficient production or equitable consumption were not starkly evident.

Markets were small and localized. They were indeed characterized by many sellers and many buyers, so that no one was able to dominate the process of price setting. The wants and needs of consumers were comparatively basic and simple, conditioned perhaps by cultural standards—but not stimulated by deft and incessant advertising. You could say the consumer was sovereign.

The technologies to produce such basic and simple goods were straightforward, calling for only modest investments of capital. It was not difficult for individual craftsmen to purchase the common tools, furniture, and rather small increments of raw materials with their personal savings and credit. Much production was thus organized on the basis of proprietorship. Putting together a woolen mill or a foundry could call for a pool of capital that exceeded the financial assets of any one entrepreneur, so several would pool their savings and credit to form a partnership; and that form of business organization was commonplace as well. The multiplicity of producers visible here is necessary for a system of free markets to deliver its societal benefits.

When still larger pools of capital were necessary, say for building a canal, the colonies and later the states were willing to charter corporate structures. The charters were strongly circumscribed as to purpose, operation, financing, and lifespan—typically twenty years, rarely more than fifty. They were revocable for cause, and shareholders in the corporations faced personal liability for corporate misconduct. Firmly under the control of the chartering body, eighteenth-century corporations, too, were institutions in the service of society. Only about two hundred had been chartered by the end of the 1700s, and dissolution at the end of the charter period was routine.[12]

---

12. See Richard L. Grossman and Frank T. Adams, *Taking Care of Business: Citizenship and the Charter of Incorporation* (Cambridge, MA: Charter, Ink, 1993). This slim and modest pamphlet is cited extraordinarily widely.

By the end of the next century, however, American corporations had achieved legal status as citizens, their rights protected by the Constitution. Charters could now be granted—and were—in perpetuity and for open-ended purposes. Combines, trusts, and monopolies dominated markets, seriously distorting the symmetry of Adam Smith's system, in which both buyers and sellers were numerous. All this became a major issue of political reform, but the corruption of free-market capitalism had begun. We will revisit this theme in chapters to come.

The free-market system, however, with all the virtues articulated by Dr. Smith was closely approximated at the time the Constitution was written and ratified.

Aristocratic Paternalism: A Reasonably Accurate Description of Political Affairs in the Late 1700s

Free-market capitalism has a substantial basis in U.S. history, but majoritarian democracy does not. Majoritarian democracy was rendered impossible, by ingenious constitutional design, but it remains a popular myth to this day.

Most Americans today would like to believe, or do, that their system of government is "democratic," that a government "of the people, by the people, and for the people" is not just rhetoric. A more sophisticated rendition speaks of "representative democracy," in which the people select some agents, expecting them to serve society as a whole. In practice, however, most issues of public concern are too contentious to be resolved in the interests of the whole society, so a majoritarian standard is adopted instead: The agents should serve the interests of a majority.

Such governments are visible today, but ours is not one of them. The Founding Fathers, with skill, ingenuity, and deliberation wrote a constitution that foreclosed the possibility of majoritarian democracy.

Majoritarian democracy requires a set of political institutions in which the views of a majority can be expressed, accommodated, and implemented. It is not enough simply for a forum to be provided, a forum in which an isolated and independent elite can attempt with the best of intentions to speak and act in the interest of society at large or even in the interest of a perceived majority. That could be called governance by divination, or it might be called aristocratic paternalism, but that is what the U.S.

Constitution established, and it was the documented intent of the Founding Fathers to do so.

We will inspect the details of what they did, but to provide a point of reference let us look at a political system in which a majoritarian view can be expressed, accommodated, and implemented. What would it look like?

It could look very much like the parliamentary system operating in Great Britain today.

Majoritarian Democracy: What It Looks Like

Majoritarian democracy is possible only if a majority can be identified, given voice, and mobilized. Then there must be a way for the majority to establish and maintain a controlling claim on the machinery of government.

For this to happen, there must be a controlling concentration of power available for a majority of citizens to capture. The British parliamentary system offers such a concentration in the office and in the person of the prime minister. The incumbent is the titular and de facto head of the controlling political party, the majority leader in the legislative branch as a consequence, and simultaneously the chief executive of the British government.

As chief executive, the prime minister can propose a statutory policy response to a public problem he or she perceives. As majority leader of the legislative branch simultaneously, the PM is typically assured that it will be enacted. Then, functioning as the principal executive officer once more, the prime minister sees to its faithful and vigorous administration.

That is a great deal of political power concentrated in a single place, and the contest for its capture is characteristically lively. Let us see how the contest is prosecuted.

Elections in Great Britain are disarmingly simple affairs. In every voting district, or "constituency," as they are called, it seems citizens are making only one choice: Who, among the candidates, will be their "MP," their member of parliament, their representative in the House of Commons. Only the names of the candidates appear on the ballot, but in fact the voters are choosing a prime minister and a very explicit package of public policy as well. The names of their prospective MPs are surrogates for several more and profound matters of choice.

Prior to an election in Great Britain, the political parties decide a number of critically important items. First, the leaders of the parties are elected by the members. This is not just a simple administrative matter, because one of the party leaders so chosen will be the next prime minister of Great Britain. Next, a "programme" is constructed, a passionately debated agenda of public policy proposals, typically a listing of legislative solutions to the jointly defined problems of the day. The Labour party, for example, might propose nationalizing the coal mines to ease an energy shortage; the Conservatives might propose breaking the coal miners' union instead. The programmes of the parties stand in stark substantive contrast to one another; they are long on explication and short on platitude. They are listings of political promises that will be delivered, to the letter, should the party be successful in the election, because each candidate will campaign on the programme explicitly and promise to support it. Finally, some housekeeping matters of candidates and their respective constituencies are resolved, and eventually election day arrives.

In each constituency voters are indeed asked only to choose a single prospective member of Parliament. But they know that a vote for a Labour MP also constitutes a preference for the Labour party's leader to be the prime minister. And they know that a vote for a Labour MP is an endorsement of the Labour party programme. Their vote is pregnant, indeed: It expresses simultaneously a preference for the constituency's representative to the House of Commons, a prospective prime minister, and a detailed, explicit package of public policy. When the votes are tallied, one party has won (normally) a majority of seats in the House of Commons. The majority of British voters has been identified, given voice, and mobilized, and its controlling claim on the machinery of government is lodged very quickly.

The leader of the victorious party, having won his or her seat in Parliament, visits Buckingham Palace, there to be appointed prime minister by the monarch. Returning to Commons, the PM submits the party's programme to a vote, the successful outcome of which, given the members' loyalty to their party leader, is guaranteed.

The astute reader will have noticed two very sensitive provisos. The party leaders must indeed win their seats in Commons, and the members of their parties must remain loyal to them. Both are met with a feature of British government Americans find peculiar.

There is no residency requirement: You don't have to live in Swansea East to represent that constituency. You can apply to the national parties to run in any one or several constituencies of your choice. The party leadership prepares "approved lists" of prospective candidates for each constituency, from which the local party organization picks the person to run. The party leaderships thus control to a large degree who will run where, and this gives them a powerful means of maintaining discipline in the party ranks.

The party members whose professions of loyalty are most frequent and strong are offered "safe" constituencies—those with long records of supporting the party. The Right Honourable Tony Blair, current prime minister of Great Britain, represents the Sedgefield constituency. It is likely that Sedgefield has voted Labour for the past four hundred years. That takes care of the first proviso: The prospective prime minister will be elected. Those of lesser enthusiasm are offered less certain constituencies. And those Labourites who have offended the party leadership in terminal fashion will be offered constituencies where Conservatives have prospered for four hundred years. Fealty to both party and leadership remains uncommonly strong, assuring the second proviso.

Clever but unknowing MPs might choose to disagree with the party leader only after a successful campaign. Whereupon the membership might well encounter another of the prime minister's powers, often invoked when the party membership becomes surly, contentious, and unruly. The prime minister can call for a new election at will. A new election iterates the process of programme construction and assignment of representation.

The membership of the party is not without its own capacity to terrorize, however. Prior to any vote in the House of Commons, the position of the majority leader is utterly clear. If a few of the majority members disagree with their leader, they will have a lot of support among the minority members who disagree by definition. And any time a vote in Commons contradicts the wishes of the majority leader, a chilling description appears in the media: The leader has "lost a vote of confidence." The "government" has been "toppled," and a new election must be called forthwith. The process of a new election also calls for a new vote in each party to identify and elect the party leadership: No sitting majority leader is guaranteed a contract extension. The prime minister, then, can be toppled and subjected to scrutiny by a surprisingly few members of his or her own party.

The British system of majoritarian politics is also tested by the impartiality of time. A new election must be called within five years of the previous one, regardless of who is satisfied, or dissatisfied, with whom.

The system is essentially unicameral. The concurrence of the House of Lords is not necessary to the passing of British law. Furthermore, the British court system does not wield the power of judicial review, and so cannot void a law by ruling it unconstitutional.

The prime minister's power is awesome and singular. There may be other ways to design a system of majoritarian democracy, but one that works extremely well is to provide a majority with the opportunity to capture a controlling concentration of political power.

Such a majoritarian government, however, is fragile indeed; its vulnerability to recall and reconstitution is acute and unrelenting, and its accountability is clear and complete. But this jeopardy is of great virtue in assuring the sovereignty of the people. Their institution of government will always remain in their service: It cannot recruit or co-opt the people into the service of itself.

A delicate, vulnerable, majoritarian system presupposes a conviction about the people: They are capable of transcending their welfare as individuals to discern and to nurture the common good, the public good, the res publica writ large. The parties will write and the voters will choose a programme they all believe to be in the interests of the nation at large, and not one that favors just their own faction.

Suppose you didn't believe this. Suppose you doubted the capacity of human nature to rise above self-interest and factionalism. Suppose you harbored a great anxiety about a "tyranny of the majority" and felt the minority would be unsafe and insecure in its grip.

Suppose you were James Madison, in Philadelphia, in 1787.

The U.S. Constitution: The Ingenious and Systematic Foreclosure of Majoritarian Democracy

James Madison and many of his colleagues were indeed suspicious of majoritarian democracy. Some historians allege that it was Shays's Rebellion a year earlier—an angry gang of agrarian debtors in Massachusetts openly defying the political dominance of urban creditors—that illuminated the dangers in rule by majority. The debtors outnumbered the creditors in Massachusetts, and they might not focus, if given political power, simply and directly on the welfare of the commonwealth at large. Maybe they would seek to cancel their indebtedness.

Madison preferred to trust in an isolated and mechanistic government. He seemed determined to invoke Rousseau's contemporary observation: "Keeping citizens apart has become the first maxim of modern politics."[13]

The champion of "republican virtues," on the other hand, of a democracy based on ruggedly independent citizens and their capacity for seeking a higher public good, was Thomas Jefferson. Unfortunately, he was serving as ambassador to France during the Philadelphia conclave, and majoritarian democracy would therefore have no vigorous advocate.

Few of the Founding Fathers could be identified as agrarian debtors, and Madison's Virginia Plan carried the day. We will inspect its particulars shortly.

A case can be made that the Founding Fathers adopted a constitution to protect and advance their own economic interests.[14] As creditors, holders of public securities, land speculators, and investors in shipping and manufacturing, they stood to benefit if a new government could marshal a number of powers. Preventing the inflation of the currency would protect the value of their debt instruments; taxation authority to refund the public debt in full would secure their bonds bought at par and produce huge profits on those bought at discount; their land claims in the West would appreciate smartly if a U.S. military presence enforced them (that is, if the Indians were displaced); and manufacturing called for tariff protection.

Some of these advantages appeared immediately upon ratification; others took a few years; none failed to materialize. And not

---

13. Quoted in Daniel Kemmis, *Community and the Politics of Place* (Norman: University of Oklahoma Press, 1990), p. 18.

14. See Charles Beard, *An Economic Interpretation of the Constitution of the United States* (New York: Free Press, 1986). Originally published in 1913, the book has generated a sizable literature of criticism and countercriticism.

one was challenged or compromised by anything approaching a majoritarian democracy. Clearly, the motives of the Founding Fathers might be debated, but not their product. The preclusion of majoritarian democracy embodied in the Constitution has proven to be impregnable.

If the key to majoritarian democracy is a controlling concentration of political power subject to capture, what would an intentional and ingenious preclusion look like? Even a soul of limited imagination would hit soon on a strategy of dispersal, to shatter the concentration of political power and scatter it as widely as possible in both space and time. That way, it would be impossible for a "majority" of any stripe to capture all the pieces and sweep them into a cohesive corpus of governance.

There were already visible thirteen governments—in the states—exercising considerable political power. That was a good start on dispersion. The Constitutional Convention was merely considering a fourteenth. Even so, the fourteenth government could become a powerful one. How, then, to scatter political power at the federal level was an intriguing problem for the Founding Fathers.

An effective way to begin is to provide an unbridgeable cleavage between the executive and the legislative functions. The U.S. president will serve only as the chief executive, and not concurrently as the controlling leader in the legislative branch. An effective way to continue is to establish a bicameral legislature. Every law will have to be passed twice, once in each chamber.

But a "majority" might conceivably "capture" the bicameral legislature. So to enact any law, the Congress will have to seek a final approval by the president, who is under no compulsion, given the power of the veto, to provide it.

Perhaps the majority has succeeded in capturing the presidency as well. So the Supreme Court will have the power of negating any law, by declaring it unconstitutional. (In fact, judicial review was established by Chief Justice Marshall, some might say arbitrarily, in *Marbury vs. Madison* in 1803. It was not a feature of the Constitution, but its impact on the dispersion of political power cannot be overlooked.)

But perhaps the majority might succeed in adding the Supreme Court to its collection of swept-up political power. A second-tier strategy takes effect: Power will be dispersed not only structurally, but across time. The president will be elected for four years; the senators for six; the representatives for two; and justices will serve for life.

But perhaps the majority is persistent. A third-tier strategy appears: Power will be dispersed among constituencies. Voters from all thirteen states will elect the president; for that office alone there will be a national constituency. Senators will have statewide constituencies. The constituencies of congressmen will be limited to residents of the congressional district only. The justices of the high court will be appointed by the president, so they will have no identifiable constituency of voters at all.

The challenge to the majority has long since become insuperable, but the Founding Fathers are not yet satisfied. Next they place a pair of filters between the people and their federal government.

Only representatives will be elected directly by the voters. The state legislatures, filter #1, will elect senators, and the president will be chosen by the electoral college, filter #2. Neither senatorial nor presidential candidates' names will even appear on the ballot cast by the man in the street.

The cliché is apt. Women cannot vote. Neither can those who are not white. Neither can those under twenty-one. Neither can those who do not own property.[15]

At ratification, the European-descent population was roughly four million people. Just $2^{1}/2$ percent of them—some 100,000 white male property owners over twenty-one years of age—were qualified to vote.[16] The final barrier to majoritarian democracy was profoundly simple: Only a tiny minority of the American people was allowed the most rudimentary participation in public

---

15. The Founding Fathers considered voter qualifications, but chose to let the Constitution remain silent on the matter. It was not a bold stroke for democracy: They left the issue for the states to decide, and the states had already installed those qualifications.

16. Derivation of figures: Leonard D. White, in *The Federalists: A Study in Administrative History* (New York: Free Press, 1965), lists the population at 4,000,000 (pp. 1–2). Daniel Hellinger and Dennis R. Judd, in *The Democratic Façade* (Pacific Grove, CA: Brooks/Cole, 1991), state that 5 percent of the males were enfranchised (p. 89). If half the population was male, 5 percent of 2,000,000 is 100,000.

affairs. The majority was systematically, deliberately, and totally excluded.

We do not and cannot have majoritarian democracy in the United States. The American majority is indeed silent, by deliberate, ingenious, and durable Constitutional intent. Instead, several tiny subsets of the entire population—a few voters, the state legislatures, and the Electoral College—were empowered by the Constitution to install their own "separated powers" into the workings of government, essentially independently, until the structure was complete.

No one, therefore, was responsible for the totality of government. That meant the totality was accountable to no one. This was true in April of 1789, when federal governance was initiated under the new Constitution, but it caused no overtly consequential damage to the American people for many years. It is still true today, and the damage is accumulating in every sector of public affairs. The reasons for the difference will unfold in pages to follow, but a government that cannot be held accountable by the governed is a loose institutional cannon of the first rank.

If the majority could not rule, who did? Conclusively, it was America's class of patricians, the de facto aristocrats, the executives and legislators of the new federal government. They were drawn from the highest strata of wealth, education, intellect, achievement, and experience, which may be why great public damage was avoided. These people to a man, and again the cliché is apt, were possessed of acute senses of noblesse oblige, at least according to orthodox history. They had in mind always the welfare of the nation at large. James Madison may have denied the ordinary citizen's ability to divine the common good, but he doubted not at all his own capacity to deliver it.

The dispersed nature of the federal structure was notably successful in keeping the citizens separated from their government, and separated as well from each other. Community was beyond reach.

To call this democracy is offensive to all but the most untutored in their history. At best it was a paternalistic aristocracy. No more than one in forty citizens could vote. Only the nation's elite were put in office. Thereafter there was utterly no citizen access to its deliberations, and the totality of the federal government, as we have seen, was accountable to no one.

Democracy and community were not necessary to foster the general welfare of society: Collectively, the individual pursuit of private gain would do so instead. Here is how Daniel Kemmis explains it:

> Republicans [Jefferson and his sympathizers] believed that public life was essentially a matter of the common choosing and willing of a common world—the "common unity" (or community), the "public thing" (or republic). The federalists [Madison, Hamilton, and others] argued that it was possible—in fact it was preferable—to carry on the most important tasks without any such common will-ing of a common world. Individuals would pursue their private ends, and the structure of government would bal-ance those pursuits so cleverly that the highest good would emerge without anyone having bothered to will its existence. It was no accident that this approach to public life was put forward by people who were centrally inter-ested in creating optimal conditions for an expanding commercial and industrial economy. The federalist plan of government was exactly analogous to Adam Smith's invis-ible hand, which wrought the highest good in the market even though none of the actors were seeking anything beyond their own individual interest. Smith introduced the concept of the invisible hand into economics in 1776. Twelve years later, Madison introduced it into politics.[17]

In the economic and political realms of the late 1700s, the uninhibited pursuit of private gain would assure the welfare of society at large. Not democracy, not community, only freedom.[18]

No one could foresee where the reliance on private gain would

---

17. Kemmis, *Community and the Politics of Place*, p.15.

18. In 1965, a well-regarded book appeared in the scholarly literature of politi-cal science, called *The Intelligence of Democracy* (New York: Free Press, 1965). Through a process of "partisan mutual adjustment," American democracy, the book argued, achieved a socially optimal state of affairs without any cen-tralizing authority to coordinate conflict. It did this through the self-inter-ested bargaining between interest groups. The book displayed Smith's the-ory of a free-market system applied explicitly to political affairs. The author, Charles E. Lindblom, was an economist at Yale.

lead. But before a century had elapsed, the characterization of the American economy shifted dramatically from the small and numerous agrarian yeomen, so highly regarded by Jefferson, to the commercial and industrial enterprises so highly regarded by the Federalists, which grew to unprecedented size and power. This could happen because the nature of citizenship would be altered radically when a new species of citizen was created. Within the century ahead, citizens in the countryside and citizens in the cities would be joined, in the freedom to pursue private gain, by the Northern Pacific Railway, Carnegie Steel, Standard Oil, and other corporate citizens with uncommon, indeed inhuman, features.

These "citizens," their descendants, and others like them would embody and energize the overshoot of American capitalism and American politics. They would fashion license from freedom.

The Federal Lands from 1788 to 1891

Assembling the Federal Lands Empire

Most of the English Crown grants to the colonies extended westward as far as the Mississippi River. After ratification, the states drew their own western boundaries generally at the limits of white settlement, assigning their westward claims beyond to the new federal regime. This was the "original public domain," and it consisted of 237 million acres.[19] These lands were reconstituted eventually as Ohio, Indiana, Illinois, Michigan, Alabama, Mississippi, Tennessee, Wisconsin, and a respectable piece of Minnesota. They account for 12.2 percent of the total area of the continental United States today.

The next transaction was twice that size. Much has been written about Thomas Jefferson's delight with farming and farmers. He was convinced that wholesome "republican virtues" of honesty, morality, and civic responsibility flowed from independent

---

19. The numbers and dates to follow were taken from the classic works *The Federal Lands: Their Use and Management,* by Marion Clawson and Burnell Held (Lincoln: University Press of Nebraska, 1957); *The Federal Lands Since 1956: Recent Trends in Use and Management,* by Marion Clawson (Washington, DC: Resources for the Future, 1967); and *The Federal Lands Revisited,* by Marion Clawson (Washington, DC: Resources for the Future, 1983).

citizens working the land. Secure in their labors and their property, only such citizens could come together into a larger community and pursue consciously a general welfare or a common good. The structure of the Constitution resulted from a contradictory philosophical view, as we have seen. But the behavior of the citizenry—pushing westward, raising concurrently barns and families—must have given Thomas Jefferson great hope. His singular anxiety is easy to imagine: When the expansion of agriculture reaches the Mississippi River, what then?

His singular response had to await his presidency in 1803. He sent $15 million to France, and bought the rest of Minnesota; all of Nebraska, Arkansas, Missouri, North Dakota, South Dakota, and Iowa; almost all of Kansas and Oklahoma; most of Montana and Wyoming; and a good quarter of Colorado. The Louisiana Purchase added 560 million acres to the federal lands empire.

No future president matched the magnitude of Jefferson's achievements in real estate investment, but his impetus continued. In 1819 a successor bought Florida from Spain for $6 million. California, Nevada, Utah, Arizona, half of New Mexico, and a third of Colorado were purchased from Mexico in 1848 for a total of $16 million, although it took armed conflict to demonstrate to the Mexicans the wisdom of selling. The rest of New Mexico and Colorado, and chunks of Oklahoma, Kansas, and Wyoming were bought from the state of Texas for $15 million in 1850. Three years later the southern border of Arizona was expanded by 19 million acres in another $10 million purchase from Mexico. Oregon, Washington, Idaho, and the remainder of Montana and Wyoming were added to the public domain by negotiating with Great Britain in 1846. In 1867 the federal government bought Alaska from Russia for $7 million and change. Finally in 1898, overriding the vigorous protest of Queen Liliuokalani, Hawaii was simply "annexed" as a "possession."[20]

Over a period of ninety-five years, with an out-of-pocket

---

20. This was done at the behest of the corporate sugar plantations in Hawaii, which shipped the bulk of their output to the mainland United States. With annexation, their production was rendered domestic and no longer subject to import duties.

expenditure of $69 million, 1,848 million acres were bought or otherwise acquired from France, Spain, Great Britain, Mexico, Russia, the citizens of Texas, and the monarch of Hawaii. These acquisitions account for 80 percent of the nation's total land area today. By any measure a bargain.

Dividing the Spoils: Redistributing the Federal Lands

It was a bargain by any measure but the Native Americans'.[21] From the territory of the Seminoles to the land of the Aleuts, cultural appraisals, traditions, and institutions of land tenure were swept away. In their place was created a federal lands empire, a "public domain" defined by another culture in altogether different ways, and for altogether different purposes. Once redistributed, the land would no longer be used fundamentally for the sustenance of life and community, but for the propagation and accumulation of private wealth—thought to be the progenitor of the common welfare in the United States. An unfettered market economy and the Constitution would see to that.

What this meant in practice was turning the citizenry loose on the existing wealth of a continent.

There was one slight but significant exception. National defense was seen, evidently, to be a public good. In an era of the supremacy of sea power for the conduct of foreign policy, and facing the apparently constant technology of wooden ships, some of that natural wealth had to be reserved to benefit a greater public. As early as 1799 some of it was—in the form of live oak, cedar, and pine on a series of "naval reserves," federal lands to be withheld deliberately from private acquisition. The Santa Rosa Naval Reserve near Pensacola, Florida, was especially noteworthy for at least two reasons. It displayed some early examples of deliberate forest management, and it constitutes an early example of fast political footwork in turning public assets to private gain: The federal judge for west Florida and the state's delegate to Congress were paid $9,000 for 1,400 acres they happened to own within the

---

21. A simple question illuminates the enormity of imperialism's injustice: What rights did France have, and Spain, Mexico, Great Britain, and Russia, to sell all this land? Another question illuminates our complicity: What right did the United States have to buy it?

exterior boundaries of the reserve—which the good congressman had voted to establish.

The reserves eventually totaled 264,450 acres in Florida, Alabama, Mississippi, and Louisiana. Maintaining public land in public ownership for the public good was established in public policy, a significant novelty. The practice would not surface again for three generations, but the precedent had been established. Had the development of iron shipbuilding occurred one generation earlier, however, setting aside the naval reserves might not have been necessary.

The redistribution of the federal lands did not wait until the inventory was completed. Accumulation and redistribution proceeded concurrently for the best part of a century. Land was offered for cash, initially and chronically for $1.25 per acre. When cash was short, credit was extended. The land claims given to veterans of military service were frequently resold and became the fungible bases for decades of speculation. Simple but extralegal occupation of land—squatting—was signally popular among the venturesome and vigorous but unpropertied; the Preemption Act of 1841 legalized it but also imposed the $1.25 per acre sale price. That unfortunate burden was lifted in 1862 with the passage of the Homestead Act. Altogether 288 million acres of federal lands were acquired by homesteaders.

Large grants of lands were made to the states upon entry into the Union, typically for the support of education—which accounted for the transfer of 94 million acres; or to collateralize the construction of canals, wagon roads, and other infrastructure—which accounted for 169 million acres more; or to encourage the draining of swamps—another 65 million acres, which suggests an extraordinary amount of marshland originally dotting the countryside.

Aside from the grants to the states, the general intent of the disposal laws was to transfer land to individuals and families. This accorded well with Jefferson's rugged agrarian democracy, and it was apparent in law after law that limited the qualified applicants to heads of families, widows, or single men over twenty-one years of age. And the laws specified small, subsistence-type parcels—typically 160 acres, a pattern that lasted into the twentieth century, appearing in the Reclamation Act of 1902. The General Mining Act of 1872 was also written for individual, not corporate citizens: Discoverers and claimants of mineral values were entitled to those values, without the payment of any royalties or fees to the U.S. Treasury whatsoever. Again, the claimants were envisioned to be the rugged hardscrabble prospectors of popular imagination, and the claims were expected to be correspondingly small parcels of land. The consolidation of large expanses of public land under singular control was neither desired nor anticipated.

The limiting factor to further expansion and settlement was clearly the lack of transportation infrastructure. But technical and institutional innovations occurred that offered great promise: The corporate form of enterprise, the improvement of steam railway technology, and the superior durability of steel rails compared to iron. The railroad corporation became an operational feature of the American economy, and so did Carnegie Steel.

Congress with energy and imagination exploited the opportunity, eventually deeding 94 million acres to railroad corporations to subsidize constructing the transcontinental routes. As we have seen, most of the lands have since been dispersed among livestock, mining, irrigated agribusiness, and timber corporations.

Those land transfers were for the most part executed with proper contracts between corporate entities, but large consolidations of public land took place by less savory methods, too. "Dummy" entrymen were a legend in the West. Hired by land speculators, or directly by timber companies and ranch owners, they filed claims under the various land laws, immediately to turn them over to their employers, who thereby accumulated large contiguous tracts of public land. One such scheme was masterminded by a gentleman in Oregon named Stephen A. Douglas Puter. In an act of apparently genuine contrition, conditioned perhaps by his status as an inmate at the time, he wrote a classic book, *Looters of the Public Domain,* but the lootings were far more frequent than the confessions.

The century-long frenzy of shifting public wealth into the hands of citizens failed to anticipate corporate citizenship. Certainly a coast-to-coast democracy of hardworking men and women and their families, secure in their labor and their property, manifesting virtue and a civic responsibility for the greater community, never materialized. The emergence of corporate enterprise contributed to the failure, but we need at least briefly to look beyond public land policy for some other clues.

Democracy Tries Again . . . and Again

The Limited Role of Parties and Interest Groups

Majoritarian democracy failed to emerge because the Constitution's deliberate barriers proved both effective and durable. Two attempts at circumvention were turned aside.

The first attack was the maturation of an institution of political parties. If it was not a well-structured system at the time of the Constitutional Convention, there was at least visible a political schism. The Federalists preferred and achieved a government of aristocratic paternalism. The other "party," nominally headed by Thomas Jefferson, was simply called the Anti-Federalists. As that particular focus faded after ratification, those of Jefferson's persuasion came to be known as "Republicans," a term Jefferson himself used in his inaugural address.[22]

Why did a system of parties become so popular and eventually so thoroughly institutionalized? When American citizens eventually realized their government was inaccessible to them, they must have been unhappy. Their discomfort was no doubt attenuated by what their government was doing—placing before them the wealth of a continent, either free or at irresistible discount. Still it is pleasant, in the construction of society's rules, to have one's preferences heard or accommodated. The party system was a means of achieving this.

The Constitution was silent about political parties, but citizens could easily recall the party systems in Europe and how they functioned to mobilize and empower a majority. Perhaps someone said, "Let's give it a try here." As the U.S. parties evolved, however, they had to confront the Constitution's deliberate fragmentation: The components of the governmental process had been separated thoroughly in time and space, so the parties could not

---

22. The discussion here is developed from Leonard D. White, *The Federalists,* fn. p. 51. Jefferson's "Republicans" begat, en route to the twenty-first century, the Democrats.

possibly orchestrate its control. They could capture the government neither all at once nor all in a single place.

The parties could recruit, campaign, and elect the dramatis personae in the many and varied jurisdictions, but there was no way, after the election, to exert a systematic influence on public policy. The Virginia Republicans in Congress could not bear heavily on the Republicans from Massachusetts, or vice versa, since they were campaigned and elected by totally different sets of people.[23] There was no way for President Washington to keep the Federalists from all the states in a single frame of mind or to insist on their loyalty in the manufacture of policy, since he had neither rewards nor punishments at his disposal.

The parties could not guarantee, then, the enactment and execution of any particular policy proposal. Senators, congressmen, and the president were free to propose and support any policy initiative they chose, utterly independent of party affiliation and utterly free of any systematic partisan discipline. The party system would be described forevermore, by succeeding generations of political scientists, as a "weak" one. "*Great* political parties," a contemporary political observer wrote, "are not to be met with in the United States at the present time."[24]

Via the nascent political parties, some citizens of the United States—the few who could vote—gained access to the selection and election of candidates, but they were still denied access to the process of constructing society's rules. The initiative for public policy still lay with the paternalistic aristocrats.

Having failed to gain access with their party system, the American people tried again by inventing another extra-Constitutional institution, the political interest group, which was visible by the mid-1800s. Now they could approach the patronizing aristocrats

---

23. Our "two-party" system today is far more accurately described as a 102-party system. Sharing only the names, the Republican and Democratic parties in each of the fifty states are utterly separate in terms of personnel, objectives, funding sources, candidates, and policy agendas. Every four years two more national organizations arise to elect a president—and they too are utterly separate in terms of personnel, objectives, funding sources, candidates, and policy agendas.

24. Alexis de Tocqueville, *Democracy in America* (New York: Washington Square Press, 1964), p. 64.

and register their policy preferences, speaking with united and focused voices.

The descriptive nomenclature ranges from the florid to the bland: special interests, single-issue organizations, pressure groups, stakeholders, clientele groups, interest constituencies, and simply "associations." In no other society on earth, however, do citizens band together so fiercely and so politically effectively on the basis of shared interests and attitudes. There are associations of retired persons, stamp collectors, physicians, gun owners, livestock growers, county commissioners, and hundreds of thousands more in countless categories, all of which resort to political activity at the slightest threat to the interest they share. In Washington, DC, today there is an organization called the American Society of Association Executives, a monument to 150 years of Americans indulging their propensity to consort.

By the end of the nineteenth century, the evolution of political interest groups had altered the nature of governance in the United States, in ways the Founding Fathers would have found repugnant. It was not by any means a majoritarian democracy: The Constitution continued to prevent that. But aristocratic paternalism could no longer be pursued in isolation. Governance had become a "pluralistic" democracy of politically active citizen organizations (and, as we shall see, corporate organizations, too).

Scholars of political science documented the transformation as early as 1908. Arthur Bentley wrote: "We shall always find that the political interests and activities of any given group—and there are no political phenomena except group phenomena—are directed against other activities of men, who appear in other groups, political or other. . . . The society itself is nothing other than the complex of the groups that compose it."[25]

Well into the nineteenth century it was paternalistic aristocrats who identified problems and crafted solutions utterly disconnected from the citizenry, but eventually the initiative for policy formulation was seized by the totality of the interest groups. Various groups brought problems to the attention of Congress, often

---

25. Arthur F. Bentley, *The Process of Democracy* (Cambridge, MA: Belknap Press, 1967), p. 222.

with preferred solutions. Congress then served to ratify public policy, no longer to initiate it.

The interest group system helped democratize American politics, but "democratize" is a slippery word. In coming to dominate the policy-making process, the group system provided citizens a route of direct access to government, and participating freely and voluntarily in political affairs is an element of "democracy." To that degree, the group system was a salutary institutional development.

But if democracy means "government by the people," the Constitution can claim the final round of mirth. It continues to "keep citizens apart," but now they are separated in groups, not as autonomous individuals. Each group may succeed in furthering a narrow and parochial interest, but there is still no mechanism to articulate, much less to pursue, the interest of the community at large. The "people," even if defined as a majority, are powerless to express common preferences and to have them accommodated.

The majority remains silent by constitutional design.

Portents of a New Era

Parties and interest groups—aided by an expanding franchise—served to broaden popular participation in governance as the nineteenth century closed. American political institutions were developing satisfactorily, and they were not yet overdeveloped.

In that time, small groups of citizens did not and could not profit at the expense of the common good. But that is the effect, the norm, of political pluralism today. Contemporary interest groups prey frequently on each other, as Bentley suggested, but some have come also to prey chronically on society at large—which is, by constitutional design, defenseless—and with gross injustice on society to come. Professor Bentley didn't see this at the turn of the century. Technical and institutional developments that contributed to the overshoot of American politics were not yet visible. Television campaigning, political action committees, and the corporate financing of elections come to mind.

The institution of corporate enterprise per se, however, had become starkly visible. Already a target of political regulation at the end of the nineteenth century, it would become the major causative agent of economic and political overshoot in the twentieth.

The nation's resource base was expanding as the 1800s closed, from improving infrastructure, and from new value perceptions and technologies. New resources became. Some, like petroleum, were tangible; others were less so. The cultural perception of utility in natural beauty and the tonic effect of outdoor life cannot be attributed exclusively to just a few individuals. But Frederick Law Olmsted, Henry David Thoreau, and the Hudson River School of landscape painting made noteworthy contributions to the becoming of the new scenic resources.

By 1869 such resources were firmly in the minds of some intrepid Montanans, who undertook an exploratory survey into the headwaters of the Yellowstone and Snake rivers. They were impressed with what they saw. They succeeded in impressing others and in gathering political support. Within two years a group of like-minded people took a policy proposal to the U.S. Congress. Interest group politics had supplanted the isolated aristocrats.

Among those offering support was the Northern Pacific Railroad, whose right-of-way skirted the northern boundary of the policy proposal. A large tract of land, full of natural wonders, to be held "inalienable for all time" and dedicated to "public use, resort, and recreation" might prove an unbeatable way to stimulate traffic from Chicago. This was no proprietary cobbler speaking, but corporate capitalism. President Grant signed the legislation on March 1, 1872, that created Yellowstone National Park. Three thousand square miles were set aside—nearly 2 million acres—and the law specified that "all timber, mineral deposits, natural curiosities, or wonders [shall remain] in their natural condition."[26]

The timber and minerals were made inaccessible, but what of the newly become resources of scenic beauty and outdoor recreation? The Northern Pacific stood ready to turn them to private gain, and did so for generations into the future. It proceeded to "dot the new Park with hostelries and furrow it with lines of travel."[27]

---

26. The quote, and a paraphrased description of the politics involved, is taken from Nash, *Wilderness and the American Mind*, p. 113.

27. Ibid., p. 113.

Yellowstone's designation is better seen as a unique circumstance than an abrupt reversal of one hundred years of privatizing the federal estate, but a tangible threat to that policy occurred nineteen years later. The politics of the Forest Reserve Act of 1891, as we will see in the next chapter, argued that private ownership and management of forestland was positively damaging to a wider public interest. The law was the genesis of the national forest system, which would be owned and managed by a public agency. A dash of crypto-socialism, perhaps, and other federal land agencies followed. But corporate capitalism eventually found easy means of subversion. No longer the land, but always the tangible commodity resources of the land, would continue to be privatized and liquidated. Public ownership and management would not be the least impediment to the private pursuit of public wealth.

Overt aristocratic paternalism was fading in 1891, as Americans enjoyed expanding access to the governmental process. Democracy tried to circumvent its constitutional preclusion, and in a peculiar, pluralistic, and limited way it had succeeded. But in the economics and politics of freedom, the foundations of license had been laid, and corporate capitalism would exploit the opportunity.

Chapter Three

Altering the Foundations
of License, 1891–1934

Trading Sovereignty for Abundance: The Rise of Corporate Capitalism

Responding to political distress about the malfunctioning economic system, the U.S. Congress undertook a great wave of reform legislation as the nineteenth century ended. Included was a series of laws that gradually halted the transfer of federal lands into private ownership. The first was the Forest Reserve Act of 1891, and the last was the Taylor Grazing Act of 1934. Timber, forage, water, and minerals continued to be freely accessible to citizens both sentient and corporate, but a substantial alteration in the foundations of license was accomplished: The land itself would be held as common property.

Along the way, however, the sovereignty of American consumers was relinquished, as free-market capitalism gave way to corporate capitalism. In exchange, consumers were provided with a cornucopia of goods and services unparalleled in history, and it must have seemed a decent bargain.

Free-market capitalism requires that citizens should be discrete human beings with finite lifespans. A parity of citizenship has to be maintained, so no single citizen can take systematic advantage of another in the ubiquitous bargaining of the marketplace. If any citizens can accumulate economic power without limit and come to exist in perpetuity as well, they will enjoy an absolute advantage, and that will render meaningless the ability of free-market capitalism to optimize social welfare.

Such citizens appeared. For decades during the nineteenth century, corporations lobbied and litigated with vigor and eventually with victory to be treated as any other citizen.[1] The brilliance of their success is enshrined in a Supreme Court case of 1886, *Santa Clara County v. Southern Pacific Railroad,* which held that a corporation was indeed the equivalent of a natural, flesh-and-blood citizen, and therefore enjoyed the protection of the Constitution and the Bill of Rights. The ability of society to control its corporations, so jealously constructed and enforced for better than a century, came to an abrupt end. (We will examine corporate existence in some detail below.)

As more and more corporate citizens joined the pursuit of private gain, they succeeded easily in constraining the freedom of the markets. Flesh-and-blood citizens faced fewer and fewer corporate producers from which to buy consumer goods, and to which to sell their productive resources—typically their labor. As the freedom and the sovereignty of consumers diminished, free-market capitalism was simply overwhelmed by corporate capitalism.

Corporations constrain freedom in the "producer goods" markets by exiting those markets at will. Capital needs can be met by retained earnings, to avoid the financial markets. Raw material markets are meaningless for vertically integrated corporations: Instead of buying calfskins in the hide market, you simply buy a cattle ranch and grow your own. And domestic labor markets are avoided today when the entire manufacturing process, say, is relocated to a *maquiladora* across the border in Mexico.

---

1. See Richard Grossman and Frank T. Adams, *Taking Care of Business: Citizenship and the Charter of Incorporation* (Cambridge, MA: Charter, Ink, 1993).

The impact of corporate citizens on consumer goods markets has been no less severe, but a seductive outcome masked the loss of individual sovereignty: The output of consumer goods in both quantity and variety rose to exceed anything in history. Living standards skyrocketed, stoked by levels of per-capita consumption never before imagined.

To make this possible, the resource base had to be expanded dramatically, and the corporate citizens did that. Coupled to the incentives of capitalism for innovation, and to the political stimulation of private gain, the expansion of scientific and technological capabilities was breathtaking. So too was the expansion of the nation's resource base, accordingly.

Copper became a critical resource in the rapidly expanding production, distribution, and application of electrical energy. The technology of steel fabrication transformed both marine and terrestrial transportation. Powering the ships and trains, the steam engine redefined coal as a source not only of thermal energy, but now of mechanical energy in large and concentrated quantities. The mechanization of agriculture, manufacturing, mining, and milling could not have taken place without it. At the beginning of the period, petroleum catapulted from neutral stuff to resource, and by the end of the period it was indispensable; steam power was rapidly displaced by internal combustion engines.

Thus a rapid expansion of the T variable, the technology variable, induced a rapid expansion of the nation's resource base. But the U variable—the perception of utility—influences the resource base, too. So long as wants and needs were stable and autonomous, as we saw in the last chapter they were during colonial times, the resource base would be limited to those substances needed to fulfill them. But if wants and needs could be enlarged, the resource base could expand to accommodate them, simply by applying the new technologies or developing yet newer ones. For the first time in human history a deliberate stimulation of wants and needs was undertaken during this period.

There were a number of reasons for this, but one stands above all others. As we will scrutinize soon in greater detail, mass production techniques were developed early in this period, and by its end they were commonplace. But mass production was pointless unless mass consumption followed, and that could be assured, it was discovered, by mass marketing through mass communication media.

As the twentieth century began, the mass media were print media. The great city newspapers soon carried advertisements for Ivory Soap, Quaker Oats, and Hire's Root Beer,[2] and if all the city papers across the country carried the same ads, a national market could be developed for soap, breakfast foods, and soft drinks. As national magazines proliferated, the nationalization of markets could and did continue.

Henry Ford was probably the first to understand another prerequisite to mass consumption; unilaterally, he doubled the wages of his labor force, to enable those who built his cars to buy them. This lesson was less apparent to other corporate producers, but not to their labor forces. During this period, unionization and collective bargaining drove wages up, assuring sufficient buying power in the mass markets.

Advertising was a conscious effort to create perceptions of utility, and rising incomes provided the capacity to indulge them.

National advertising and the development of new technologies called for large concentrations of capital, and the growth and development of American corporations exploded. Small logging operations could not bring together sufficient capital accumulations for the huge steam-powered Lidgerwood Interlocking Skidders, or to build logging railroads. The Weyerhaeuser corporation found it easy. Prospectors with picks and shovels could scarcely develop the hardrock mines of the Anaconda Copper Mining Company. And in the production of consumer goods from toasters to automobiles, corporate enterprise blossomed as well. The corporation became the dominant form of business enterprise.

During this period the transformation of free-market capitalism to corporate capitalism was completed. Sentient citizens could no longer roam the markets seeking the best bargains they could strike. Now they confronted corporate citizens who were not inclined to bargain and didn't find it necessary. The corporate citizens could and did dominate the markets for producer goods,

---

2. These were some of the first "brand names" advertised as such. See "Advertising" in *Microsoft Encarta 1997 Encyclopedia,* 1997, the Microsoft Corporation.

and they were learning how to manage the markets for consumer goods.

In time, American consumers would no longer go to the market to get what they wanted; they would go there to learn what they wanted. The prudent, austere, careful, and rather simple consumption patterns that lasted from colonial days well into the nineteenth century would be transformed by the institution of advertising into the high-consumption throwaway lifestyle characteristic of the twentieth.

The corporation provided abundance, but in the markets consumer sovereignty disappeared.

Confronting Corporate Capitalism: A New Mission for the Federal Lands

Corporate capitalism was liquidating the nation's forested estate as rapidly as market forces would allow. Left behind were devastated mill towns and wastelands of stumps and logging debris, which bred astonishing fires. In 1871, some 1,182 people were killed when 1.2 million acres burned near Peshtigo, Wisconsin, and 418 more died near Hinkley, Minnesota, in 1894. The practice of "forest devastation" became a potent political issue, and it was not an isolated concern.

As the nineteenth century was winding down, the corporate pursuit of the American Dream was generating pathologies only the dim-witted could fail to see.

The employment of eight-year-old girls in textile mills or equally young males in the coal mines became, in sequence, a standard practice, a social disgrace, and another national political issue. Child labor and forest devastation were only two examples of corporate excess. The marketing of tainted food and drugs was another. The conscious "restraint of free trade" was, too, as corporations formed combines and trusts, and entered into collusive agreements to do so.

How could these things happen in "free-market capitalism"? According to Adam Smith, and presumed by the Founding Fathers, not only individual welfare but a social *optimum optimorum* was to flow from the unconstrained pursuit of private gain. Had something misfired along the way to the twentieth century?

The Corporate Citizen

The Smith model of a free-market economy depended on a rough equality of numerous buyers and sellers to guarantee parity in the marketplace, in fact to guarantee the freedom of the market. No single party could dominate, or even materially influence, the market as a whole, so that all the many participants could move freely to their locus of best advantage. The discipline of such a competitive system is harsh: Mortality among proprietary producers is high, but the sovereign consumers prosper, secure in their knowledge of quality products efficiently made.

With the emergence of corporate capitalism in the nineteenth century, fewer and larger producers came to characterize more and more markets. It takes little analytical brilliance to see the dangers this posed for free-market capitalism. With fewer and fewer corporate sellers in the markets for consumer goods, the bargaining power of the consumers is increasingly compromised. And with fewer and fewer corporate buyers in the markets for producer goods, the sellers there—typically the sellers of labor—were exploited as well, with neither compassion nor restraint. Something was indeed misfiring. The markets were no longer free.

The modern corporation, i.e., after *Santa Clara County*, is a marvelous creature of institutional ingenuity. Chartered by a state government, it becomes a legal persona with rights, privileges, and obligations that are utterly independent of any human being: The corporation is as ephemeral as an angel, or a demon. It can enter contracts of any sort, it can incur and redeem debt, it can buy, hold, and dispose of property of any kind, it can be taxed or relieved from taxes, and it can be damaged and sue for relief, or be sued by others for damage it might incur. All these transactions can occur either between corporate entities or between corporations and real people.

Modern corporations bear little resemblance to the corporate builders in earlier times of canals and toll roads. Colonial charters typically limited the lifespan of the corporation. Modern charters typically do not: The corporation is established "in perpetuity." Colonial charters typically and strongly delimited the purpose of the corporation—to build a canal, for example. Modern charters typically do not: Most empower the corporation to undertake virtually any enterprise and to change what it undertakes at will. (A company once called the Catheter Corporation of America now makes and markets toothpaste.) Finally, colonial charters held stockholders personally liable for corporate misdeeds, and modern charters certainly do not: The stockholder's liability is limited to the value of his or her holdings.

A peculiar citizen has indeed appeared in the marketplace. The modern corporation is immortal and boundlessly versatile. Through acquisitions of or mergers with other corporations, it is capable of limitless growth. Modern corporations have become uncontrolled, uncontrollable, unaccountable, and lately transnational concentrations of economic and political power unprecedented in human history.

Neither Adam Smith nor the Founding Fathers ever saw one.

The oldest and largest of the great corporate structures so visible in the economy today gained their status of invincibility only after decades of secular evolution. In the nineteenth century, they began as extensions of the personalities of the "captains of industry" enshrined in the folklore of commerce: John D. Rockefeller, Jay Gould, Andrew Carnegie, J. Pierpont Morgan, Jay Cooke, James J. Hill, and others. These men felt a great deal of ownership in their corporations by virtue of retaining large, often controlling blocks of common stock in their own names, and in this respect early corporations differed little from proprietorships: Ownership and management were fused. As a consequence the "captains" were subjected to at least a degree of accountability. They enjoyed personally and directly the pleasures of their corporation's success or endured the pain of its failure.

Their corporations as a matter of legal definition lived on, and in time they would turn for corporate leadership to the nation's growing pool of MBAs and lawyers. Not charismatic but professional managers eventually rose to the leadership positions in American corporations. Ownership and management were separated, and the last source of corporate accountability disappeared.

Not so for corporate power. In its purest and most common form, corporate power is maintained by lodging in one person the roles of chief executive officer and chairman of the board of directors.

The board of directors serves two purposes: Ostensibly it represents the stockholders' interests, and it is alleged to be the source of corporate strategy and policy making. It serves, in other words, a legislative function, so that naming one person to be the chief executive and simultaneously chairman of the board creates, in a commercial setting, the equivalent of a prime minister. A single locus of enormous power is created. It is not, however, subject to capture by a majority in any sort of election.

The professionalized managements of large modern corporations play immensely powerful roles in the affairs of our society and in the character of our culture. At their disposal are the bulk of society's productive factors—invested capital, highly skilled labor, and in recent times huge pools of liquid assets, or "money." Thus is conveyed not only the obvious economic power, but also enormous political influence: The magnitude of corporate financing of political campaigns has become a national scandal. Corporate managements of today are as insulated from the citizens of the nation as the "paternalistic aristocrats" were in the late 1700s, and the decisions they make are no less important. We will revisit this issue of corporate power and autonomy in chapters to come.

As the consolidation of production into fewer and fewer corporate hands continued in the late 1800s, the canon of economic behavior regarding efficient production was at least adequately fulfilled.

Legend has it that Eli Whitney first applied the concept of interchangeable parts, boosting production efficiency in a truly revolutionary way. The next logical step did, too: arranging sequential assembly into a production-line configuration.

The combination of specialized labor, interchangeable parts, and sequential assembly was a recipe for the manufacturing of products literally en masse, but it posed a serious problem. The potential for overproduction became real, immediate, and acute. The appearance of a solution must have been slow and sporadic, but it would have profound and malign impacts on the American society, on the biophysical environment, and on the federal lands in the years to come.

Corporate enterprise would have to recast the entire character of the consumer-goods marketplace to ensure that mass production would be counterbalanced with mass consumption. The marketplace of sovereign consumers, independently expressing their autonomous preferences would have to be reorganized and regimented so that common, identical preferences would be registered, without deviation and without interruption. To exploit the potential of mass production, a homogeneous high-consumption society would have to be crafted. The way to do this was to aim common messages of education and influence about the benefits of consumption, and common persuasive themes about standardized products, to the consumers en masse indeed. Today we call this "advertising," and no other economy on earth has done so much with it.

Mass marketing would depend on mass communication, and that would depend on the development of mass media technologies. Newspapers, magazines, and books abounded in the late 1800s, empowering the few to speak to the many, but they depended on mass literacy to be effective. The advent of compulsory education assured a society able to read, but in the twentieth century that ability was rendered irrelevant. Radio advertising suggested the possibility and then television advertising confirmed it: A lucrative market could as well be illiterate.

Whatever else might be said of corporate enterprise, it cannot be faulted for inefficient production—or for failing to transform a nation from prudence into profligacy.

But what about the other social imperative of a provisioning system, the canon of equity? Much has been written about the corporate excesses that had accumulated by the late 1800s. Child labor, tainted foods, shoddy products, sweatshops, appallingly unsafe and unsanitary working conditions, and the trend toward combines, trusts, and monopoly finally became intolerable. Inequities by any measure abounded.

Included in this inventory was the destructive clear-cutting of the federal-lands forests in Michigan, Wisconsin, and Minnesota, the issue that was finally denoted as "forest devastation." Since the demand for lumber products was expanding rapidly as settlement crossed the treeless plains; and since the lake states pineries were a ready source of supply; and since the expanding rail network soon connected the two; and since there was literally no legal means of acquiring public timber resources for cutting, the lumber mills simply helped themselves. It was not petty larceny: 394 million board feet of white pine were cut along the St. Croix River in the decade of the 1840s, for example, authorized by the law of supply and demand, perhaps, but not by any other.[3]

To redress these inequities the American people late in the

---

3. Quoted in Paul W. Gates, *History of Public Land Law Development*, written for the Public Land Law Review Commission, 1968. See p. 537. Gates refers to Agnes M. Larson, *History of the White Pine Industry in Minnesota*, Minneapolis, 1949, but says, "Mrs. Larson offers as her only source for the table, A.D. Cooke of the U.S. Surveyor General's office in St. Paul."

1800s abandoned Adam Smith and the market system, no longer so free. They turned to public policy instead. Using the novel institution of the political interest group, they achieved, for the federal lands, an astonishing alteration in the foundations of license. We will look shortly at the details.

American corporations learned to play a political game, too. These abstract citizens took a different approach to gaining access. Instead of creating political interest groups, the corporations captured a political party and transformed presidential politics.

Initially, there had been no corporate hesitation to play both sides of the street, contributing to either party or both. James J. Hill of the Great Northern, for example, gave $10,000 (in today's currency, say about $200,000) to Grover Cleveland's Democratic campaign in 1892, and with excellent foresight. It was Cleveland's attorney general, Richard S. Olney, who ingeniously used the Sherman Anti-Trust Act against Eugene Debs and the Pullman strikers in 1894—and eventually broke the strike with U.S. Army troops. Democrat Cleveland was no friend of labor. But then Hill switched his support vigorously to the Republicans in 1896.

Hill's move was not fickle. That was the year the parties staked out the policy stances and crystallized the clientele axes that endured for many years. The Republicans would represent corporate capitalism. The Democrats would represent the consequentially disadvantaged.[4]

The Republican nominee, Congressman William McKinley, had risen to prominence by sponsoring a stiff increase in the protective tariff, of huge benefit to corporate America. At the convention, the party also adopted an unequivocal stance on the gold standard, of no less benefit to corporate America.

Cleveland's power base had been the bloc of "gold Democrats" in the Northeast, primarily the New York bankers. But at the Democratic convention, the agricultural southern and midwestern factions, the silver miners from the West, and working-class people everywhere—disadvantaged by both the high tariff and the

---

4. The overshoot of American politics lay eight or nine decades in the future. This partisan distinction would remain visible until then, when the Democratic party veered sharply to the right, unable to forgo the corporate financing of increasingly expensive television campaigning.

gold standard—nominated William Jennings Bryan, a Nebraskan of distinctly anti-corporate persuasion.

The alignment of the nation's two economic strata with the two political parties had never been so clearly drawn.

The campaign of 1896 was extraordinary in other ways. It marked the emergence of a political boss with national stature— Mark Hanna, the Ohio capitalist—and it displayed three innovations of Hanna's that would characterize presidential politics for generations to come. One was superb grassroots organization. By the time of the national convention, McKinley's nomination was the merest of formalities, so thoroughly had Hanna canvassed the state organizations for prior and binding commitments of delegates. Another was the first use of mass media advertising in political campaigns. Hanna printed and distributed 120 million copies of 275 different pamphlets, written not only in English but also in German, Polish, Yiddish, Italian, Swedish, and other languages.[5] And the last was the willingness to raise and spend breathtaking amounts of money, which both of the activities above absorbed in great quantity. Official records list Bryan's campaign costs at $675,000 and McKinley's at $3,350,000.[6]

It was an important election for corporate interests to win, and their tactics were less than wholesome: James Hill and Mark Hanna pressured corporate boardrooms again and again for the financial resources necessary, and company after company clarified for its employees that a Bryan victory would mean locks on the factory doors the following day. McKinley won, and the strategic policies so vigorously sought by American corporations—high protective tariffs and the gold standard—were established.

But this was constitutional, not majoritarian politics. Corporate capitalism could still be opposed through interest group action, and it was. Great ad hoc coalitions could achieve surprising victories. Corporate enterprise was vanquished in the child labor issue, for example, by a combination of organized labor and

---

5. See Matthew Josephson's companion classic, *The Politicos: 1865–1896* (New York: Harcourt, Brace and World, 1963). p. 699. This book was published originally in 1938.

6. Ibid.

the well-orchestrated, articulate, and humane mothers of the country.

As the practice of interest group politics evolved, a new view of the role of government emerged. Corporate capitalism had interfered with free markets in structural ways; the American people sought equity by interfering in political ways. Government regulation of the market process came to be sought and appreciated widely, a development over which later, conservative economists would suffer great intellectual dyspepsia. They would write books harshly criticizing the period and the practice of regulation, with such lurid titles as *The Birth of a Transfer Society,*[7] and *Capitalism and Freedom,* the classic by Milton Friedman.[8]

This is not to say that the institutional changes had been trivial. Thomas Jefferson and James Madison both would have been amazed at the reworking of economic and political processes the nation had accomplished in a span of ten decades.

---

7. See Terry L. Anderson and Peter J. Hill, *The Birth of A Transfer Society* (Palo Alto, CA: Hoover Institution Press of Stanford University, 1980). Anderson, Hill, and other "free-market economists" find deplorable the nineteenth-century emergence of interest groups making claims against each other. Doing so, they argue, involves the transfer of property without compensation and hence is very unattractive at the outset. But the resources expended to effect transfers are otherwise unproductive, and thus constitute social waste in addition. Society should depend instead on the market to effect transfers, they assert, a far more efficient mechanism of exchange. Theirs is a clever, academic spinning of theory, rendered fundamentally irrelevant in the messy world of reality. Anderson and Hill understand the beguiling symmetry of Adam Smith's market system far better than they understand subsequent de facto history and the quantum shift represented by the institution of incorporation. If children can be bought from their parents in a system of markets, to labor thereafter twelve hours a day, there is something wrong with the system, not the parents.

8. Milton Friedman, *Capitalism and Freedom* (Chicago: University of Chicago Press, 1962). Professor Friedman celebrates the freedom in the marketplace for neckties, which allows consumers to choose any color they wish. Otherwise, the majority-rule property of politics would impose a common color on everyone. His casting of politics in a majoritarian mode erects a straw man of heroic proportions and displays Professor Friedman's ignorance of constitutional history. His formula for the prevention of majority rule is virtually congruent with what the Founding Fathers did, in fact, design. Such fetching naivete did not handicap Professor Friedman's service in the Reagan administration as chairman of the Council of Economic Advisors: Indeed, it may have been required.

Sylvan Prosperity and the Corporate Threat: The Ideological Underpinnings of a Policy Shift for the Federal Lands

The first concerns about the rapid exploitation of American forests were voiced by the scientific community. The issue of forest devastation was joined, but it was never clearly delimited or defined. Did forest devastation mean only that trees were cut down? Did it refer as well to the frequent occurrence of subsequent wildfires blazing through the logging debris left behind? Did it truly suggest that the nation's forests were being transformed into utter wastelands, never again to support the growth of trees?

The rapid cutting of American forests was conspicuous even to scientists in Europe, but the situation initially aroused curiosity, not concern. In 1842 a French naturalist simply saw an opportunity for research: "M. Boussingault . . . expresses his opinion . . . that extensive clearings [of forests] lessen the amount of rain which falls in a given district; and he expresses a hope that the vast changes going on in America will not be allowed to pass away without affording materials for placing this matter on a sure basis."[9]

The proper weighting and evaluation of human impact was another element of interest. One writer thought it was conspicuous, but comparatively insignificant:

> The changes produced by the agency of civilized man . . .
> though not of great importance when compared with
> those which result from the unceasing operation of natu-
> ral causes, are interesting to the naturalist. . . . In . . . the
> United States . . . such changes have occurred with great
> rapidity, converting, in a few years, uninhabited forests to
> countries having the aspect of regions long inhabited by
> civilized man.[10]

---

9. *The Penny Magazine* of the Society for the Diffusion of Useful Knowledge, Vol. 11 for 1842, London: Charles Knight and Company, pp. 502–503.

10. John William Dawson, "On the Destruction and Partial Reproduction of Forests in British North America," *Edinburgh New Philosophical Journal* 42 (October 1846–April 1847). Edinburgh: Adam and Charles Black, pp. 259–271. Note the invisibility of 18 million Native Americans.

This benign judgment was sharply challenged by a book whose influence would come to dominate the politics of forest devastation. In May of 1864, simultaneously in London and New York, George Perkins Marsh's book *Man and Nature; or Physical Geography as Modified by Human Action* was published.[11] His argument was this:

> Nature, left undisturbed, so fashions her territory as to give it almost unchanging permanence of form, outline, and proportion. . . . [12] But man is everywhere a disturbing agent. Wherever he plants his foot the harmonies of nature are turned to discords. . . . [13] The ravages committed by man subvert the relations and destroy the balance which nature had established between her organic and her inorganic creations; and she avenges herself upon the intruder, by letting loose . . . destructive energies, hitherto kept in check. . . . [14] Man has too long forgotten that the earth was given to him for usufruct alone, not for consumption, still less for profligate waste.[15]

Marsh's exemplary landscapes were those around the Mediterranean Sea. He was the ambassador to Rome for twenty-one years, when foreign policy was less demanding of its adminstrators. At some leisure he studied the barren hillsides around the Mediterranean, and, reading in two dozen languages, he studied as well in the region's libraries. He synthesized a sequence of misfortune and consequent results: Strip away the forests, expose the topography to accelerated soil erosion, and there would appear "bare ridges of sterile rock" in the highlands and a "luxuriance of aquatic vegetation that breeds fever and more insidious forms of mortal disease" in the lowlands. Choked harbors and stalled commerce follow, and finally "the earth is rendered no longer fit for the habitation of man."[16] Marsh was well aware of the rapid clearing of forests in the United States, and here was a theory capable of predicting the outcome: Sterile rock, pestilential swamps,

---

11. George Perkins Marsh, *Man and Nature; or Physical Geography as Modified by Human Action,* centennial edition (Cambridge, MA: Belknap Press, 1965).
12. Ibid., p. 29.
13. Ibid., p. 36.
14. Ibid., p. 42.
15. Ibid., p. 36.
16. Ibid., p. 187.

human habitation made unfit. The evil of human activity would destroy the nobility of balanced nature, and humanity would suffer: It could be called the Marsh syndrome.

Even the most casual reading of the book, however, reveals gross inconsistencies. For Marsh was also a respectable, if amateur, engineer. He applauds a potential canal from the Mediterranean to the Dead Sea, 653.3 feet lower in elevation, anticipating a virtual recreation of the garden Eden when some three thousand square miles of "evaporable area" are added to the region. He can scarcely contain his enthusiasm for diking the North Sea in Holland and constructing the Suez Canal—"the greatest and most truly cosmopolite physical improvement ever undertaken by man."

Man and Nature fails to distinguish which human activities are "ravages committed by man" turning nature's harmonies to discords, and which are "cosmopolite physical improvements." But clearly the ideology of conservation, congealing in the nineteenth century and surviving as environmentalism today, adopted only Marsh's pejorative view of humanity and the corollary thought that humanity is somehow distinctly separate from "nature."

The separation is deeply ingrained in Euro-American culture, made explicit in our language. That which is "natural" is free of human influence, while artifacts and influences of human origin are deemed "artificial." We will explore in subsequent chapters the mischief this cultural separation causes, and we will look at some implications of overcoming it.

Marsh did not originate the notion, but neither did he equivocate. Charles Scribner, his publisher, was piqued about this and queried Marsh in a letter, "Does not man act in harmony with nature? And with her laws? Is he not a part of nature?" Marsh replied:

> No, nothing is further from my belief, that man is a "part of nature" or that his action is controlled by laws of nature; in fact a leading spirit of the book is to enforce the opposite opinion, and to illustrate the fact that man, so far from being . . . a soul-less, will-less automaton, is a free moral agent working independently of nature.[17]

---

17. Marsh, *Man and Nature,* p. xxiv. David Lowenthal edited the text of the Belknap edition of Marsh's book, from which these quotes are drawn. The exchange of correspondence between Marsh and Scribner is recalled in Lowenthal's introduction.

His jaundiced judgment was unmistakable in speaking of forests: "the too general felling of the woods has been recognized as the most destructive among the many causes of the physical deterioration of the earth."[18] Then he brought the Marsh syndrome home: "It is certain that a desolation, like that which has overwhelmed many once beautiful and fertile regions of Europe, awaits an important part of the territory of the United States."[19]

Not all the contemporary reviews were enthusiastic. One raised the issue of mankind's role and noted: "He seems to forget in his large conclusions that to preserve the forest is in many cases to narrow the space allotted by Providence to the growth and maintenance of mankind. Finding 'tongues in trees' he allows them to speak somewhat too loudly in their own behalf."[20]

That reviewer did what fewer and fewer would do in the future: He read the entire book carefully and noted Marsh's ambivalence about man's agency. He concluded, "There is what we may best describe as a want of *back-bone* to the volume."[21] (The italics are in the original.)

Nevertheless, *Man and Nature* was rewritten, republished, or reprinted in 1865, 1867, 1869, 1871, 1874, 1877, 1895, 1898, and five times more in the twentieth century. The publishing history of the book demonstrates that it was widely distributed, and the influence was large by any standard. Turning forests through human improvidence into sterile wastelands and pestilential swamps was powerful imagery, and as the finer inconsistencies of *Man and Nature* were overlooked or forgotten, the Marsh syndrome would alter profoundly the politics of license.

The rapid deforestation was soon noticed by domestic periodicals. An 1871 article asserted:

> At the present increased rates of consumption, it is believed that the timber now growing in the lake states

---

18. Ibid., p. 189.

19. Ibid., p. 201.

20. Anon., *The New Edinburgh Review or Critical Journal* 20 (1864), Article VI, "Man and Nature; or Physical Geography as Modified by Human Action, by George P. Marsh," pp. 464–500. The quote here is on p. 478.

21. Ibid., p. 467.

will be all cut and marketed within fifteen or twenty years. . . . It is generally admitted that an equal demand upon our redwoods in the future, as has been made during the past, will obliterate them from our shores within the course of a few years only.[22]

The *New York Times* echoed this sentiment: "California has, perhaps, 500,000 acres of forest now, of which fully one-half has been cut away within the last two or three years."[23]

F. L. Oswald, a physician, made a "plea for our forests," relying on both passion and contemporary medical science. Deforestation causes the spread of deserts, Dr. Oswald explained, because, in his words, "forests produce rain."[24] Human populations are decimated as deserts spread, because diseases, once held in check by "the disinfecting influence of forest air," rise to epidemic proportions. In the "Valley of the Quadalquivir," Oswald reported, "a population of 7,000,000 shrank to a million and a quarter sickly wretches. . . ." Deserts, famines, pestilence Oswald saw, "and all this change is due to the insane destruction of forests."[25] His debt to Marsh was not acknowledged, but he had diagnosed the syndrome, adding sickly wretches to the list of symptoms.

Oswald proposed a novel remedy: a political intervention. He urged protection in law for "the woods of all the upper ridges in hill countries." A similar suggestion came from Harvard. Professor Charles S. Sargent, a botanist there, was probably more knowledgeable about U.S. forests than anyone else writing at the time. Sargent noted that forests provide public values that transcend or at least supplement their private value as commodities, and said forthrightly that federal control is necessary where "the forests . . . cannot long survive the wasteful and shortsighted

---

22. Taliesen Evans, "Western Woodlands," in *Overland Monthly* 6 (1871). San Francisco: John H. Carmany and Co., p. 225.

23. *New York Times*, October 21, 1874, p. 4.

24. F. L. Oswald, M.D., "The Climatic Influence of Vegetation—A Plea for Our Forests," in *Popular Science Monthly* 11 (May–October, 1877). New York: Appleton and Co., p. 4.

25. Ibid.

methods of individual management. . . ."[26] Do we see Professor
Sargent here calling corporate capitalism to task?

George Perkins Marsh left no doubt. Addressing the "rotten-
ness of private corporations," he wrote:

> I shall harm no honest man by endeavoring . . . to excite
> the attention of thinking and conscientious men to the
> dangers which threaten the great moral and even political
> interests of Christendom, from the unscrupulousness of
> the private associations that now control the monetary
> affairs, and regulate the transit of persons and property, in
> almost every civilized country. More than one American
> State is literally governed by unprincipled corporations,
> which not only defy the legislative power, but have, too
> often, corrupted even the administration of justice. . . . I
> believe the decay of commercial morality, and I fear of the
> sense of all higher obligations other than those of a pecu-
> niary nature . . . is to be ascribed more to the influence of
> joint-stock banks and manufacturing and railway compa-
> nies . . . than to any other one cause of demoralization.[27]

Then as now private enterprise also had its passionate defenders, and political intervention to them was unthinkable. "The
Government of the United States," one such partisan proclaimed,
"has no more concern in holding or managing forest property
than it has in working its unoccupied wheatfields." Continuing his
paean, the writer continued:

> Individuals can grow timber, and take care of it when
> grown, better than the Government, and the less the Gov-
> ernment mixes itself up with business of this nature, the
> better. . . . The forests of Michigan or Louisiana may be
> exterminated, as have been those of New England, with-
> out seriously affecting the nation as a nation. Such forests
> will grow again if profit can be found in growing them.[28]

---

26. Charles S. Sargent, "The Protection of Forests," in *North American Review*
    135 (October, 1882).

27. Marsh, *Man and Nature*, p. 51.

28. "A National Forest Preserve," *The Nation: A Weekly Journal* (New York:
    Evening Post Publishing Company), September 6, 1883, p. 201 ff.

No free-market economist could have said it better.

Soon some finer distinctions were drawn. "If the forests were to be used instead of destroyed," *Century* magazine argued in 1886, there would be no insurmountable problem:

> But the American woodman does not understand the distinction. . . . All the Western mountain forests should be withdrawn at once from pre-emption or sale—a step which would not, of course, prevent the government from deriving a considerable revenue, in time, for the sale of timber which could be spared.[29]

Perhaps the commodity resources could be made available while the land remained in public ownership. It would take eleven years to accomplish this in statute, but that would be the direction federal land policy would take. The pursuit of private gain could continue.

Congress in 1876 had established in the Department of Agriculture a Division of Forestry to study the general situation of forests and forestry. By 1886 the division was the de facto forum for the debate about forest devastation and a clearinghouse for proposed solutions. The chief of the division was a naturalized German professional forester, Bernhard Eduard Fernow. Born in 1851 to an aristocratic family in Prussia, he was a well-educated, perceptive, and rather scholarly man. In time he proved, somewhat in violation of his inclinations, to be a consummate political operative, in revolutionizing federal land policy.

Fernow found Marsh's book provocative and sound. "An extensive literature on the subject of forest benefits has now accumulated," he wrote. "But I do not intend to rehearse these often-cited arguments, which are so well elaborated in George P. Marsh's classical book, *Man and Nature*." Instead, Fernow wrote in *Popular Science Monthly* what became his own standard treatise and policy position.[30] Always proud of his citizenship, he under-

---

29. Joseph Edgar Chamberlain, "Will the Land Become a Desert?" in *The Century Illustrated Monthly Magazine* 31, New Series vol. 9 (November1885–April 1886). New York: The Century Company, pp. 532–536.

30. B. E. Fernow, "Our Forestry Problem," in *Popular Science Monthly* 32 (November 1887–April 1888). New York: D. Appleton and Co., pp. 225–236.

stood the nuances of American institutions with extraordinary sophistication:

> Our difficulties lie mainly in the unique manner in which our country has been settled, and in the spirit of our institutions, which is too prone to resent interference with private rights, even where the common interest seems to call for such. In Europe government is so regarded as to give wider scope to its action, and not only are government forests and forestry permissible and natural, but government interference, if for the interest of the general welfare, is borne less impatiently.

He wrote with grace and understatement, but Fernow overlooked a central fact: The Constitution had precluded by design and with inordinate success the systematic articulation of the "general welfare." The general welfare would result automatically from free citizens boundlessly exercising their "private rights." Fernow was focused, however, on the fundamental difficulty that had arisen: The Founding Fathers had not anticipated corporate citizens, and could not have imagined the social costs they would incur.

Fernow then went on to explain the Marsh syndrome and concluded with a resolute call for action:

> From this hurried view of the relation which the forest cover of the earth holds toward the economies of Nature, it should appear that more than a private interest must attach to it; that, whenever men are aggregated as a nation or a government for the protection of the public against the willfulness of the few, the care of the forest should receive earnest and timely consideration, and, if necessary, legislative action. . . . Let the United States Government, which still holds some seventy million acres of the people's lands in forests, . . . set aside . . . and manage them as a national forest domain.[31]

An editor for the *New York Times* was impressed and wrote an editorial on May 3, 1889, entitled "The National Forest," warmly

---

31. Ibid.

advocating the idea. Another followed on August 24 of that year, praising the "Division of Forestry of the Department of Agriculture, and at its head . . . a capable man, Mr. E.B. [sic] Fernow, zealous in his duties and fully appreciative of their importance." Then Professor W.R. Fisher, writing in *Nature* magazine, condemned the "utter absence of a State forest policy in the United States" and roared, "How long will the rulers of the United States shut their eyes to the appalling waste of the resources of their country which is still rampant? . . . all European experience points to the necessity of State forests."[32]

European experience would soon guide the way in the United States.

The Politics of Confronting Corporate Capitalism

Passing of the Forest Reserve Act in 1891 exemplified the operation of American political pluralism at the close of the nineteenth century: Overt aristocratic paternalism had been overtaken and left behind.

There was no need to marshal a majority. Doing so was then, as it continues to be now, a constitutional impossibility. To alter or initiate public policy, a special interest group needed only to convince a handful of key legislators, for by now Congress had put in place its complex and durable system of standing committees. Great deference was paid them: A "do pass" recommendation to a full chamber was rarely overridden.

The interest group's task was made easier in the absence of opposition. Corporate capitalism did not participate visibly in the resolution of the forest devastation issue, because other issues bore down more directly and heavily: child labor, the purity of food and drugs, protective tariffs, the gold standard, and antitrust sentiment. But the reorientation of the federal lands was very much a part of countercorporate reform, and the politics were typical.

The Interest Groups

In 1845 a physician, Dr. Franklin B. Hough, was admitted to membership in the American Association of Geologists and Nat-

---

32. W. R. Fisher, "Forestry in North America," in *Nature* 40 (January 15, 1891). New York: MacMillan and Co., p. 48.

uralists. Three years later, the organization broadened its outlook and adopted a new name, the American Association for the Advancement of Science (AAAS).

Darwin's *Origin of Species* appeared in 1859 and, among other cultural traumas, it fostered the growing intensity of interest in science. Othniel C. Marsh addressed the AAAS in 1877 to proclaim: "To doubt evolution . . . is to doubt science, and science is only another name for truth."[33] The association certainly shared that view, along with a conviction that discoverable natural laws could and should serve as a guide to morally right behavior. Technical forestry would be presented as a scientific enterprise to the AAAS in a few short years, by Bernhard Fernow, and would assume this mantle of righteous truth.

Another physician, Dr. John Aston Warder, joined the association in 1851, indulging as Hough did an interest in horticulture, botany, and natural history. In 1875 Dr. Warder formed, in Chicago, the American Forestry Association, the first interest group to focus exclusively on the forest devastation issue. By 1889 it had merged with or absorbed a number of like-minded groups to become an effective political force with a truly national membership. (The American Forestry Association survived until the 1990s, when, after years of declining membership and increasing reliance on corporate financing, it adopted the trendy but oblique name of American Forests, and lapsed into self-serving irrelevance.)

In 1889 there was a substantive policy objective to be won. Forest devastation had to be halted and reversed, and two interest groups stood ready. In the American Association for the Advancement of Science a small group of men was interested in the issue, and in the American Forestry Association nothing else mattered.

The Ideologies

Dr. Franklin B. Hough and the AAAS came to represent one of two policy stances in the forest devastation issue.[34] Theirs began

---

33. Paul F. Boller, "New Men and New Ideas," in H. Wayne Morgan, ed., *The Gilded Age: A Reappraisal* (Syracuse, NY: Syracuse University Press, 1963), p. 237.

34. The differentiation of two distinct strands of thought or definitions of forestry is discussed in a dated but rather charming way in Herbert A. Smith, "The Early Forestry Movement in the United States," in *Agricultural History* 12, no. 4 (October 1938).

with a "forest culture" bias, an emphasis on tree planting, and made a generally passive prescription. It developed into a "data-and-demonstration" approach, and it relied on science, not surprisingly: The collection and dissemination of scientific data would lead to the morally correct handling of forestland. Thomas Meehan read a paper at the 1874 annual meeting of the AAAS that reiterated the virtue in tree planting and forest culture, insisting that the private sector, explicitly not the government, should carry out the program.[35] A "Report of the Committee on the Preservation of Forests" was presented at the same meeting. The report paraphrased—a stern critic would say it plagiarized—*Man and Nature* in describing the irreversible consequences of the "destruction of forests": floods, erosion, sterile wastelands. (It is cheerfully silent about sickly wretches.) It prescribes liberal doses of data dissemination by the government but cautions that "operations of planting and management must . . . be left to private enterprise."[36]

John Aston Warder and the American Forestry Association held a different view, which called for public ownership and professional management. Warder had been the U.S. Commissioner for Forestry and attended the World's Fair in Vienna in 1873. He came home impressed with European forest policy, and wrote a one-hundred-page report, forthrightly staking out a strikingly different approach than "data-and-demonstration":

> The increasing scarcity of timber within the first century of the nation's history and that in a country famous for the richness and value of its sylva, and for the extent of its woodlands, is a subject that calls for the most serious consideration of the statesman, and perhaps for the interference and care of the government.[37]

That was a truly radical proposition to make; happily, it was buried in a House of Representatives report, where it could be

---

35. See pp. 37–45, *Proceedings of the American Association for the Advancement of Science,* 23rd Annual Meeting, held at Hartford, Connecticut, August, 1874. Published by the Permanent Secretary, 1875.

36. Ibid., p. 42.

37. Quoted in S. T. Dana, *Forest and Range Policy* (New York: McGraw Hill, 1956), p. 87.

ignored, but as it was being filed away in 1876, a young man was stepping off a ship in Philadelphia. In large measure, he would be responsible for exhuming it.

Fernow, the Catalyst

The bridge between the ideologies and the two interest groups as well was Bernhard Fernow.[38]

Fernow had attended the forest academy at Muenden, studying under the eminent German forester Gustav Heyer. The classic forestry Fernow learned was rationalized by the mercantilistic economy, stratified society, and cameralistic politics of Germany in the seventeenth and eighteenth centuries—institutions colossally at odds with the freebooting capitalism and ostensible democracy of the United States in the ninteenth century. State ownership and a rigid adherence to a sustained-yield cutting budget, determined and enforced by public professional foresters, were its central tenets.

Fernow's arrival in 1876 was not by accident. He may have attended the American Centennial Exposition in Philadelphia, and indeed there was an exhibit about forestry manned by Hough and Warder. There is no record of the three foresters—one professional and two avocational—making contact until six years later. Fernow's priority was a young Philadelphia woman named Olivia Reynolds whom he had met on the Continent.

Miss Reynolds's charms deserve far more credit in the history of North American professional forestry. It would be thirty years before Fernow returned to Germany, and then only for a brief visit. Instead, he chose to forgo a sizable inheritance of forestland in Prussia, to become a U.S. citizen, and to seek successfully Olivia's hand in marriage. Thereafter he headed the federal forestry agency for twelve years, catalyzed the passage of the Forest Reserve Acts, founded the first American school of forestry and the first in Canada as well, and established the patterns and format of professional forestry existing still in both nations.

In 1876, however, there was not yet a palpable need for a pro-

---

38. The standard biography is Andrew Denney Rodgers III, *Bernhard Eduard Fernow: A Story of North American Forestry* (Princeton, NJ: Princeton University Press, 1951). Much of the exposition to follow comes from this book.

fessional forester. Fernow worked as a scribe in a law office. Then he invented a scheme for electrically reclaiming the tin from tin cans and learned the uncomfortable difference between technical and economic success. His next venture was less capital-intensive: He taught German. Then he was an assistant bookkeeper in a hardware firm. Finally in 1879, after his marriage to Miss Reynolds, Fernow was hired by an iron works firm, Cooper, Hewitt and Company.

The web of personal relationships, not always visible to but ever critical in the dynamics of interest group politics, began to form. Fernow's position was arranged by a friend of his wife's family, a consulting engineer often retained by Cooper, Hewitt named Rossiter Raymond. He had served with John Aston Warder as another commissioner to the Vienna Exposition in 1873 and was likewise familiar with European forestry. Raymond was a good friend of Abram S. Hewitt.

Hewitt, a Democratic congressman from New York and one of the partners in the firm, had served in 1876 as chairman of the Democratic National Committee. This contact would prove valuable to the reform of federal lands policy—and to Bernhard Fernow.

Fernow managed a charcoal-fired iron furnace in Slatedale, Pennsylvania, for Cooper, Hewitt. He corresponded with John Birkinbine, editor of the *Journal of the U.S. Association of Charcoal Iron Workers*. Birkinbine was impressed with Fernow's argument for sound, sustained-yield management of forests to stabilize the iron industry—it would assure a supply of charcoal—and published a number of Fernow's papers. Birkinbine would serve later as president of the Pennsylvania Forestry Association, which established the first major forestry periodical. *Forest Leaves* first appeared in 1886 and served well the publicity needs of the forest reform movement.

But before that, in 1882, Birkinbine sent Fernow, representing his journal, to a forestry meeting in Cincinnati. There, six years after landing in Philadelphia, Fernow met Hough and Warder in person. The old amateurs and the young professional had intersected, and Fernow's activities in the reform initiative intensified from that time on.

In 1883 Fernow left Cooper, Hewitt and moved to New York. Here the persona of Abram S. Hewitt takes on a certain poignance in the career of the young forester. Grover Cleveland, the former mayor of Buffalo, New York, was elected president in 1884, the first Democrat in twenty-four years. Hewitt was not only Fernow's prior employer, but, as congressman from New York and former chairman of the Democratic National Committee, he knew Cleveland intimately. Within two years, Fernow was appointed by President Cleveland to be the chief of the Division of Forestry in the Department of Agriculture.

Except for two overriding factors, the appointment smacks of partisan patronage. First, Fernow was uniquely qualified for the task, as the nation's sole forester with professional credentials—in glaring contrast to his predecessor in the forestry agency, a Congregational minister. And second, Fernow was a lifelong Republican. He had good friends in strategic locations, but he was no partisan hack.

Now Fernow had a forestry platform, and for a long time he'd had a program: the need to constrain the periodic harvest of timber by its periodic growth;[39] the beneficial effects of a protected forest on hydrologic conditions;[40] and the need for state regulation or outright ownership.[41]

The last element was the genesis of the abrupt turnabout in federal lands policy, and Fernow was candid about it. In a speech to the AAAS, he argued:

> The forest resource is one, that under the active competition of private enterprise is apt to deteriorate and in its deterioration to affect other conditions of material existence unfavorably; the maintenance of continued supplies, as well as of favorable conditions, is possible only under the supervision of permanent institutions, with whom present profit is not the only motive. It calls preeminently for the exercise of the providential functions of the State to counteract the destructive tendencies of private exploitation. In some cases restriction of the latter may suffice, in others ownership by the State or some smaller part of the community is necessary.[42]

---

39. Ibid., p. 124.

40. Ibid., p. 98 and passim.

41. Ibid., p. 92 ff.

42. Quoted in Dana, *Forest and Range Policy,* p. 86.

That played well to the American Forestry Association. According to his biographer, Fernow also held the conviction that the scientific and economic laws undergirding forestry were universally appropriate,[43] and that would appeal greatly to the American Association for the Advancement of Science. Fernow would manage brilliantly to orchestrate his political support into a policy-making success.

Legislating the Forest Reserve Act

By the late 1800s the secular development of political institutions had relocated the initiative for the formulation of public policy. It had shifted from the paternalistic aristocrats isolated in Congress to the spectrum of interest groups, where problems were identified and prospective solutions crafted, to be taken thereafter to Congress for ratification in law. Such was the case precisely with forest reform.

In 1873 the American Association for the Advancement of Science appointed a committee for "bringing to the notice of . . . Governments . . . the subject of protection to forests. . . ."[44] Franklin B. Hough was its chairman. He spent most of the winter in Washington, asking Congress to create a commission of forestry to investigate, document, and publicize the facts of the forestry situation—in other words, data and demonstration. There was not a word about nationalizing forestland.

Congressman Mark H. Dunnell of Minnesota, sensitive to the heavy cutting occurring in his state, introduced reform legislation, but it died in the 43rd Congress. When the 44th convened, Hough was back and so was Dunnell. The bill was introduced again but stalled in the Committee on Public Lands. In August, Dunnell appended the bill's substance to an appropriation act for fiscal year 1877—to this day a favorite tactic to circumvent a reluctant committee—and it sailed into law.

This was a crucial step in the reform of federal land policy. Because of it, we hold today 673 million acres of federal land as common property, and it was done with a parliamentary gimmick. No majority had willed it. No majority was even aware of it.

---

43. Ibid., p. 98.

44. See p. 10, Section B, *Proceedings of the American Association for the Advancement of Science,* 22nd meeting, held in Portland, Maine, August, 1873. Published by the permanent secretary, 1874.

In November of 1876, at an annual salary of $2,000, Hough was appointed commissioner of forestry to pursue the forest investigations. He would be succeeded in time by Nathaniel H. Egleston, the Congregational minister, who would yield the position to Bernhard Eduard Fernow. About a year after Hough was appointed, he submitted a 650-page report. It contains five enthusiastic references to "the admirable work by our countryman, George P. Marsh,"[45] a great appreciation for data-and-demonstration, and a lot of practical tips about tree planting.

For the time being, the more aggressive and radical approach to the forest devastation problem—public ownership and management—would have to simmer in John Warder's American Forestry Association, and in the keen mind of Bernhard Fernow, then laboring at his iron furnace in Pennsylvania.

In 1883, Fernow became the secretary of the American Forest Congress, and he was quick to learn the dynamics of interest group politics. "The newspapers were good to us and we kept them supplied with trumpet blasts before the AFC meetings and glowing accounts of what was achieved," he wrote. "I learned then the power of the press and the names and methods to conjure with. The gospel spread!"[46]

By 1884 the American Forestry Congress, meeting in Washington, was moving quickly toward Fernow's position, even though both Hough and Egleston were there. Fernow spoke about a system of government forests that would ultimately "pay its own expenses from the sale of ripe timber." And F.P. Baker, one of Egleston's employees—he now had three—outlined the specifics of a professionally trained career service to administer such forests. There was no dissent, but much "enthusiasm and earnestness" instead.[47]

With the American Forestry Congress gaining strength each year, Secretary Fernow and President Warren Higley, both New Yorkers, undertook to form a state group, the New York Forestry

45. F. B. Hough, *Report upon Forestry* (Washington, DC: Government Printing Office, 1878), p. 309. Other references to Marsh appear on pp. 76, 80, 268, and 334. (The index, in contrast to the absence of a table of contents, is remarkably comprehensive.)

46. Rodgers, *Bernhard Eduard Fernow,* p. 79.

47. Ibid., p. 92.

Association in 1885. It did not ultimately survive, but Abram S. Hewitt was there, and it was shortly afterward, apparently, that he recommended to President Cleveland Fernow's appointment to the Division of Forestry.

"In 1886," Fernow wrote later, "having resisted the tempter for half a year, because a politician and not a forester was needed for the position, I accepted the call to take charge of the forestry work in the Department of Agriculture."[48] His dues were paid in full, but his plan for a system of national forests, professionally managed, would take another eleven years to put in place. The politics of interest group pluralism was halting and inefficient in Fernow's day, when the players were amateurs. They had been trained in medicine, botany, and forestry, not the law. Fernow spoke with high volume, much truth, and great prescience when he admitted to inappropriate credentials.

Shortly after his appointment, he began drafting a piece of legislation that came to be known as the Hale bill. It was a complete package: A system of land classification and reservation of permanent public forests to be administered by a corps of professional managers. (Drafting legislation in executive agencies deviated markedly from the practices the Founding Fathers emplaced. In time, it would become routine.) For an amateur Fernow did a creditable job.

In 1888, Senator Eugene Hale from Maine introduced Fernow's package. The most radical provision—nationalizing the forests—was enough to kill it in committee. Support for the bill was concentrated almost exclusively in the East, where federal lands and resource values had already been privatized. Unalterable opposition centered in the West, where such opportunities remained.

In 1889 Fernow spoke to the American Association for the Advancement of Science, assembled in Indianapolis, on "The Need of a Forest Administration in the United States." The two ideologies might have collided, but the association was so impressed with Fernow's argument that an ad hoc committee was appointed to scrutinize it carefully. Chaired by the AAAS president, T.C. Mendenhall (Fernow was appointed secretary), the

---

48. Ibid., p. 108.

committee was no splinter group of tree-planting political conservatives. Indeed, it repudiated the data-and-demonstration approach as insufficient and adopted Fernow's package essentially intact.

The Mendenhall Committee and the American Forestry Association drafted a joint memorial to both Congress and President Benjamin Harrison. It called for reserving the forested federal lands from private acquisiton, and for an interim committee to study and propose legislation for subsequent administration, thus separating the major elements of Fernow's program. In April, Harrison agreed to the proposal and sent it to Congress on January 20, 1890. Representative Mark Dunnell, whose rider had established Hough's position fourteen years earlier, introduced appropriate legislation.

Neither Dunnell's legislation nor the Hale bill, Fernow's complete package, passed during the session, but the most radical departure from existing policy, the idea of forest reserves, was made into law in a wholly unexpected and capricious way.

An altogether unrelated land reform bill, the General Revision Act, had passed both houses in slightly different form and was in conference committee in early March of 1891. In a midnight meeting, Interior Secretary John W. Noble, apparently acting independently, inserted an amendment simply granting the president the authority to withdraw forest reserves from private entry. The new Section 24 was a long and grammatically incorrect sentence, and it failed to specify any use of the reserves or any form of administration.

The amendment violated the congressional rule prohibiting the addition of new material in conference committee, but there it was. When the conference committee bill was presented orally, four days prior to adjournment, hardly anyone in either chamber was aware of the truly radical provision in Section 24. The conference bill was enacted, and President Harrison signed it the next day.

The obscure, arguably illegal Section 24 eventually became the best remembered feature of the law, which historians chose eventually to call the Forest Reserve Act of March 3, 1891.

Thus a long chain of citizen participation in interest group politics culminated in a bizarre parliamentary stroke. Fernow himself had to speculate on what had happened in that midnight meeting: "I do not know who drafted the exact clause, but I know it would never have been inserted if we—that is, those who were actively carrying on the forestry propaganda—had not educated the Secretary of the Interior to the propriety of this move."[49]

Within the next two years, Presidents Harrison and Cleveland used the law to withdraw about 18,000,000 acres of federal land from private entry. The century-old policy of transforming public lands into private property was confronted, and so was corporate capitalism.

The achievement was not widely appreciated. A year and a half after the Forest Reserve Act was enacted, the *New York Times* was still calling for forest reservations to be established,[50] and almost two years elapsed before the editors realized the legislation had passed.[51]

The Federal Lands as Public Lands

Fernow could not yet retire to a life of scholarly, academic respite from his political exertions. First he had to put in place the rest of his package: the public—and scientific—management of the reserves.

It was a difficult task, made more so by the voices of anxious curiosity that arose when many Americans, not excepting some elected to the Congress of the United States, learned what had happened on March 3, 1891. There was no little talk of repealing Section 24. If the reserves were to survive at all, some means of rationalizing them, and of managing them, had to be provided, and soon.

Twenty-seven bills respecting the forest reserves and their administration were introduced between 1891 and 1897. Hardly anyone could agree on anything until a group of scientists was established to study the situation and to make recommendations. The president of the National Academy of Sciences, Walcott

---

49. Ibid., p. 155.

50. "The Forest Lands," *New York Times*, September 27, 1892, p. 4.

51. "The New Forest Reserves," *New York Times*, February 27, 1893.

Gibbs, appointed a "Forest Commission," which undertook the inquiry. Eventually, the commission filed its recommendations: not about use, not about administration, but only about creating more forest reserves.

On February 22, 1897, President Cleveland proclaimed some 21,000,000 acres of new reserves, more than doubling the existing system.

Congress nearly had a seizure. In the tumult that followed, even another rider to an appropriation bill was possible. Senator Richard Pettigrew from South Dakota tacked it on this time, to the "Sundry Civil Expenses Appropriation Act for Fiscal Year 1898," which was signed into law on June 4, 1897. It directed that the reserves were to be established only to secure "favorable conditions of water flows, and to furnish a continuous supply of timber for the use and necessities of citizens of the United States." The secretary of the interior was directed to establish rules and regulations for the use and protection of the reserves.

Most of Fernow's program was left unspecified, but none of it was overtly prohibited, and the idea of nationalizing forested land had survived.

Within the year, Fernow left to organize a school of forestry at Cornell, and Gifford Pinchot took his place in the Division of Forestry. The position still called for a politician, not a forester, and Pinchot met that standard with distinction. His credentials in forestry were a bit suspect, anyway—he had "studied with" some eminent European foresters but had not completed a certification program.

Pinchot succeeded eventually in having the forest reserves transferred to his jurisdiction in the Department of Agriculture; in having his agency renamed the U.S. Forest Service; in recasting the forest reserves as "national forests"; in expanding the size of the system to about 150,000,000 acres; and in growing his staff and budget, over an eight-year span, from 11 people and $28,520 to 1,391 employees and $1,195,218, respectively. That is consummate bureaucratic politics. In 1898, the Division of Forestry sported (by including Pinchot) 2 professional foresters. By 1905 there were 153.

Nationalizing the forestland proved to be a popular innovation in federal resource policy. It could well be called crypto-socialism:

public ownership and management in fact, but unacknowledged as such.

Perhaps the next most spectacular example, both chronologically and in eventual magnitude, was in the "reclamation" of arid lands. Two competent books describe the socialization of irrigated agriculture in the West. One is Donald Worster's *Rivers of Empire,* which speaks of irrigation in the "local subsistence mode" to describe what might have been: small-scale, indigenous irrigation technology applied by resident farmers using exclusively their own labor and essentially their own capital. The words "hardy yeomen" come to mind, and Jefferson's agrarian democracy might have occupied at least some of the arid West had that mode of irrigation obtained. Instead, a "capitalist-state mode" was put in place; the financing, engineering, construction, and bureaucratic operation of a colossal and complex irrigation system by the federal government, to the stratospheric advantage of the capitalistic, typically absentee, and eventually corporate landowners. On the land is not an agrarian democracy but a rigidly stratified "hydraulic society" of shamefully differentiated incomes: Whole families of resident aliens laboring on hands and knees, while the beneficiaries of subsidized agribusiness drive Cadillacs across the desert.

Cadillac Desert is, in fact, the title of Marc Reisner's book. It is the empirical companion to Worster's cultural and institutional history, describing the manic drive to spread the costs of irrigation across society at large while capturing a highly concentrated stream of benefits.

Tragic social injustices and degraded western landscapes resulted from the Reclamation Act of 1902. The act appeared to favor the small landowner residing on the land, as no more than 160 acres could be irrigated by any one owner, and the ten-year, zero-interest loans for the projects seemed designed for small, independent operators, too. But, in fact, the act created a tool of plunder for the wealthy and the corporate.

The primary beneficiaries early in the irrigation game were not quite the stature of Rockefeller, Carnegie, Morgan, and Hill, but they were regional counterparts with similar instincts and skills. In California, Moses Sherman, Henry Huntington, and Edward Harriman (railroads); Joseph Sartori and L. C. Brand (banking);

William Kerckhoff (electric utilities); Edwin T. Earl, Harry Chandler, and Harrison Gray Otis (newspapers) banked millions speculating on San Fernando Valley land, made immensely valuable when the California Aqueduct was built from the Owens Valley to Los Angeles. *Cadillac Desert* chronicles their achievements.

There were also immortal citizens, corporate citizens, growing larger and politically influential. They would have reclamation policy and law amended, to nullify the residency expectation and the acreage limitation, and to extend the repayment period fourfold. Such citizens as the Prudential Life Insurance Corporation, Chevron Oil, Getty Oil, and Shell Oil; Tenneco, and the Southern Pacific Railroad would come to own and operate irrigated farms occupying hundreds of thousands of acres, all watered by the Bureau of Reclamation.[52]

Crypto-socialism turned out to be not as effectively, or as openly, and certainly not as uncomfortably countercorporate as it seemed in the 1890s. The land or the irrigation works may have been socialized, in the proximate sense of public financing, ownership, and management. But the resource values of the land—the timber, the water, the minerals, the forage—could be and would be in wholesale terms separated from the land, liquidated, and privatized. The peculiar pattern was becoming clear. Federal lands socialism was quite acceptable so long as two conditions were met: It could never be identified with that word, and it had to result in gratifying profits to its corporate beneficiaries.

But the pattern had been set of maintaining the lands in public ownership. There were more national forests on the way, under the provisions of the Weeks Act in 1911, authorizing the repurchase of abandoned private land. There were more national parks forthcoming; after its creation in 1916, the National Park Service was ever anxious to expand. There were wildlife refuges created on federal lands, and in 1934 the Taylor Grazing Act codified the last fugitive resource, the open-range forage. In large measure, after that, there were no more transfers of public land to private hands.

---

52. See Marc Reisner, *Cadillac Desert* (New York: Penguin Books, 1986), pp. 285 ff.

The deliberate creation, between 1891 and 1934, of a common estate of federal lands was part of the evolution of American economic and political institutions. The period witnessed substantial change, even progress. Per-capita consumption was rising sharply, driven by phenomenal increases in agricultural and industrial productivity, though grave inequities in distribution remained. Life expectancies were extended, educational achievement nationwide was growing, nutrition and public health improved. In the political sphere, civil rights were more reliably assured: The abolition of overt human slavery was the most dramatic example. Women won the right to vote, many property qualifications were withdrawn, and senators were elected directly. Interest groups provided avenues of citizen access to the policy-making process, and a well-developed party system orchestrated the elections. Civil disturbance was rare, and when it was suppressed by military force, as in the Pullman strike, it did not escalate to large-scale sympathetic rioting. Even during the Great Depression, when social stresses were probably at their zenith, we experienced neither famine nor insurrection. The institutions of provisioning and rule-making were evolving.

Far more atrophied than the slowly and painfully improving status of women and African Americans was the plight of Native Americans. The bald racism of the Founding Fathers' days seemed not to diminish, seemed not to be open for inspection, even for description, far less for criticism.

Bernhard Fernow was singularly, ironically, perhaps surprisingly responsible for introducing into Euro-American institutions an axiomatic feature of Indian cultures—the idea of land held in common for the common good. His writing, his speeches, and his accomplishments in public policy bespoke his commitment to the transcendental welfare of the people at large, to that of the individual, either animate or corporate. He never used the term "tribe," however; he would have found that distasteful in the extreme, because his perception of Native Americans was typical of his time.

In the summer of 1886, at "the invitation of a generous and public spirited friend," Fernow traveled to the territory of Arizona and spent weeks studying its mountains, canyons, forests, mineral and forage resources, institutions, history, and potential for settlement. He addressed the National Geographic Society in Washington the following February 5, in a speech entitled "The Forests and Deserts of Arizona." The talk was subsequently published in the society's periodical. Fernow, whose non-native mastery of English was the equal of Joseph Conrad's, spoke with uncommon clarity, but also with the common idiom of his culture:

> Arizona . . . the earliest discovered of the western territories and yet the last to pass from the redman's dominion and the least developed; the land of a high prehistoric civilization, of cave dwellers and cliff-dwellers, and of the peaceful agricultural Hopi and Pima, and yet until a decade ago terrorized by the most warlike of the Indians, the Apache. . . . From 1863, when the territory was segregated from New Mexico, to 1874 the history of Arizona is written in blood. It took a hardy man to run the risk of tomahawk and scalping knife in order to benefit from the rich mineral discoveries. . . . The successful campaigns of General Custer, however, broke the war spirit of the Indians and led to the treaty of 1874, when these Indians were placed on reservations. . . . Since the Apache Indians, with their cunning leader Geronimo, were removed to Florida in 1886 the peaceful progress of the territory is assured. . . . Three centuries and three score years of history! Yet the beginnings of civilization and of the development of the territory date back hardly a score of years, and it is only a little over a decade since a really peaceful progress has begun—since the marauding Apache has been removed![53]

Fernow was immersed in his culture—he was not an evil man—and his comments are distasteful now because that culture

---

53. Bernhard E. Fernow, "The Forests and Deserts of Arizona," in *National Geographic* 8 (July–August, 1897), pp. 203–226. Fernow's biographer, Andrew Denney Rodgers III, cited many times above, describes this speech and footnotes the article in his book, published in 1951. Rodgers describes only Fernow's fascination with the botanical features of Arizona, apparently finding Fernow's language about the "marauding Apache" unworthy of comment. Rodgers was certainly not unique in his time: In 1958, the Eisenhower administration's interior secretary, Fred Seaton, undertook a policy of "termination" of the Indian reservations and cultural assimilation, beginning with the Winema in Oregon.

has at least inched forward. But clearly, in establishing 673 million acres of commonly held land, the "dominant culture" socialized that which had been socialized for millennia—the commonly held land of Native Americans.

After Fernow's success in initiating an identifiable common estate—random, lucky, messy, discontinuous success—we didn't know how to make the land held in common serve a common purpose. Our cultural history failed us, so we directed the European institutions of property rights and private wealth against those "public" lands—subsequently to strip, as we have done, are doing, and are about to complete, the resource values from the land, to be liquidated and privatized.

But the land endures. It will recover in time if we leave it alone, and faster if we invest in restorative techniques. Far more significantly, and posing a far greater challenge, the land remains as common property. Our institutions of common use, of common enjoyment, of sharing a common habitat, however, are still ill perceived, ill defined, and ill developed. We are little more comfortable with the word *tribe* than Fernow was. Shaping and articulating institutions of commonality and community are the challenges that lie ahead, and they are far more difficult than the task of land restoration.

First in history, however, we will have to try something else. We will have to apply science, investment, and technique to the "management" of the federal lands, according to the canons of professional practice.

Chapter Four

A Prelude to Overshoot:
Professional Management for
the Federal Lands, 1934–76

Coping with Scarcity amid Escalating Abundance

As corporate capitalism gathered momentum in the twentieth century, it succeeded in nationalizing the markets for more and more consumer products, until it dominated nearly all of them. In exchange for their sovereignty as consumers, citizens were served up an unprecedented abundance of consumer goods. There were two drivers: the corporations' success in developing new technologies that transformed more and more neutral stuff into useful resources, and their corollary success in triggering new perceptions of utility. They created a high-mass-consumption society and developed a resource base to support it.

The American economy probably achieved full development between 1934 and 1976. There emerged the potential for all citizens to enjoy a decent and dignified standard of living. That so many did not (and still do not) was a matter of distributive injustice, not a scarcity of resources or the inadequacy of production. In the midst of increasing abundance, a general strategy of professional management that was better suited to cope with resource scarcity was installed on the federal lands. The misfit of strategy and circumstance would eventually cause a series of controversies, detailed later in this chapter.

In the history of federal lands, 1934 and 1976 are landmark years. In 1934, the Taylor Grazing Act created federal Grazing Districts and established the Grazing Service to administer them. That law thus extended deliberate, public, and professional management to the expanse of public domain that had not been dedicated earlier as national parks, forests, or wildlife refuges.

The law was explicit, however, in specifying management of the Grazing Districts "pending final disposal." That meant that Congress was not yet ready to abandon the privatization policy, but with the exception of some last and desperate attempts at homesteading in Alaska in the 1950s, privatizing federal lands came to a de facto conclusion.

Finally, in 1976, the practice came to a statutory end. The Federal Land Policy and Management Act made permanent the public ownership of the Grazing Districts and mandated for their management the professional principles of sustained yield and multiple use. There was little opposition to the legislation. The users of all the federal lands had become hugely indifferent about ownership. You don't have to own the land, they had discovered, to hijack the timber, forage, water, and minerals, to dump the external costs on society at large, and to be subsidized in the process.

A pattern had emerged in winding down the privatizing of federal lands: classify or categorize the land, proclaim its retention in public ownership, create a federal agency to oversee it, and trust the management professionals therein to pursue the greater public interest.

The agencies today are the Forest Service, the National Park Service, the Fish and Wildlife Service, the Bureau of Land Management (née the Grazing Service and the General Land Office), and the Bureau of Reclamation. And the professions are forestry, wildlife biology, range management, and irrigation engineering. (The National Park Service has no dominant core profession. It has managed nevertheless to generate a coherent doctrine of park administration that we will investigate later.)

All the professions would display, eventually, a scheme of equilibration: Their "management" activities sought to assure a perpetual supply of timber, or grass, or water, or fish and game animals. They would do this by bringing the periodic use or harvest of each renewable resource into equilibrium with its periodic increment of growth.

Most of the professions had to be invented. The exception was forestry, which was instead imported, in the mind of Bernhard Fernow.

The First Equilibrators: Foresters, Forestry, and Sustained Yield

Fernow's forestry was classical European, sustained-yield, timber-management forestry. If the aggregate volume of all the trees in the forest increased by 100 board feet each year, for example, then 100 board feet could be cut each year, indefinitely. The "cut" might be in the form of a single tree containing 100 board feet, or of two trees each containing 50, but the yield could be sustained in perpetuity.

This sustained-yield paradigm of timber management defined the profession, and in forestry schools it was taught as holy writ. Fernow founded a school of professional forestry at Cornell, and Gifford Pinchot soon had another underway at Yale; the curricula were cast in the same Germanic tradition.

Professional forestry was developed in the aristocratic-mercantilistic political economies of western Europe in the 1700s, and of Germany in particular. It was almost perfectly suited to that institutional context. Mercantilism was a form of political-economy in which the welfare of a strongly centralized state was paramount. Given a strong state, the welfare of the citizens was assured, since the primary hazards were external and foreign: threats from the trade and often the military of other mercantilistic nations. A large and chronically positive trade balance would ensure a continuing flow of hard currency into the state treasury. Thereupon, a persuasive military and naval force was made financially possible, in an age when warfare was a popular tool of foreign policy.

Note the importance of seapower, and the corollary importance of merchant shipping. Ships were singularly critical to the welfare of the state, and ships were made of wood. They had been so constructed for a dozen centuries and would continue to be for at least another dozen decades. The absolute and strategic significance of forests, and forestry—and foresters—had never been so lofty, nor would it ever be again.

Mercantilism was characterized by a *scarcity* of resources, a *stability* of institutions, and a derived *certainty* about the future.[1]

The most troublesome feature was the specter of resource *scarcity,* but to deal with it, a nation could choose among five classic strategies of response: develop more of the domestic supply; discover more; import more; rely on a technical substitute; or limit consumption. All but one of these were foreclosed for Germany in the 1700s, however.

The options of development and discovery were beyond reach in a country long settled. There were neither unknown nor untapped forests to be drawn into production. Importing forest resources was physically possible but was nullified by the canons of mercantilism. Positive trade balances were sought at all costs—explicitly including the higher prices that domestic transactions might impose.[2] A fourth scarcity-avoiding strategy—technical substitution—was also rendered ineffective.

The German economy, designed to enhance the welfare of the state, rewarded producers for their craftsmanship, economy in the use of materials, and product durability. The mousetrap to build was one of exquisite quality, proven efficacy, and anticipated long life. There was no incentive to innovate, to design a mousetrap with new and superior mechanics; and if innovation is not rewarded, there is not likely to be much. For a thousand years or more, ships had been built of wood, for example. There was no systemic stimulus to develop alternative technologies.

In terms of the resource equation, $R = f(S,U,T)$, the technol-

---

1. The discussion to follow owes much to the Harvard Conference on Forest Production offered in the 1960s at the Harvard Forest near Petersham, Massachusetts. Consisting of two weeks of lectures, readings, discussions, and field trips during the days, intensified discussions and informal whiskey sipping in the evenings, it was an exhilarating experience of intellectual challenge and stimulation. The director of the forest at the time was Dr. Hugh M. Raup, and Dr. Ernest M. Gould was the forest economist on the staff.

2. See John Fred Bell, *A History of Economic Thought* (New York: Ronald Press, 1953), p. 112.

ogy term T was not a variable in mercantilistic Germany, but a constant. Given an unchanging agenda of wants and needs in the society at large—to be argued below—the utility or U variable was a constant as well. With technologies and utility perceptions frozen, the S term itself becomes a constant, and now we must write R = S: The resource and the substance are equivalent. Let us call this an "inventory concept" of resources. For the circumstances of Germany in the eighteenth century, it meant that resources were finite and limited—or scarce—and their conservative management and utilization were mandatory.

The final response to resource scarcity—limiting consumption—was the only one possible, and that's what the sustained-yield policy did.

Timber was a biological, or flow resource, not a mineral or stock resource. Its yield could be sustained unendingly if each year's consumption did not exceed each year's aggregate growth. So long as the sinking or rotting away of German shipping was no greater than the growth of German forests, there could always be a German fleet. For forest resources, at least, sustained yield was a perfect solution to the problems posed by mercantilism.

The characteristic of *stability* in eighteenth-century German institutions also can be inferred from elements in the resource equation. If technology was unchanging, it was therefore stable, by definition. The wants and needs of consumers were largely historical, indigenous to the culture, essentially unstimulated and unmanipulated, and therefore largely stable as well. (There was no ceaseless barrage of mass-media entreaties to seek constantly more and newer personal gratifications.)

Empirically, the secular stability of production, consumption, and culture was far less than absolute, or we would witness still a German flotilla of merchant and naval vessels made of wood. By comparison to the twenty-first century, however, the case for stability in Germany in the 1700s can rest.

Any system that is stable is also certain. Its trajectory and future condition are predictable, and that makes long-term planning a secure exercise. The professional forester's plans must be long term, indeed. Trees grow very slowly. Speaking casually of "rotations" of a century or more, to designate the interval of sustained-yield cuttings, was easily justified three centuries ago in western Europe.

Limiting the periodic cutting to the periodic growth of a forest was inescapable under the conditions of scarcity. And projecting that management regime a century ahead was appropriate for a stable system with a certain future. Thus was professional forestry rationalized, constituted, taught, and imported into the United States via Bernhard Fernow's lively mind.

During his tenure as director of the forestry school at Cornell, Fernow undertook to do what no one else had done: He applied technical, scientific forestry to a tangible, vibrant, and altogether too visible, real American forest. He did so on a 30,000-acre demonstration forest the state legislature had provided the school, in the Saranac Lakes region of the Adirondacks. The forest displayed a vigorous stand of hardwood species, seriously offensive to Fernow's commercial sense of silviculture; the coniferous softwoods, pine and spruce, were much more highly valued in the marketplace.

No one should have doubted his intentions. Forestry, in Fernow's own words, was a "technical art, wholly utilitarian, and not, except incidentally, concerned in esthetic aspects of the woods; it is engaged in utilizing the soil for the production of wood crops, and thereby of the highest revenue attainable. To make the soil produce the largest amount of the most useful wood per acre is the foremost aim of forestry."[3]

Fernow saw the hardwood trees as inferior species, not the "most useful" at all. So he set about clear-cutting them and planting instead pine and spruce, which grow more happily in full sunlight than in the shade, say, of a sugar maple.

He was undertaking a *timber-type conversion* and initiating *even-aged management* for the coniferous trees, in a scheme of *area regulation*. These italicized terms and their meanings existed as abstract images in Fernow's mind. (Kindred professional foresters today can summon them to mind, too.) His perception of objective reality was conditioned by these images, but the objective reality was simple enough. Fernow was cutting down all the hardwoods—which meant virtually all the trees.

Fernow would learn, as his professional descendants would

---

3. Quoted in Andrew Denney Rodgers III, *Bernhard Eduard Fernow: A Story of North American Forestry* (Princeton University Press, 1951), pp. 305–306.

have to learn, that objective realities could be perceived in vastly differing ways.

However useless the sugar maple might have been in Fernow's mind, it was highly regarded in the Adirondacks, particularly in the autumn, for its contribution after all to the "esthetic aspects of the woods." So proclaimed many of the residents of the Saranac Lakes region, who appreciated those aspects, and who misconstrued completely in their untutored way what Fernow was attempting to do. To them it seemed that Fernow's clear-cuts were simply denuding the mountainsides, and they used that term in their protests.

Fernow and his profession, who and which had been drafted into the politics of forest devastation as the solution, now stood accused of perpetuating the problem. Fernow protested vigorously the accusations, sought vehemently to explain to unknowing citizens the nuances of professional practice, and proceeded with a certain righteous but gracious defiance to extend his clear-cuts. I am the expert, the professional, he justifiably claimed. Trust me, he naively asked.

They did not. Fernow later claimed it was two wealthy bankers from New York, owners of estates near his demonstration forest, that did him in, but Governor Benjamin Barker Odell vetoed the appropriation bill for the College of Forestry at Cornell. It closed its doors forever in 1903.

Governor Odell explained his actions this way:

> the operations of this College of Forestry have been subjected to grave criticism, as they have practically denuded the forest lands of the state without compensating benefit. I deem it wise, therefore, to withhold approval of this item until a more scientific and more reasonable method is pursued in the forestry of the land now under control of Cornell University.[4]

Fernow went on to a distinguished career in forestry education in Canada, and professional forestry began a long, painful exercise in learning. The beauty of the forest, when perceived

---

4. Ibid., p. 315.

and articulated by society at large, or even subsets (not excluding wealthy bankers), becomes a scenic resource—just as pine and spruce as timber resources had been created from neutral stuff in prior years and as a wilderness resource would be in the future.

Foresters would have to learn that cultural appraisals of the biophysical environment cause resources to become. Other renewable resource management professions would have to learn this also, and they would all have to realize that the engine can run both ways: Resources could cease to be—long before their physical exhaustion and return to the category of neutral stuff.

All this would cause a professional trauma: Equilibration schemes—sustained yield in its several manifestations—would have to be abandoned as utterly unworkable in a dynamic society.

Equilibration in a Context of Change: A Recipe for Convulsion

Neither the protesters in the Adirondacks nor Forester Fernow could have known how prototypical their respective activities were. Three generations would pass before their episode was replicated, and until then the misfit between equilibration schemes and institutional dynamism would not be conspicuous again.

Fernow avoided trouble just as long as his notion of sustained yield was kept an abstraction. No one complained at all during the Sturm und Drang of forest reform; it was only when Fernow set out to sustain the yield of real spruce and pine trees, in a real forest appreciated otherwise by real people for its natural beauty that he ran head-on into dynamic institutions.

As the schools of professional forestry proliferated—sixteen in the first decade of the century and some four dozen now—sustained yield was taught with undiminished fervor, Cornell's experience notwithstanding.

Until after World War II, however, little cutting was done on the federal lands. The nation met its needs for commercial timber largely from the private lands of the forest products corporations, and the public forests were held in a custodial status.

Fernow's initial good fortune was replicated for his professional successors: Hearing no criticism of their sustained-yield paradigm in the abstract, the foresters enjoyed a great measure of esteem. When it came time to apply the practice in real forests, however, the problem of differing perceptions arose again, and so did the strident protest. A scheme born in scarcity wrought havoc in a context of abundance.

Sustained yield, we saw, was exceptionally well suited for the conditions of scarcity displayed in western Europe in the 1700s. The "inventory" concept of resources made sense, and it was described in a contemporary book that dominates conventional thinking still.

Thomas Robert Malthus, the English cleric, philosopher, and sometime economist, published his *Essay on Population* in 1798. An inventory concept of resources was apparent in the *Essay*, but it was made explicit only in much later years when a "Malthusian equation" was distilled from its pages:

$$\text{Standard of living} = \frac{\text{Resources}}{\text{Population}}$$

As the population grows inexorably, pressing on a fixed resource base, standards of living must plummet, according to Reverend Malthus. Each citizen's slice of the collective pie must get smaller and smaller. This is an explicit representation of resource *fixity*, and with any population growth at all it becomes an explicit representation of resource *scarcity*.

Such a model of scarcity rationalized the sustained-yield strategies of professional resource management, as we have seen. It also forms a fundamental assumption of modern environmental thought, and complements the separation of humanity from nature, proposed by George Perkins Marsh. When we speak of "natural resources" simply as petroleum, metallic ores, salmon, timber, and water, we are invoking the inventory concept of resources. Humanity depends on such "natural resources," which are fixed in either physical quantities or rates of growth—and hence are scarce.

We have seen in passing another way of looking at the relationship of humanity to its biophysical environment: The Native American view, which sees not separate entities, but a single borderless existence. An academic replication is the idea of a single "biosocial system" in which humanity and the biophysical environment are not only interrelated, but also interactive, interdependent, and in a constant state of mutual adjustment. We will elaborate this further on, but we have brushed against it in the functional concept of resources. When $R = f(S,U,T)$, we proclaim that both "natural" elements (S) and the human elements (U and T) are required for "resources" to exist.

An excellent example is the wilderness resource. The standard history of the issue is Roderick Nash's work, *Wilderness and the American Mind.* It describes Aldo Leopold's collaboration with Arthur H. Carhart in persuading their Forest Service superiors to withhold large areas of national forestland from any sort of development. It could well be said that Leopold and Carhart were among the earliest to perceive a wilderness "utility."

In the first such action, the Gila Wilderness Area was designated on June 24, 1924, by District Forester Frank C.W. Pooler. The Gila Wilderness encompassed 574,000 acres in New Mexico, some 897 square miles, and not surprisingly it accommodated Leopold's vision of what a wilderness should be: "a continuous stretch of country preserved in its natural state, open to lawful hunting and fishing, big enough to absorb a two weeks' pack trip, and kept devoid of roads, artificial trails, cottages, or other works of man."[5]

Leopold's expectation of wandering on horseback for two weeks would be sorely tried in future years when wilderness designation was applied to far less expansive properties. The Pelican Island Wilderness in Florida covers .0086 square miles, some 5.5 acres. Squared off, that's 490 feet from one side to the other.

Wilderness and the American Mind chronicles a textbook example of resources "becoming," to repeat Zimmerman's choice of words. If neutral substances become resources by cultural perceptions of prospective utility, supplemented by the technical

---

5. Quoted in Roderick Nash, *Wilderness and the American Mind* (New Haven, CT: Yale University Press, 1967), p. 186. In a footnote on p. 206 of Nash's otherwise credible volume, he recounts Robert Marshall's accomplishments as a vigorous hiker. Marshall was another giant in the history of the wilderness resource, perhaps even literally. According to an account Nash quotes by Marshall's brother George, he often hiked thirty miles in a day, apparently, not rarely forty miles in a day, and on several occasions seventy miles in a day. If George Marshall and Roderick Nash are not among the less discriminating of recorders, brother Robert must have flirted with superhumanity. To cover seventy miles in a day—given four hours off for rest and nourishment—he would have had to maintain a pace of $3^1/2$ miles per hour for twenty hours. That is vigorous hiking.

means for capturing that utility, then Nash's book shows the "wilderness resource" in just that light.

There were at least three different historical perceptions of wilderness. Once in human history, say in biblical years, Nash explains, "wilderness" was a fearful place. The "wilderness" into which Christ entered was neither 490 feet square, nor considered a pleasant setting for a two weeks' pack trip. Later, in the American West, wilderness was a challenge, and great folk heroes were made of those who "tamed" it. Eventually, Leopold and Carhart articulated the social appreciation for the recreational, perhaps spiritual values to be gained in experiencing landscapes apparently unoccupied by humans or their artifacts.

In the case of the Gila Wilderness, however, the land had been unoccupied for just thirty-eight years. By 1924, it had been only that long "since the Apache Indians, with their cunning leader Geronimo, were removed to Florida in 1886. . . ." But now a different culture was appraising the land with different values and utilities in mind. For this culture, such land had become the "wilderness resource."

The biosocial construct of "resources" is displayed here with a great deal of clarity. The spontaneously occurring substance is the apparently unoccupied, undeveloped land. The value or utility is the refreshing experience of visiting that land or the psychic satisfaction of knowing it's there. The technology, in Leopold's time, had to do with saddle and pack animals—which have been almost completely displaced today with high-tech backpacks, space-age tenting, freeze-dried foods, and specialty clothing derived from petroleum or recycled plastic bottles.

Note the distinction in the quote from Leopold between land "preserved in its natural state" and the "artificial trails, cottages, or other works of man." The distinction was maintained, as we have seen, in the statutory definition of wilderness: "where man is a visitor who does not remain." Wilderness is thus a biosocial resource defined in terms that separate humanity from nature.

That specific inconsistency has caused very little mischief, but failing comprehensively to adopt a biosocial view can cause a great deal. To define resources as functions of biophysical and social elements is to express the unity of a single system of humans in their biophysical environment, a unity axiomatic to Native American cultures. It accommodates the dynamism in our economic and political institutions, which effect substantive changes in our resource base. Indeed, at the cost of our sovereignty as consumers, substantive changes have provided abundance.

Let us stylize our political economy as democracy/capitalism, to contrast it with the aristocracy/mercantilism of eighteenth-century Germany, and see what happens thereafter to the properties of scarcity, stability, and certainty. Those features of the older set of institutions made sustained yield necessary; their absence in the new set make it absurd.

Democracy/capitalism begins with a contrary assumption: It is the welfare of the individual not the welfare of the central state that is the primal objective. Assure individual well-being, and the health and vigor of the state will follow. The invisible hand will see to that, through constitutional means, or through the grand homeostasis of the market system. (We are stylizing here.)

All the escapes from resource scarcity that were beyond the reach of aristocracy/mercantilism have been available to democracy/capitalism, and the most effective escape still is.

The option of "discovering more" was played out with glee and handsome accumulations of private wealth for the better part of two centuries, and in spite of the late socializing of 673 million acres. Timber, water, minerals, forage, arable land unprecedented in productivity, hides, fur, and fish, coal, oil, and gas were there to be discovered, transformed if necessary from neutral stuff to resources, to be reduced to possession, to be liquidated, and they were. Though the "discovery" option is winding down, that liquidated wealth is intact still—but now in private hands, not the public's.

The jury is still out regarding the option of "developing more." The development of timber resources on federal land was a primary controversy of the late twentieth century, and so was petroleum development on the north slope of the Brooks Range in Alaska. Physically the development option is still open; the only threat to its closure is political. Those with environmental credentials argue for closure. Corporations with financial stakes in the outcome disagree. Republican administrations openly favor the latter, while Democrats differ only by offering incantations of environmental sympathy. With respect to the federal lands, the development option will close when there is little left to be plundered.

The option of "importing more" is scarcely discouraged by a nation that displays bipartisan euphoria for the General Agreement on Tariffs and Trade, the North American Free Trade Agreement, and the World Trade Organization. Some see GATT, NAFTA, and the WTO accords as multinational corporate hunting licenses for the most exploitable labor pools and biophysical environments anywhere on the planet. It is difficult to disagree, but the globalization of the resource base adds immeasurably to our domestic abundance.

The "substitution" option in democracy/capitalism is the most potent escape from resource scarcity. Precisely because capitalism is so competitive,[6] the search for lower production costs and superior products is unending. Innovation is hugely rewarded and a great deal takes place, in the quest for better ways of doing things (production technologies) and better things to do (novel products).

The search for better ways of doing things expands the T variable. We can build yachts not only of solid wood, but also of plywood panels, and of steel, ferroconcrete, fiberglass, and aluminum. The abundance of substitute technologies, each using a different substance, or S variable, is the equivalent of abundant resources for the construction of pleasure craft. There is no consumer good or service for which this circumstance of abundance fails to hold.

The search for better things to do, for novel products, creates and multiplies the "utility" variable, and thereby is capable of calling into service substances that were previously neutral. The development and adoption of the automobile is perhaps a good example. It offered a new utility: personal transport at unprece-

---

6. Competition, in a fully developed economy, in which consumption is "optimal," might take place between the producers of any particular good. It need not be and it typically is not price competition: Model for model, Fords and Chevrolets are identically priced. The competition takes place in "product differentiation," in the efforts to persuade the consumer that one automobile confers on the owner perhaps more sex appeal than the other. In overdeveloped economies, which display the pathology of hyperconsumption, the significant competition a producer faces is not from competing producers of a given product, but from competing products. Consumers already have an "optimal" supply of automobiles, so the threat to the marginal Chevrolet is not a Ford, but a comparably priced motorboat. "Competition" has come a long way since Adam Smith.

dented velocities. The useless by-product of kerosene production, gasoline, was pressed into service, and the energy resource base expanded. When the perception of utility is force-fed by mass marketing via the mass media, the consequent expansion of the resource base is awesome. We have been driven to hyperconsumption this way, and hyperconsumption is scarcely possible without a hyperabundance of resources to support it.

To forestall the reader's need for involuntary leaps of faith, a tangential elaboration is necessary here.

The case for abundant resources is indisputable when resources are defined at the end point in the chain of production processes and not, as is commonly done, at the beginning. This can be better understood if the word "input" is substituted for "resource," a practice not unusual among economists.

A standing tree is an input, a resource, to a logging company. The output is a log, which becomes an input, a resource, to a sawmill. The mill's output is, say, dimension lumber, which becomes the input to the construction of wood-frame housing. The final output is the house—the point at which production ends and consumption begins.

At this point, the consumer-goods point, "resources" are most appropriately defined by and for a society. At this point the range of alternate technologies, each with its prescribed substance, is the widest, and resource abundance is consequently at its greatest. For every consumer good, there is a wide range of optional technologies and allied substances.

Favoring this point of definition is not to proclaim resource abundance in some cornucopian sense, to rationalize thereafter the greatest binge of consumption in the history of the planet. Distributive injustice aside, American people are already engaged in that, doing physical disservice to themselves and to the biophysical environment, not excepting the federal lands. They do so to the primary benefit of the corporate agents of production.

We should define resources at this point because it should always be the welfare of the citizens in society that is paramount, not the welfare of the institutional agents of service, which is to say the producers. Even economists appreciate the sovereignty of the consumer.

Adopting the orthodox point of definition, which is not the end but the beginning of the production chain, we are forced to assume the viewpoint of the corporate producers. Scarcity appears to them when they commit capital to a particular technology, and technology to a particular product.[7] That freezes both the U and the T, and the producer relies on a single S, or substance—which appears scarce. Then the inventory concept of resource holds: $R = S$. For a Champion International sawmill, only logs serve as resource inputs.

A widespread, cultural assumption of resource scarcity is of wondrous benefit to corporate producers. It engenders much concern and hand wringing and fosters an apparently sympathetic willingness to be gouged by extortionate pricing. None of this is necessary, because society at large does not share in the rigors of scarcity: There are numerous options always available. We can build houses with Champion International lumber, all right, but also with steel studs and panels, with concrete, with bricks or blocks, with adobe, with straw bales, with tamped earth, with geodesic domes of aluminum and fiberglass. (Each competing resource, furthermore, is fighting vigorously for market share.) We need to know that our resources are more than sufficient to meet our needs for housing, food, energy, and psychic well-being, in order to choose intelligently among them—and, more important, to retain the initiative for choice.[8]

To see this from a different angle, already encountered, we do not have a production problem. The problem of distributive injustice is severe, but if production is not constraining, neither are resources.

From the citizen-consumer's standpoint, and from society's standpoint, both the utility and the technology elements are quite variable, and the functional definition holds true: $R = f(S,U,T)$.

---

7. This stubborn reality is not invisible to corporate managements. The Philip Morris Company, as if to acknowledge that its historic tobacco products are lethal, has moved aggressively into the processing and marketing of foodstuffs.

8. The conscious rejection of breeder reactors in particular, and increasingly the rejection of nuclear energy in general, are just such intelligent choices. Uranium is becoming neutral stuff once more. Choices of this sort should remain social, not corporate, decisions, and they are made possible only by the abundance, from a social perspective, of resources.

We can then substitute the f(S,U,T) for the R in the Malthusian equation, and this is the result:

$$\text{standard of living} = \frac{f(S,U,T)}{P}$$

This relationship can be described as an abundance model, and resources defined as functions instead of inventories have expanded at a far greater rate than population. Living standards rose dramatically until a fully developed economy was achieved. We have environmental problems today not because per-capita consumption is sufficient or because the economy is fully developed. They exist because per-capita consumption is oversufficient, hyped to excess; because the economy is overdeveloped. The biophysical problems of the environment are fixable, but far more consequential and seemingly intractable are the social problems of inequitable distribution, in our own country and on a global scale. If resources are abundant, there is no physical reason for underconsumption anywhere.

Resource abundance does not constitute an invitation to gorge; it provides the freedom and imposes the responsibility for choosing wisely which spontaneously occurring substances to use—and which to avoid.

A vast reordering of resource policy for the federal lands is overdue. Such a transformation needs to be undertaken from a social perspective—in which resources are abundant—and to pursue a general condition of public well-being. In the past we have crafted public policy using an assumption of resource scarcity—which only producers face—and have handicapped the general welfare, accordingly. That is why this chapter is building the foundation for an alternative approach.

The abundance of resources for the production of goods and services today, in both the absolute terms of physical quantities and the relative terms of conceivable need, is beyond dispute. The options of discovery, development, importation, and substitution are omnipresent, and, in various ways, their adoption is stimulated if not mandated by our economic and political institutions.

Scarcity has long since disappeared as a rationale for applying sustained yield strategies. For many reasons implicit in the paragraphs above, so has stability. The high volatility of production technologies and product characteristics induces a high degree of instability in consumption patterns. Without stability in the system, there can be no certainty of the future.

Foresters can clear-cut a forest and plant another in a textbook application of sustained yield, as Fernow did, expecting that neither utilities nor technologies will change before the forest matures, a century or more into the future, expecting that society will want the same forest then as it does now, expecting that resources are immutable in form and function. But they had better not.

All the rationalizing elements of sustained yield—scarcity, stability, and certainty—are contradicted, in the political economy of democracy/capitalism in the twenty-first century. The dynamic nature of our institutions is beyond question, so the application of equilibrating schemes, as Fernow's unfortunate example demonstrated, is likely to produce convulsions.

The Diffusion of Equilibration: Other Professions, Other Agencies

The convulsions in the federal forests did not arise until the foresters took sustained yield from their textbooks and applied it on the landscapes, well past the midpoint of the twentieth century. In the meantime, the other renewable resource management professions were invented, and each of them adopted its own scheme of equilibration.

The towering figure in the development of wildlife biology is Aldo Leopold. The range of this man's thinking and the grace and power of his writing are without equal in the American conservation movement. We have seen his seminal contribution, his virtual invention of the wilderness idea. Leopold is also applauded for articulating an ethical responsibility in the treatment of land. Less well known, because it is more narrowly focused, is Leopold's revolutionizing of wildlife biology. Within the profession, however, his impact is acknowledged and acclaimed.[9]

---

9. In a classic in the field, Durward Allen relies with explicit appreciation on Leopold's pioneering thinking. See Durward L. Allen, *Our Wildlife Legacy* (New York: Funk and Wagnalls, 1954).

In the early years of wildlife management, the animals themselves were the focus of attention. Since female deer were directly
responsible for the reproduction of the species, good management prohibited the shooting of does. That constituted essentially the entire strategy of game management, until Leopold
made some astonishing suggestions. The controlling factor was
probably not the safety and survival of the females, but the health
and vigor of the species' habitat—the totality of food and water
availability, escape and thermal cover, breeding, birthing, and
rearing sites, etc.

The reproductive capacity of the herd, it became apparent
from field research, was sufficient to overstock virtually any conceivable level of habitat quality. Without the hunting of does—
"antlerless deer" was the euphemism—the herd would overstock
its range, inflicting long-term damage to both the habitat and,
consequently, the production of deer.

A "carrying capacity" was calculated for the range of each deer
herd. If this population was not exceeded, a sustained yield of
deer could be assured in perpetuity. Equilibrating strategies were
worked out and implemented in state fish and game agencies
across the country, and applied to other species as well.

The game managers suffered a fate similar to Fernow's when
they insisted on the harvest of antlerless deer. Hunters accus-
tomed to "buck laws" revolted. They were caught up still in the
assumed need to protect the females—now disproven. Once
again, the objective facts were subject to differing interpretations,
and the controversy boiled for a decade or more.

For the administration of the federal grazing districts, the systematic practice of range management was worked out and
offered as a degree program in western universities. The working
strategy was closely related to that of wildlife biology. A carrying
capacity of livestock could be calculated, again using a habitat
datum. "Range condition and trend" were the constraining data.
If the condition was bad and the trend was down, permittees were
granted fewer "AUMs"—animal-unit-months—and had to
reduce the size of their herds accordingly. Only in such a way
could a sustained yield of grass be assured in perpetuity.

Yet another convulsion. The livestock operators were no less
inclined than Fernow's tormentors to undertake political inter-

vention, and more than one intransigent district manager was forced out of his job.[10]

In each of these cases of controversy, professional managers were taking the long-term, sustained-yield view. Their clients disagreed, seeing something else in the objective realities of the situations. We need not anoint heroes or condemn villains to see that static equilibration strategies, extended over perpetual time horizons, do not fit well in cultural circumstances of volatility and ferment.

The controversies eventually subsided. In the case of deer hunting, they were strongly localized since it is the state agencies, not the federal land managers, that exercise jurisidiction over hunting and fishing. Hunters gradually saw the wisdom of managing habitat instead of animals, and came largely to support the biologists' views—probably because they shared the assumption that deer would always be a desired game animal, and sustained yield made sense. In the time since the controversies, however, which peaked in the early 1960s, the popularity of deer hunting has declined severely, and in many parts of the nation today, deer have become neutral stuff once more.

In the case of range management, the controversies subsided for a different reason. It was not the range conservationists' success in educating their clientele, the ranchers. Rather, it was their good sense to take a patient and gradual approach to improving condition and trend. They did what they could when they could, and inched ahead. The strategy paid off until 1946. In that year, the director of the Grazing Service found himself squarely in the center of an intractable situation. The House demanded that he raise grazing fees. The Senate, sufficiently persuaded by Senator Patrick McCarran from Nevada, demanded he lower them.[11] The director couldn't do both, nor could he comfortably opt for neither. In the face of his dilemma, Congress decided to terminate

---

10. The standard reference is Phillip O. Foss, *Politics and Grass* (Seattle: University of Washington Press, 1960).

11. To this day, below-market grazing fees constitute a notorious subsidy to the livestock industry.

the agency. It did so by combining it with the General Land Office to form the Bureau of Land Management.

We can discern equilibration strategies in the other federal resource agencies as well.

The National Park Service has no identifiable resource profession with a value agenda. It developed an agency philosophy, nevertheless, but has backed itself into an ideological cul-de-sac. Much of its contemporary management posture dates to the "Leopold Report" of 1963, which resulted from an inquiry into elk management in Yellowstone Park. Starker Leopold, Aldo Leopold's son, chaired the committee that undertook the study. After addressing the empirics of the elk situation, the report looked further afield, to the entire national park system:

> As a primary goal, we would recommend that the biotic associations within each park be maintained, or where necessary recreated, as nearly as possible in the condition that prevailed when the area was first visited by the white man. A national park should represent a vignette of primitive America . . . observable artificiality in any form must be minimized and obscured in every possible way. A reasonable illusion of primitive America could be recreated, using the utmost in skill, judgement, and ecological sensitivity. This in our opinion should be the objective of every national park and monument. . . . Above all other policies, the maintenance of naturalness should prevail.[12]

The report's distaste for "artificiality" is confounded by the strange datum, "first visited by the white man." That leaves the Leopold Report open to either of two serious criticisms. Was there no human occupancy and use of the land prior to white visitation? We have dealt with that cultural arrogance earlier. Or, accepting prior use, are there quantum distinctions in the nature of human occupancy? Are Native American people "natural"—or are they simply "primitive?" Is only "the white man" capable of doing

---

12. Quoted here from John C. Hendee, George H. Stankey, and Robert C. Lucas, *Wilderness Management*, 2nd edition, revised (Golden, CO: North American Press, 1990), p. 307.

"artificial" things? These intractable questions were not raised in the report, and the Park Service has yet to face them squarely.[13] The Park Service to this day has tied itself tightly into conceptual knots with the Leopold Report. It practices "natural management" with messianic vigor and virtue, which is to say it will do nothing "artificial." Alston Chase, writing about this philosophical stance in his book *Playing God in Yellowstone,* can scarcely contain his apoplexy.[14] And Chase wrote just before the 1988 summer when one-third of Yellowstone exploded in fire. That was the predictable (and predicted) consequence of the altogether "artificial" suppression of forest fires in the park for more than half a century. Having changed its mind about fire suppression after the Leopold Report, the Park Service ignored its responsibility for the powder keg it had built and decided thenceforth to "take what nature gives us." In the textbook on wilderness management the concept of "carrying capacity" is a central theme.[15] It is adopted in the Park Service practices of restricting backcountry use to some predetermined quantitative number each day, or metering the numbers of people who are permitted to float the Colorado River through the Grand Canyon, or rationing the annual ascents of Denali. In this manifestation of sustained yield the consumption of these experiences is arbitrarily limited to "sustain" their availability. Thus does yet another federal agency equilibrate with enthusiasm, but to date there has been no controversy. The clientele groups seem to share the assumptions of fixity and scarcity and accept the limitations with gracious and righteous self-denial.

There is one more agency to inspect, the Bureau of Reclamation. The defining professionalism in the agency is the civil engi-

---

13. The report's rigid ideological separation of humanity from nature continues the mischief of George Perkins Marsh discussed in chapter 3.

14. Alston Chase, *Playing God in Yellowstone: The Destruction of America's First National Park* (New York: Harcourt Brace Jovanovich, 1986). Chase discusses the wild oscillations in Park Service management philosophies. There is much to criticize about the imposition of professional dicta on agencies' value agendas, but at least they do serve to unify and stabilize management approaches.

15. Hendee et al., *Wilderness Management,* p. 187 ff.

neering of great hydraulic structures, but nestled therein is another scheme of equilibration.

The original idea of "reclamation" was to facilitate the settlement, presumably by Jeffersonian yeoman, of public lands that were too dry to support conventional agriculture. John Wesley Powell's idea of "commonwealths" in the arid West was probably the source of the thinking. Decentralized semiautonomous democracies of hard-working irrigation farmers, organized on the basis of drainage basins, was the prospect. But it was contradicted, finally, by the "irrigation centralizers," to adopt Donald Worster's term (and his telling argument), who were interested not in democracy. To further their own commercial interests in manufacturing, finance, and transportation, they sought the rapid economic development of the West instead.

The Newlands Bill, which became the Reclamation Act of 1902, was a triumph for the centralizers, and Worster's theme has proven out in the decades since. Far from promoting the family farm and agrarian democracy, the Bureau of Reclamation has encouraged and supported corporate agriculture (e.g., the Central Valley Project) and urban development (e.g., the Central Arizona Project) almost exclusively. In doing that, the Bureau transformed the western rivers into lakes and much of western agriculture into a stratified culture of corporate agribusiness millionaires and alien immigrant labor, legal and otherwise.

Only once was the Bureau threatened, but it was a physical, not a political threat.

The issue was not the failure of Teton Dam in Idaho in 1976, even though eleven people died and thirteen thousand head of livestock were lost. The bureau survived that mishap with public relations rhetoric and the symbolic severing of a few engineers' heads. But in 1983 the Colorado River attacked the bureau's Glen Canyon Dam, with the serious intent of washing it away and breaking completely free thereafter, all the way to the Gulf of California. It might have meant the end of the Bureau of Reclamation.

Glen Canyon Dam is located in Arizona, just a few miles upstream from Grand Canyon National Park—through which the last free-flowing segment of the river still runs. The epic battle between the river and the dam, for three days in late June of 1983, was an unconditional standoff.[16]

The dam was built by the Bureau of Reclamation, but the only land that Glen Canyon irrigates, that it has "reclaimed," is a patch of grass about the size of a football field, at the base of the dam structure, put there purely for landscaping. For Glen Canyon is what is known as a cash register dam. It is a single-purpose hydro-electric installation intended only for producing revenue to balance off the irrigation dams the bureau operates elsewhere at great financial loss.

The equilibration scheme in the operation of cash register dams is dicey. In order to maximize power generation and hence revenue, you want to catch and hold in your reservoir any inflows, however erratic they may be. But you need enough storage capacity ahead of time, so the trick is to anticipate those inflows. In the arid West, to grant the bureau its due, the facility and reliability of doing that are sometimes fleeting and slight.

The flow of western rivers is almost exclusively a function of winter snowfall and the rate at which it melts. This is particularly true of the Colorado River system, with its headwaters high in the snow-burdened western slopes of the southern Rocky Mountains, while its course traverses some of the most sere and forbidding deserts on earth.

Snowpack, at least, is not difficult to measure, and the bureau tracks it carefully, drawing down its reservoirs in years when it is heavy, maintaining fuller pools when it is not. At cash register dams, though, the bureau is not aggressive in its drawdowns. Since the play at such dams is water to power to money, you don't want to spill before you really must.

A large snowfall late in the season is particularly ticklish. You've been keeping your pool as high as you can, but now there's an additional load you hadn't expected up there in the mountains, and you can't draw down your reservoir overnight. Time, not just storage capacity, now becomes critical, and the last thing you

---

16. A chilling account of the near-disaster in 1983 appeared in the December 12, 1983, issue of *High Country News*, pp. 10–14, in a story entitled, "How Lake Powell Almost Broke Free of Glen Canyon Dam," by T.J. Wolf. The account to follow draws heavily on that source.

want is a deluge of warm spring rain that accelerates the runoff dramatically.

In a normal season, Glen Canyon Dam impounds in Lake Powell 6.7 million acre-feet of water produced in the runoff season, from April to July. In 1983 it had to contend with 14.6 million. Lake Powell has a shoreline that is longer than the entire West Coast, but it cannot contain that much water.

Spillways are designed into dams to handle unusually heavy water flows, typically by dumping them over a notch in the top of the dam onto a reinforced sluiceway, to form an impressive but harmless waterfall. A spillway so designed is an open-air conduit, and its unconstrained, low-pressure hydraulics are simple and benign.

At Glen Canyon, there were two spillways, but neither of them overtopped the dam. Instead, they were tunnels bored into the red Navajo sandstone of the canyon walls on either side of and upstream from the dam. Lined with reinforced concrete, they slanted down and beneath the dam, emptying at river level below. A 41-foot tube is a sizable piece of piping, but it is still a pipe, and when water flows through it at 120 miles an hour, its constrained, high-pressure hydraulics are complicated and fierce.

For twenty years after Glen Canyon was completed, the spillways were never used. But then the heavy warm spring rains hit the late snow in the Rockies.

A normal high flow through Glen Canyon Dam is about 25,000 cubic feet per second in the summer, when every air conditioner in Phoenix is running at capacity. On June 27, 1983, the engineers at Glen Canyon were dumping in desperation 92,000 cubic feet per second out of Lake Powell, into the turbine penstocks of the dam, down the four 8-foot emergency tubes of the river outlet works, and through both spillways. The whole dam was shaking, audibly rumbling, as chunks of reinforced concrete the size of automobiles thundered in the spillway tunnels and rocketed out the exits high into the air. That was distressing, an indication that the spillway tunnels were cavitating and their concrete linings eroding.

Then the huge chunks of debris and the frothing water both turned brick red, and mere distress escalated into whimpering terror. Now the concrete linings were breached, and the water was blasting away the soft red Navajo sandstone "bedrock" on which the dam rested, literally undermining it. The river was trying to squirm under the dam.

The dam itself was in no danger of breaking; it was a curved gravity dam, with more than adequate strength. If the fracturing and washing of the sandstone went far enough, however, the dam would rip loose from its abutments and foundation and become one huge rolling boulder, forming the most fantastic rapid anyone had ever witnessed in the Colorado River.

The situation was beyond rational or intuitive assessment. The violation of engineering and design parameters was horrendous, and evident with each shudder of the structure. There was utterly no way to measure or monitor what was happening beneath the footings of the dam in that soupy maelstrom of melted snow from the Rocky Mountains and red sandstone from the desert.

What next? The prospect is a colossus of disaster, unapproached certainly in the history of civil engineering, probably in the history of human construction.

First, the river rafting parties in the Grand Canyon experience the white-water adventure of the millennium. Then, other fantastic rapids appear downstream from the Grand Canyon a few hours later, when Lake Mead drinks Lake Powell, and Hoover Dam is the next to quiver and yield. And then Davis Dam, Parker Dam, Headgate Rock Dam, Palo Verde Dam, Imperial Dam, Laguna Dam, and Moreles Dam follow in lockstep. If the dikes breach, the Salton Sea in California rises to levels unseen in geologic ages; and if they hold, the desalinization plant at the Mexican border is rinsed into the Gulf of California.

A domino metaphor leaps to mind, but that ignores the cumulative effects of the fury. A chain reaction comes closer, since the stored water in each successive reservoir is added to the flood as each dam fails. Below the shambles of Moreles, decades of accumulated runoff from the Colorado River watershed hunt for a way to the sea.

The quick and sequential destruction of nine mainstem dams on the Colorado River would constitute the greatest and most rapid single dissipation of public capital in the nation's history. The loss of life and private property would be massive.

The combat between dam and river was deadlocked for three days. Then on June 29, the classic dilemma of immovable objects and irresistible forces was sidestepped. The runoff into Lake Powell was reported to be peaking, and the spillway gates were inched down to reduce the dumping to 87,000 cubic feet per second. In subsequent days the flow was reduced to 61,000, then 51,000 cfs. Temporary flashboards first of plywood then of steel plates were installed on top of the spillway gates to gain eight feet of storage capacity in Lake Powell. On July 23 the spillway gates were closed, and the flashboards held. At eight feet over full pool elevation, the surface of Lake Powell stood just seven feet below the crest of Glen Canyon dam, but from there it receded. So did the terror.

Repairing the battleworn spillway tubes took more than a year, $15 million, and ten thousand cubic yards of concrete. If you had that much concrete to build a sidewalk four feet wide and three inches thick, it could be fifty-one miles long.

One wonders if the bureau could have survived, as an agency, a disaster of that prospective magnitude, one that it escaped by a matter of days, perhaps hours, and for the want of a few more acre feet of snowmelt. Not just the agency, but the whole rationale of centralized water development, federal reclamation policy, and the premises and stature of civil engineering would have been up for scrutiny and criticism. Trusting federal resource assets to the knowledge and skills of professional managers might have seemed a mighty error, and the corrective measures would have been traumatic.

That is indeed conjecture. What is clear is that, by the mid-1960s, across the spectrum of federal lands resource professionals were applying their scientific, engineering, and managerial skills in forestry, wildlife biology, range science, wilderness management in the national parks, and water development. To a greater or lesser extent, they were applying strategies of equilibration, and they were encountering perceptions of their activities at odds with their own.

The causes of the grumbling had something in common, and that was their novelty: They represented change. It was the imposition of sustained-yield forestry that caused Fernow's misery; the initiation of "antlerless deer" hunting that ruffled the hunters; and the first application of the carrying-capacity limitation that annoyed the livestock operators. New techniques and policies stood in contrast to existing practices.

But quickly imposed novelties could be expected in the unique effervescence of American institutions, in which change took place so rapidly. Only a few decades prior to Fernow's difficulties there was no such thing as a vacation home in the Adirondacks. In the interim, scenic resources had become. Female deer became a huntable resource when the biologists insisted on their utility. And the domestic livestock operators transformed what was to them the neutral stuff of western grasses into a forage resource with their technology of open-range grazing and cattle drives. And all the while, because of the urging of the Constitution and of "free enterprise," American corporations happily created new perceptions of utility and new technologies, propagating a dynamic context of abundance.

The equilibration schemes of the resource professionals, ôn the other hand, were suited perfectly to static conditions of scarcity. It is little wonder the grumblings arose. The misfit of professional paradigm to empiric circumstance was never articulated, but something was amiss.

None of the disagreements escalated to the scale Fernow endured: having his enterprise obliterated. Even in the case of the Grazing Service, merger proved superior to termination, and in the other episodes survival was never an issue. The misfits were insufficiently apparent, not yet acute.

Suppose, however, Glen Canyon dam had rolled over, sending Lake Powell to begin the piling-on of the eight additional mainstem structures. After the catastrophe, in the silence and the sorrow and the mist and the mud, a misfit between professional practice and empiric circumstance would be apparent indeed. A post mortem response could take many forms, but it is at least likely that the bureau would expire and the nine dams would never be rebuilt. The Cadillac drivers in the Imperial Valley would screech for relief, and Phoenix would howl for salvation, but no tax dollars and not much sympathy would flow. Things have changed, people would say, we don't need those dams now, and maybe we never really did. Whatever they gave us, we can do without, and maybe we'll be better off anyway. In a context of abundance, we don't need to cope with scarcity.

A Unified View Emerges, but a Convulsion Is Replayed

The Unheeded Messages of Aldo Leopold and Black Elk

In 1949 Oxford University Press published Aldo Leopold's work *A Sand County Almanac and Sketches Here and There*. For the next forty years it was widely read by resource management professionals, highly praised, and significantly ignored.

Leopold spoke about land as commodity and land as community, and strongly endorsed the latter. A long quote is in order, because Leopold was the first to express, in the dominant culture, a concept of land interaction that would emerge, and needed to, as the twentieth century ended.

> THE COMMUNITY CONCEPT
>
> All ethics so far evolved rest upon a single premise: that the individual is a member of a community of interdependent parts. His instincts prompt him to compete for his place in that community, but his ethics prompt him also to co-operate (perhaps in order that there may be a place to compete for).
>
> The land ethic simply enlarges the boundaries of the community to include soils, waters, plants, and animals, or collectively: the land.
>
> This sounds simple: do we not already sing our love for and obligation to the land of the free and the home of the brave? Yes, but just what and whom do we love? Certainly not the soil, which we are sending helter-skelter downriver. Certainly not the waters, which we assume have no function except to turn turbines, float barges, and carry off sewage. Certainly not the plants, of which we exterminate whole communities without batting an eye. Certainly not the animals, of which we have already extirpated many of the largest and most beautiful species. A land ethic of course cannot prevent the alteration, management, and use of these "resources," but it does affirm their right to continued existence, and, at least in spots, their continued existence in a natural state.
>
> In short, a land ethic changes the role of *Homo sapiens* from conqueror of the land-community to plain member

and citizen of it. It implies respect for his fellow-members, and also respect for the community as such.[17]

This is probably the first assertion by an Anglo-American writer of humanity's relationship to the biophysical environment that is congruent with the Native American view. Compare Leopold's words to those of Black Elk, a holy man of the Oglala Sioux:

> My friend, I am going to tell you the story of my life, as you wish. . . . It is the story of all life that is holy and is good to tell, and of us two-leggeds sharing in it with the four-leggeds and the wings of the air and all green things; for these are children of one mother and their father is one Spirit. . . .

> Is not the sky a father and the earth a mother, and all living things with feet or wings or roots their children? [It is]. . . . the earth, from whence we came and at whose breast we suck as babies all our lives, along with all the animals and birds and trees and grasses.[18]

Half a century later Leopold's assertion is only beginning to take hold in the thinking of the resource management professions, and it sits like a ticking bomb in the curricula of their professional education programs. Those curricula are altogether dominated by science, and science cannot accommodate either ethics in general or "respect" in particular, not to mention humility and reverence—explicit in Native American thought, implicit in Leopold's.

Leopold's thinking expressed in *Sand County* seems a quantum jump from his earlier definition of wilderness, in which he drew a sharp distinction between man and nature. Here he bolts from Marsh's explicit separation in *Man and Nature*, from the biblical

---

17. Aldo Leopold, *A Sand County Almanac and Sketches Here and There* (New York: Oxford University Press, 1949), pp. 203–204 (paperback edition).

18. See John G. Neihardt, *Black Elk Speaks: Being the Life Story of a Holy Man of the Oglala Sioux* (Lincoln: University of Nebraska Press, 1961), pp. 1–3.

view of "dominion," and from the orthodoxy of his culture. Leopold's thinking represents a "paradigmatic shift" of the first order.[19]

Certainly he spoke with clarity about his preferred redefinition of professional forestry. Again a long quote is in order:

> Careful scrutiny reveals a single plane of cleavage common to many specialized fields. In each field one group (A) regards the land as soil and its function as commodity-production; another group (B) regards the land as biota, and its function as something broader. How much broader is admittedly in a state of doubt and confusion.
>
> In my own field, forestry, group A is content to grow trees like cabbages, with cellulose as the basic forest commodity. It feels no inhibition against violence; its ideology is agronomic. Group B, on the other hand, sees forestry as fundamentally different from agronomy because it employs natural species, and manages a natural environment rather than creating an artificial one. Group B prefers natural reproduction on principle. It worries on biotic as well as economic grounds about the loss of species like chestnut, and the threatened loss of the white pines. It worries about a whole series of secondary forest functions: wildlife, recreation, watersheds, wilderness areas. To my mind, Group B feels the stirrings of an ecological conscience.[20]

There is a subtle inconsistency here in distinguishing between nature and artifice while arguing for community, but Leopold provides with humility and tact his own exquisite defense. He is no more "writing" an ethic than Moses "wrote" the Decalogue (the comparison is Leopold's), but simply attempting to chronicle an evolution of social thought.

Leopold discusses a similar cleavage in the wildlife field in

---

19. The term *paradigmatic shift* is Thomas Kuhn's, describing how the sciences progress: not by the slow accumulation of marginal knowledge, but by imaginative leaps to new visions. See his *Structure of Scientific Revolution* (Chicago: University of Chicago Press, 1970).

20. Leopold, *Sand County Almanac*, p. 221.

which "for Group A the basic commodities are sport and meat; the yardsticks of production are the ciphers of take in pheasant and trout." He also saw a cleavage in agriculture, between high-input farming and organic farming.

Type B forestry—and range conservation, and wildlife biology, and certainly the Type B management of western rivers—would be a long time in arriving. It would be faintly visible as the twentieth century faded, but only after society at large had marked what the Type A professional equilibrators had otherwise accomplished: overcut forests, overgrazed grasslands, depleted salmon runs, and rivers turned into slackwater.

None of the resource professions set out to achieve such dismal results. Their static schemes were overcome by the dynamics of change and eventually by economic and political overshoot, but there was more to it than that. The history of professional resource management is one of extreme reductionism that guaranteed cabbage-patch forestry and the meat-market management of fish and game. The management of trees, grasses, wildlife, water, and even recreation developed as singular and separated specialisms.

Textbooks, coursework, and baccalaureate degree programs evolved in each specialty: forestry (traditionally, that is, timber management), wildlife biology, range conservation, hydrology, and outdoor recreation. Professional societies and associations emerged in each specialty, and so did research bases, journals of specialized literature, and eventually Ph.D. programs. (And each specialty adopted the rational calculus, traditions, and quantification of science.)

The larger society followed suit, in organizing effective interest groups around the independent resources. Associations of cattlemen, wool growers, loggers, miners, lumber manufacturers, pulp and paper interests, irrigators, appreciators of wilderness, skiers, campers, birders, hunters and fisherfolk, hydropower enthusiasts, white-water river runners, off-road vehicle owners, mountain climbers, and snowmobilers congealed around typically singular perceptions of utility and value.

The Congress may have set the pattern by creating separate and singular agencies to handle each renewable resource. Many argue that the Forest Service is in the business primarily of commercial timber production. The BLM is often called the

Bureau of Livestock and Mining for substantially good reasons. The national parks are devoted to recreation. The Fish and Wildlife Service has a narrowly defined mission. The Bureau of Reclamation's myopia about water impoundments is legendary. Neither the agencies nor their respective clientele groups looked very far past the borders of their parochial, single-resource interests.

Only Leopold in isolation and Black Elk as an agent were speaking in comprehensive, integrative, interdependent terms, while the fissuring and reductionism continued and accelerated. Academic forestry subdivided into forest growth and yield, forest entomology, forest fire science, forest engineering, forest silviculture, forest measurements, forest economics, forest products, forest grazing, forest policy, forest genetics, forest management science, forest pathology, forest wildlife habitat, forest recreation, forest hydrology, forest ecology, forest soils—all of them rooted in science, always and everywhere more science.

Meanwhile, the clientele groups fissured into finer and finer subdivisions on the bases of technique—skiers according to downhill, cross-country, or snowboard preferences—or single species, to be satisfied only, it seemed, with unlimited quantities of trout or ducks.

In the profession of forestry and in the federal agency devoted to it, the Forest Service, a seminal idea appeared in the 1930s that might have counteracted the reductionism. It was "multiple use," the notion that forested land could be used for timber production, certainly, but also for wildlife habitat, for domestic grazing, for watershed protection, and for outdoor recreation.

The literature of multiple use was rich and varied and occasionally characterized by controversy.[21] The debate centered on the nature of the multiplicity: Were the uses to be undertaken simultaneously on every acre, or could they be segregated instead into adjacent single-use allocations, under the jurisdiction of a "multiple use" agency?

---

21. A very modest contribution, written with the smug flippancy of a young assistant professor, appeared after "multiple use" was encoded in the Multiple Use Sustained Yield Act of 1960. See R. W. Behan, "The Succotash Syndrome, or Multiple Use: A Heart-Felt Approach to Forest Land Management," in *Natural Resource Journal* (October 1967).

Had the former argument prevailed, both profession and agency might have adopted decades sooner Leopold's integrated system view. To achieve multiple uses simultaneously, acre by acre, would have required the anticipation of interactive effects, and in the evolving study of forest ecology there was a foundation for anticipation. In the evolving study of forest economics, joint-production theory pointed out promising directions for managerial analysis and decision making. The intellectual structures were available to transform Leopold's vision into Type B practice.

But the argument for simultaneity did not prevail. Multiplicity was pursued through adjacency instead, because that minimized the threat to the primacy of sustained-yield timber production. David Clary argued this persuasively in his book *Timber and the Forest Service*.[22]

Multiple use thus became merely a policy of land use, not the revolutionary new technique of professional forestry practice it might have been. Any use of forestland that was profitable intrinsically, or could be made so by subsidy, was encouraged. Multiple use had nothing to do with ecology, but much to do with the epidemic plundering of public assets that appeared in the decades to come.

Leopold would not live to see his progressive thinking adopted. He died in midlife fighting a brushfire on his neighbor's land, a tragedy for his family, his profession, and for the federal lands. Had his voice continued and had his Type B concept prevailed, much of the environmental damage on the federal lands might have been avoided. Instead, the Type A approach dominated the thinking of the professionals, the behavior of the agencies, the agendas of the interest groups, and the strategies of the resource-extracting corporations.

However, the Forest Service was in some respects a notable departure from this norm. The admiration in the Forest Service for "multiple use," even though restricted to the adjacency application, led it in time to embrace seriously all the renewable

---

22. David A. Clary, *Timber and the Forest Service* (Lawrence: University Press of Kansas, Development of Western Resources Series, 1986). Clary makes a stern case that the messianic idealism of professional forestry in preventing the social disaster of a "timber famine" never wavered in the agency's single mindedness over sustained-yield timber production.

resources, their management professions, and their peculiar manifestations of sustained yield. The timber resource dominated the
agency's thinking, its budget, and its activities, but intramural
advocates for the other resources over time were emplaced and
finally empowered.

Limiting the periodic harvest of a renewable resource to its
periodic growth is the fundamental dictum of sustained yield, but
it can take at least two forms. The benign and conservative form
sets the harvest level according to the spontaneous (some might
say "natural") periodic increment of the resource. A bolder, more
vigorous approach applies capital to the resource, to stimulate
production "artificially." This approach holds an immense appeal
to resource managers with exaggerated anxieties about scarcity,
and it appeals immensely to those of the Type A, cabbage-patch
persuasion. *Maximum* sustained yield would be limited only by
the biological capacity of the land to absorb productive capital
inputs.

As the second half of the twentieth century got underway, the
bold form of sustained yield was pursued enthusiastically by the
federal resource agencies. After WWII, the budget floodgates of
public capital opened, and the maximizers of sustained yield went
on a binge of dam construction, rangeland "improvement," recreation facilities development, road building, and clear-cutting. Single-resource agencies, cheered on by their single-resource clientele groups, undertook Type A management activities with
unprecedented capability.

Labeled "intensive management" in the Forest Service, the
enthusiasm led to "a conspiracy of optimism," as historian Paul
Hirt described the period.[23] The allowable cut, later to be called
ASQ, or "allowable sale quantity," became a function of the
budget for "timber management." And what timber management

---

23. Paul W. Hirt, *A Conspiracy of Optimism: Management of the National Forests
Since World War Two* (Lincoln: University of Nebraska Press, 1994). Hirt's and
Clary's books make good companion pieces. Clary (see note 22) describes
the obsession with timber scarcity of the professional foresters in the agency;
Hirt describes the political consequences of naive capital-intensive forest
management and how it benefited enormously not the forest but the forest
products industry. Much of the story to follow in the next few paragraphs is
paraphrased from Hirt's book.

meant, in the postwar years, was the conversion of complex biological systems, the old-growth forests of the West, into simplified timber plantations. It is not physically easy to effect such a conversion.

First the forest must be developed with timber access roads. Then the old trees must be removed to make way for the new trees, presumably superior in terms of species and genetic character. Removing them all at once, a practice known as clear-cutting, proved to be irresistibly efficient. The forest industry was pleased to proceed, if only the agency could measure, mark out, appraise, advertise, and administer the timber sales with dispatch. That called for increasing timber management budgets.

It was in the agency's interest to seek increasing budgets. It was in the industry's interest to offer political support. Neither was laggard in pursuing its interests. It was in the Congress's interest to grant the increasing budgets, because the returns to the U.S. Treasury in the form of stumpage payments, the top management of the Forest Service argued, could well exceed the budget allocations for timber sale preparation and road construction.

The success of the conspiracy of optimism between the agency, its industrial beneficiary, and Congress, was no less than grandiose. In the quarter century after World War II, timber harvests from the national forests essentially quadrupled, from a bit more than 3 billion board feet per year to nearly 12 billion. To reach and remove the timber, a network of roads was built that finally totaled some 342,000 miles, almost seven times the aggregate length of the interstate highway system.[24]

The next tasks in transforming forests into plantations aren't nearly so exciting. Site preparation, planting, seeding, tending, protecting, and thinning operations appealed to the professional sensibilities of the Type A foresters, but not to the forest industry and not to the Congress. Appropriations for those elements of timber management were chronically scant. Year after year, agency foresters asked for budgets that were "balanced" between the extractive tasks of timber sale preparation and road construction, and the stewardship tasks of forest regeneration, nurture, and protection that would "sustain" the yields in the future. There

---

24. Ibid., p. xxiii.

was no immediate payoff from such activities for either the forest industry or the Congress, and the balance was never remotely approached. Token amounts for stewardship placated the foresters and served to blunt any accusations of congressional irresponsibility, and in time the agency foresters stopped complaining.

The Forest Service did to the western forests, finally, what the Bureau of Reclamation did to the western rivers. With mighty applications of public capital, the richly diverse riverine and forest systems were transformed into single-purpose engines for the production of private wealth. All the federal resource agencies— including the Park Service with its billion dollar program of redevelopment called Mission 66—invested capital to benefit private and almost exclusively corporate interests. The plunder of public assets was heavily subsidized. Only one of the agencies, however, would incubate the massive conflict and controversy that erupted in the late 1960s, to traumatize the federal lands community for the succeeding decades.

That distinction fell to the U.S. Forest Service. As we have seen, the Forest Service behaved in many respects like the other single-resource agencies. By virtue of its professional legacy and by virtue of the postwar political success of the forest industry, the agency did indeed emphasize the timber resource. But we have also seen how stoutly the Forest Service touted its policy of multiple use. In the process of hiring on the supporting professions of wildlife biology, hydrology, engineering, range conservation, and recreation management, the agency was inescapably appealing to a broader constituency. Not only were internal advocates emplaced, but external expectations were stimulated, among the whole range of alternative single-resource users. Only the Forest Service confronted a plural and contentious constituency of resource users capable of conflict within itself, and quite capable of launching a subset into a direct attack on the agency.

It turned out that simultaneous multiplicity was unavoidable. The convenience and political expediency of segregating uses into adjacent compartments were overpowered and displaced by the ecological reality of interdependence. The primacy of timber management activities, the heavy emphasis on clear-cutting and road construction, impacted heavily the concurrent ability of those same acres to graze domestic livestock, to furnish terrestrial and aquatic habitat for wildlife and fish, and to maintain an aesthetic backdrop for recreation activities.

Sustaining a yield of timber in perpetuity, the Forest Service found to its dismay, foreclosed the other potential and simultaneous uses of forest land—and each of those other uses now had advocates within the agency and clients without.

The Bitterroot Controversy: Bernhard Fernow Revisited

In Montana, in the 1960s, in the Bitterroot National Forest the timber managers were maximizing the sustained yield of commercial timber by building roads and clear-cutting. Then they carved miles and miles of terraces into the mountainsides. Doing that enabled them to mechanize the process of "artificial regeneration." The terraces provided level platforms along which to run planting machines, and furthermore, research had shown, they would trap and hold the moisture of winter snows. The survival rate of the planted seedlings was much higher as a consequence.

On the other side of the valley, the foresters pointed out, was the part of the Bitterroot National Forest designated as the Selway Bitterroot Wilderness Area. What they were doing with the terraces on this side of the valley was good timber management. Wilderness there, timber production here: We're a multiple-use agency, they said. Trust us.

The people in the Bitterroot Valley did not—not any more than the residents in the Adirondacks had trusted Bernhard Fernow. The Bitterrooters who grazed livestock, diverted water for irrigation, hunted and fished, and appreciated the beauty of the mountains saw other things, perceived other values. What seemed to the foresters to be good sustained-yield forestry looked like forest devastation to the local people. The terraces were visible for miles and drew particularly caustic criticism.

The foresters explained about planting machines, retained moisture, and good timber management. The users and appreciators of the other resources would have none of it, and neither would Guy M. Brandborg, a former supervisor of the Bitterroot National Forest. They wrote letters to the editors of local newspapers complaining, and soon a reporter for the *Daily Missoulian*, Mr. Dale Burk, codified the complaints.

Burk interviewed each of the resource users, and documented the diminished value of forage production, the stream sedimentation, the habitat damage, and the visual insult of the clear-cut and terraced mountainsides. He interviewed Brandborg, who objected in principle to the agency's aggressive, capital-intensive form of sustained yield. Burk's stories were intelligently understated, but nonetheless explosive: Timber cutting and the Forest Service in western Montana, indeed in the nation, had never been subjected to such concentrated criticism. The criticism itself—and Burk's reporting—became the topic of other stories elsewhere in the country.

A deluge of letters was sent to Montana's junior senator, Lee Metcalf. A native of the Bitterroot Valley, Metcalf served on the Senate Committee on Interior and Insular Affairs, and he took up the issue with vigor and sincere passion.

On December 2, 1969, Senator Metcalf wrote to Dr. Arnold W. Bolle, dean of the School of Forestry at the University of Montana. He enclosed a sampling of constituents' letters, and said:

> These letters reflect the writers' and my growing concern over Forest Service management practices within the Bitterroot National Forest and elsewhere.
>
> I am especially concerned, as are my constituents, over the long-range effects of clearcutting, and the dominant role of timber production in Forest Service policy, to the detriment of other uses of these national resources.[25]

Metcalf then asked Dean Bolle to make an independent assessment of the situation in the Bitterroot:

> I believe that a study of Forest Service policy in the Bitterroot by an outside professional group would be beneficial to the Montana Congressional delegation and to the entire Congress, especially the Senate and House Interior Committees. The Bitterroot is a typical mountain timbered valley and the results of such a study might well be extended to recommendations national in scope. I hope appropriate faculty members at the University of Montana will participate. If this is possible I would welcome whatever policy recommendations such a committee would offer.[26]

---

25. Author's personal files.

26. Ibid.

Dean Bolle appointed what came to be known formally as a Select Committee of the University of Montana, and informally as the Bolle Committee. From the School of Forestry were W. Leslie Pengelley, a wildlife biologist, economists Richard E. Shannon and Associate Dean Robert F. Wambach, and a professor of forest policy.[27] Gordon Browder and Thomas Payne from the College of Liberal Arts completed the committee. Browder, a sociologist, and political scientist Payne had served with Bolle for years on the faculty of the School of Administrative Leadership, which offered postgraduate study for resource professionals in state and federal management agencies.

Metcalf could not know that forestry educators nationwide had undertaken already an initiative to broaden the professional curriculum. Four years earlier, Dean Bolle had suggested such an initiative to the Council of Forestry School Executives, and he had watched with satisfaction as the Forestry Curriculum Development Project unfolded, with his enthusiastic participation and encouragement, but largely under the leadership and guidance of others.

The initiative sought to broaden the single-resource emphasis on timber management to a Type B concern for the entire forest system. Multiple use could be defined in terms of simultaneity, and professional practice could be revolutionized, but it would take much effort and time, a great deal of time.

Meanwhile, at Montana, Bolle had encouraged his own faculty to redesign its professional curriculum. A focus on "integrated forest resource management" was the result, a prototypical construction of Type B forestry. Senator Metcalf's invitation to suggest a redirection of national forest policy was an electrifying opportunity to advance the new approach to professional practice. The Select Committee was not indifferent to the opportunity, nor was it indifferent to the hazards involved.

Between the time of the Senator's request and the completion of the committee's work, the first nationwide Earth Day was declared, displaying the national scope and the intensity of the

27. The professor of forest policy found quite awkward the reconstruction of the work of the Bolle Committee that follows. Dispassionate objectivity was not possible, but the compulsion was strong to document the membership of the committee and to record a few nuances of style, contribution, and achievement.

environmental movement. Forest management on the Bitterroot National Forest was not an independent and isolated issue; the committee's findings and suggestions would be scrutinized not only by scholarly colleagues in academic forestry, but also in the harsh visibility and vigorous controversy of environmental politics.

Bolle's work was risky for another reason. Forestry schools had a long heritage of sympathy and support for the U.S. Forest Service. It is not inaccurate to say that the professional schools are institutional descendants of the agency: Gifford Pinchot founded the first durable school at Yale, and for years the master of forestry degree from Yale was the preeminent credential of professional faculties. That dominance had waned by 1970, but no forestry school had yet publicized its neutrality or affirmed the primacy of its dedication to the traditions of academic freedom and social criticism.

Bolle indulged his preference for encouragement and facilitation, instead of dramatic, heroic, authoritarian leadership.[28] His guidance often took the form of a seminal question, opening sectors of analysis and debate that might have been overlooked. Browder and Payne brought insights from their social sciences; the issue was far broader than technical silviculture, and their quiet, thoughtful analyses made that clear to the committee members from the School of Forestry. Shannon understood the particulars of the intramural and interagency politics of the environmental issue and had perhaps the most intricate network of Washington,

---

28. In a letter to the author dated July 15, 1990, Bolle explained his preference: "An interesting thought on leadership styles emerges from all this. Heroes vs. Helpers. The hero is the great man who sees the problem, decides on the conclusion, leads the charge of supporters of his cause. He gets (takes) all the glory of success or becomes the martyr if it loses. The helper, on the other hand, gets involved when he sees a problem and need for change, but his effort is to help others see and understand what goes on. Together they get the knowledge and understanding first to identify the problem and to be sure it is commonly understood. Then he helps to consider the possibilities for action to achieve needed change, helps examine and evaluate consequences of possible actions, and then helps achieve the desired action. This idea is not new, of course, but somehow the Hero-Helper words help clarify the difference. . . . The helper avoids credit for himself, always seeks to attribute it to others. I like to think of myself as in the Helper mode, and that's why this sudden honor is such a shock." The letter was written shortly after receiving one of the many accolades Bolle received later in his life.

D.C., contacts. Pengelley contributed the legacy of Leopold's appeal for an ethical relationship with land, refined with his own thinking, speaking, teaching, and writing. Wambach's incisive, analytical mind produced the first systematic criticism of the diseconomies of "intensive management," and his argument was powerful. He backed his conviction with candor when he drafted the pivotal and unequivocal statement in the committee's report: "The practice of terracing on the Bitterroot National Forest should be stopped." Thus inspired, the committee's collegial sense of commitment was galvanized, and Bolle was gratified to see its determination clarified: It would speak forthrightly.

It did. On November 9, 1970, Dean Bolle submitted his committee's work to Senator Metcalf. The first five statements of finding, in what came to be known as the Bolle Report, were candid beyond dispute:

1. Multiple use management, in fact, does not exist as the governing principle on the Bitterroot National Forest.
2. Quality timber management and harvest practices are missing. Consideration of recreation, watershed, wildlife, and grazing appear as afterthoughts.
3. The management sequence of clearcutting-terracing-planting cannot be justified as an investment for producing timber on the Bitterroot National Forest. We doubt that the Bitterroot National Forest can continue to produce timber at the present harvest level.
4. Clearcutting and planting is an expensive operation. Its use should bear some relationship to the capability of the site to return the cost invested.
5. The practice of terracing on the Bitterroot National Forest should be stopped.[29]

Findings 9 and 10 pointed at the root of the problem: the "unbalanced" budgeting that subsidized the plunder of public assets, a problem that was not unique to the national forests.

---

29. The Bolle Report was reprinted as Senate Document no. 91-115, *A University View of the Forest Service* (Washington, DC: U.S. Government Printing Office, December 1, 1970). The Statement of Findings appears on p. 13.

9. Unless the job of total quality management is recognized by the agency leadership, the necessary financing for the complete task will not be aggressively sought.

10. Manpower and budget limitations of public resource agencies do not at present allow for essential staffing and for integrated multiple use planning.[30]

When Senator Metcalf released the report on November 18, the *Daily Missoulian* ran a front-page story by Dale Burk, headlined "UM Study Condemns Forest Service Practices." That was indisputably candid, too, and it set off a chain reaction of controversy and change.

In the universe of public affairs, national forest policy is but a tiny sector, but in that factor the Bolle Report was a stimulus for change of some consequence. The epicenter of the controversy it engendered was in Montana: The local forest industry, overcoming its initial apoplexy, sent an attorney to the state capital in Helena, in a sophomoric attempt to have Dean Bolle and his committee members discharged from the university.

The impacts rippled and radiated across the nation. Stories about the Bolle Report appeared in the *New York Times*, *The Washington Post*, and episodically elsewhere, including *The Reader's Digest*. Gifford Bryce Pinchot, the son of the first and fiery Chief of the Forest Service, visited the Bitterroot National Forest with the Bolle Committee, witnessed the ravished landscape, and remarked, "This would have killed the old man." That event itself was the center of a stormy debate in the literature of conservation and professional forestry.

John Adams of the Natural Resource Defense Council queried the committee to see if the Bitterroot National Forest could be sued for violating the Multiple Use Sustained Yield Act. Jointly they concluded no, the act was probably too vague—but environmental litigation soon became a potent tool. A successful lawsuit several years later on the Monongahela National Forest hinged on the careful work of an NRDC attorney, and the "Monongahela decision" would force some major changes in the statutory basis of national forest management.

---

30. Ibid.

That would take another six years, but in the meantime, attempts at legislative reform were undertaken almost immediately. Bolle, Wambach, and Shannon shuttled to Washington and elsewhere around the country regularly, to testify and consult.

Hatfield of Oregon, no critic of the forest industry, introduced S. 350 on January 27, 1971. It was called the American Forestry Act. Metcalf countered with S. 1734 on April 30, the Forest Lands Restoration and Protection Act of 1971. After taking testimony in Washington, the Senate Subcommittee on Public Lands held field hearings in Atlanta; Portland, Oregon; and Syracuse. The industry lined up consensually in support of Hatfield's bill; the environmental community did likewise for Metcalf's. Neither passed.

Draft bills of forest reform, hearings records, a number of studies including the Bolle Report, and congressional committee reports were stacking up in Senator Herman Talmadge's Committee on Agriculture and Forestry. The committee fashioned the raw material into the Forest and Rangeland Renewable Resources Planning Act in 1974. Two years later it orchestrated the enactment of the National Forest Management Act.[31] We will consider this legislation in some detail in the next chapter, but Senator Hubert Humphrey's comments introducing the bill marked a significant milepost:

> We have had 15 years since the Multiple Use and Sustained Yield Act was passed. Much has happened, and as we look at what has transpired, the need for improvement is evident. . . . The days are ended when the forest may be viewed only as trees and trees only as timber. The soil and the water, the grasses and shrubs, the fish and wildlife, and the beauty that is the forest must become integral parts of the resource manager's thinking and actions.[32]

---

31. The legislative politics of passing these laws was detailed capably in Dennis C. LeMaster, *Decade of Change: The Remaking of Forest Service Statutory Authority During the 1970s* (Westport, CT: Greenwood Press for the Forest History Society, 1984).

32. Quoted in Charles F. Wilkinson and H. Michael Anderson, "Land and Resource Planning in the National Forests," *Oregon Law Review* 64, nos. 1 and 2 (1985), pp. 69–70.

There was Leopold's Type B forestry described on the floor of the U.S. Senate. It would be nearly as explicit in the law to be enacted. In the universities it was being debated, and in the more progressive professional schools it was being developed.

So even though "intensive management" had failed the well-meaning equilibrators, there was reason to be optimistic: A Type B approach to renewable resource management could signal healthier forests. Given wider diffusion, it could also mean healthier rangelands, river systems, maybe even parks, and perhaps a better outlook for people who used and enjoyed the federal lands.

Revolution was scarcely at hand. The *Journal of Forestry*, the professional publication of the Society of American Foresters, carried not a single word about the Bitterroot controversy, or about the varying legislative proposals. The debate was reported instead in the popular periodicals of conservation.

At the University of Montana, Dean Bolle and his committee faced some dissenters among the faculty who respectfully defended the old, Type A ways. A strident group of alumni, feeling betrayed and deserted, registered objections. Equilibration schemes in their simplicity offered such profound security; assumptions of resource scarcity were so deeply embedded in the wisdom of our culture; intensive management was so quickly, easily, and comfortably rationalized. Substantive change, always uncomfortable, frequently painful, is more likely to be evolutionary. But change was certainly on the near side of the horizon in the mid-1970s, and the future of the federal lands seemed promising. In legislation and in professional practice, the momentum was running in the right direction.

In the larger institutional context, however, there were momentums, too. A fully developed economy and a fully developed political system lumbered toward overshoot, and co-opted the promising developments in federal lands policy and in professional managerial practice. The federal lands had been damaged, but they had not yet been blighted: that would take place in the decade of the 1980s.

Chapter Five

The Economics and Politics of License: Corruption and Predation, 1976 to the Present

The Institutional Tables Are Turned

During the last quarter of the twentieth century the corruption of American capitalism and the predatory nature of American politics became visible and then conspicuous. Our institutions overshot.

Economic institutions exist to provision the community, political institutions exist to sustain it, and both should remain servants of society at large. When institutions overshoot, they become autonomous, inducting society into their service instead. Consumers are then exploited to further the interests of producers, and citizens are exploited to sustain a self-serving structure of governance. We will see some details shortly.

First we need to reconsider that economics and politics are neither separate nor independent sets of activities. The behavior of contemporary corporations belies a sharp line of demarcation. Corporations resort to politics continuously to achieve economic ends: cost subsidies, tax relief, marketing assistance, the externalization of costs, direct revenues (procurement contracts), military protection of foreign raw materials supplies, access to least-cost labor pools and minimized environmental regulations anywhere in the world, and the sub-market pricing of federal land resources.

"Free markets" are scarcely free: They are driven by public policies put in place by contemporary corporations in their own interests, and thus the economic system is conditioned by political action. Corporations utilize political action committees to dominate the financing of political campaigns, and thus the political system is conditioned by economic interests. The economic structure of corporate capitalism has captured the politics of governance, and American people have become subservient to their economic and political institutions.

We have seen the effects of overshoot on the federal lands. Too many roads and clear-cuts; too many fences, vegetative "type conversions," and water developments; too many dams in the rivers; too much development of energy resources; arguably too many marinas and resorts and overcommercialized national parks. In brief, the federal lands were assaulted with "intensive management," and it took a great deal of public financing to achieve.

Until overshoot, the financing was lacking, but during the prior decades, the technical means of intensive management had been conceived and refined in the minds of the resource professionals. Operating under assumptions of scarcity, they knew exactly what they wanted to do. They were anxious to do it, and eventually the financing arrived.

It did not arrive by accident, and its arrival was immensely profitable to the resource corporations. The provision of public capital was not orchestrated site-by-site and project-by-project in coherent communities, by on-the-ground managers interacting in good faith with interested citizens. That pattern—it could be called "bottom-up" budgeting—had existed for most of the twentieth century, but institutional overshoot strongly centralized the decisions for the federal lands in Washington, D.C. There a triumvirate of permanent and professionalized policy makers held sway. Legislators, lobbyists, and executive agency careerists undertook mutually beneficial collaborations to reach decisions and resolve disputes, not in real, tangible, and decentralized communities, but in statute and in the budget process.

That's how the public financing for intensive management arrived, and it took the form of hugely expanded, top-down programs of public investment. The benefits were concentrated on the permanent and professionalized staffs of the resource managing agencies (expanding budgets and policy space); the incumbent politicians (campaign funds) and their permanent, professionalized staffs (career security); and the resource-extracting corporations and financial institutions that had driven the political system to overshoot (money, in one form or another). The federal lands suffered biophysical damage, and society at large bore unprecedented costs.

The institutional tables had been turned.

The Overdeveloped Economy: Corrupted Capitalism

An underdeveloped economy displays inadequate per-capita production and consequently inadequate per-capita consumption. Hunger is perhaps the most vivid but by no means the only symptom. High rates of illiteracy and infant mortality are others. Individuals would be better off if they consumed more, and society would benefit. The marginal benefit of additional consumption is positive.

A fully developed economy is one in which production and per-capita consumption are optimal. The marginal benefit of additional consumption is zero.

In an overdeveloped economy the marginal benefit of consumption is negative. Production and consumption are so elevated that absolute decreases in individual and collective well-being are experienced. By any serious accounting, consumption in the range of negative marginal benefits is unfortunate and irrational, both for the individual and for society at large. It is hyperconsumption.

Hyperconsumption, on a per-capita basis, is chronic and flagrant in the United States today.

The personal and public health results of hyperconsuming red meat are matters of record. Heart disease, stroke, colon and breast cancer, obesity, and diabetes are direct consequences of excessive beef consumption; they account each year for hundreds of thousands of deaths and billions of dollars in health care costs.[1] Americans would be far healthier if the consumption of red meat were drastically reduced. But millions of acres of federal land, and hundreds of millions of dollars in federal subsidies, are devoted to its production. In the process, the federal lands continue to be overgrazed, adding environmental damage to the social costs of red meat hyperconsumption. Downstream pollution by feedlots and slaughterhouses exacerbates the misfortune.

Using public assets to damage public health and the biophysical environment simultaneously is perverse public policy.

The personal and social consequences of hyperconsuming energy are also matters of record. No other single source of air pollution in the United States comes close to the combustion of hydrocarbons, and we burn them at prodigious rates. Americans consume twice as much energy per capita as citizens of West Germany, $2^{1/2}$ times as much as the Japanese, $12^{1/2}$ times the Chinese rate, and 52 times the Nigerians',[2] incurring in the process literally incalculable costs of respiratory diseases in society and atmospheric carbon loading of the biophysical environment.

Again, we would be far better off, individually and collectively, in both social and environmental dimensions, with a drastic reduction in energy consumption. But once again we subsidize

---

1. See Jeremy Rifkin's book *Beyond Beef* (New York: Penguin Books, 1992). Rifkin chronicles the multinational corporate "beef complex," a web of economic and political structures and forces that provides a global example of corrupted capitalism. Dispatching millions of native agrarian peoples to urban poverty so their lands can be converted to corporate cattle grazing; diverting much of the world's grain production from human food to cattle feed; transforming most of the planet's rich and complex grassland ecosystems into dusty and overgrazed pastures; usurping enormous proportions of water supplies for grain irrigation and cattle watering; and then marketing to the wealthiest nations in the world a product that is demonstrably dangerous: This is not an example of institutions in the service of humanity.

2. See Alan Durning, *How Much Is Enough?* (New York: W.W. Norton, for Worldwatch Institute, 1992), p. 53.

its production with allocations of cheap federal resources and obscene tax concessions to the energy industry.[3]

The hyperconsumption of paper in the United States is a third example. American citizens consume $1^1/2$ times as much paper per capita as their counterparts in West Germany and Japan, 30 times as much as the Chinese, and 308 times as much as Nigerian people.[4] We are provided with about 680 pounds of paper per person per year; much of this arrives in the form of disposable or redundant packaging, and only the beleaguered postal carrier can estimate how much of it is junk mail.

The environmental costs of paper production are severe. The impact on the nation's forests is but the initial one. Paper manufacture is a major source of both water and air pollution. And the largest single component of solid waste is paper. Again, the costs borne by individuals and society at large are not trivial, either. Any cutting of the nation's forests, any loading of air- and watersheds with pollutants, and any expansion of landfills to accommodate hyperconsumption of paper is perverse public policy.

In the consumption of red meat, energy, and paper, the conclusions we have reached are identical and stark: Individuals, society at large, and the biophysical environment all would benefit by

---

3. An unsurpassed book about the history of the petroleum industry is Daniel Yergin, *The Prize: The Epic Quest for Oil, Money, and Power* (New York: Simon and Schuster, 1991). Yergin dispels any modicum of uncertainty about the political power of the petroleum industry, or about its utter indifference to any loyalty beyond the pecuniary. The sequence of Yergin's narrative ends with Saddam Hussein invading Kuwait, and his 781 pages of petroleum geopolitics confirms Senator Robert Dole's observation about the Gulf War: It was not about democracy, it was about "o-i-l." The multinational oil companies demonstrated their capacity to recruit the British and U.S. military forces to defend their primary sources of supply. The strategic interests of both countries and the economic interests of the companies had become inseparable, indeed indistinguishable.

A thorough but dated volume about the subsidizing of the industry, and its wholesale and willful violation of antitrust laws, is John M. Blair, *The Control of Oil* (New York: Vintage Books, 1978). Blair explains, among a great deal else, the "golden gimmick": OPEC's classifying as "taxes" the payments made by oil companies to purchase crude. Each dollar of foreign "tax" so collected is subsequently deducted, dollar for dollar, from the companies' U.S. tax liability. The net cost to the companies for crude purchased in this fashion is exactly zero.

4. Durning, *How Much*, p. 91.

absolute reductions in consumption.[5] But in each case the federal lands and the federal treasury are employed to sustain it.

Why would individuals, and society at large, undertake and continue to consume at levels that are positively harmful to themselves and to the biophysical environment? They have been victimized by capitalism turned corrupt and inducted into the service of their corporate agents of production.

Perhaps the first statement and systematic analysis of this institutional reversal was contained in a book by John Kenneth Galbraith, *The New Industrial State*. Galbraith challenges the fundamental assumption of orthodox economic thought. The consumer, he argues, is no longer sovereign. The "accepted sequence" of information flowing from consumers to producers—which we traced in chapter 1—has been reversed. In the "revised sequence," markets are managed for corporate benefit, by corporate necessity.

Instead of a "free-market" system that relies on a sovereign consumer, we have instead a planning system, but the planners do not reside in public agencies, planning what they expect will serve the public good. That would be textbook socialism. Instead, the planners reside in corporate headquarters, planning products, production quantities, product prices, and the magnitude of net revenue, according to what they expect will serve the good of the company. (The "invisible hand" took care of all these things in Adam Smith's economy.) And then they construct marketing strategies to assure that the plans will be realized. Having told the consumer what the product will be, how much will be available, and at what price, the corporate producers must see to it that the consumer will agree. That is done primarily by advertising.

Some will argue, as Galbraith's critics do, that no one can be forced to buy anything. No matter how beguiling the imagery of country club and mansion, no one can be forced to buy a luxury automobile. No matter how appealing the message of self indul-

---

5. Aside from the three examples, what other goods and services are characterized by hyperconsumption? National defense? Football games? Automobiles? Television programming? Is the hyperconsumption of suburban space the direct cause of urban sprawl? A shorter list might result if the question were "What goods and services are *not* characterized by hyperconsumption?"

gence, no one can be forced to dine on a killer diet of hamburgers and french fries. Individuals possess a high degree of freedom of choice.

The trivial rebuttal to this reasoning is best stated in the interrogative: Then why do corporations spend billions advertising? A more serious rebuttal takes a longer view. What about a process that extends not merely over a model year, but over four or five human generations? Advertising over that much time has a cumulative effect. We haven't been sold only services and products: We have been sold en route the virtue of consumption in and of itself. Our entire culture has absorbed and internalized a high and positive value of simply buying and consuming things—in sharp contrast to the cultural values of the 1800s of prudence, thrift, economy, and austerity. In the short term, only products can be advertised, which we can refuse. In the long term, a lifestyle has been constructed and imposed, which we couldn't refuse. Cumulatively, advertising has created not only a high-mass-consumption culture, but now a culture of hyperconsumption.

If it is merely easy to attribute too much to advertising, it is stupidly easy to attribute too little. Alan Durning, writing in *State of the World, 1991,* states:

> Advertising has been one of the fastest growing industries during the past half century. In the United States, ad expenditures rose from $198 per capita in 1950 to $498 in 1989. Total global advertising expenditures, meanwhile, rose from an estimated $39 billion in 1950 to $237 billion in 1988, growing far faster than economic output.[6]

What does that buy? In the United States, Durning says:

> [Citizens] live completely enveloped in advertising messages. The sales pitch is everywhere. One analyst estimates that the typical American is exposed to 50–100 advertisements each morning before nine o'clock. Along with their weekly 22-hour diet of television, American teenagers are

---

6. Alan Durning, "Asking How Much Is Enough," in *State of the World, 1991* (New York: W.W. Norton for the Worldwatch Institute, 1991), p. 163.

typically exposed to 3–4 hours of TV advertising a week, adding up to at least 100,000 ads between birth and high school graduation. . . . [Ads] are posted on chair-lift poles on the ski slopes, and played through closed circuit televisions at bus stops, in subway stations, and on wall-sized video screens at shopping malls.

Ads are piped into classrooms and doctor's offices, woven into the plots of feature films, placed on board games, mounted in bathroom stalls, and played back between rings on public phones in the Kansas City airport. Even the food supply may soon go mass media: the Viskase Company of Chicago now offers to print edible ad slogans on hot dogs, and Eggverts International is using similar techniques to advertise on . . . eggs. . . .[7]

Today, we are blasted with some three thousand advertising messages per day,[8] making the distinction between sufficiency and hyperconsumption supremely obscure.

How did we arrive at this point? By random chance (some technical innovations); by dumb luck (they worked); and by our failure to monitor the results.

Throughout history, consumption had been limited by production, but innovations in mass production led to a reversal of the roles: Production would now be limited by consumption, so it made unusually good sense to stimulate it. An upward spiral of stimulated consumption continued, mass production worked better and better, and the productive capacity of the economy eventually surpassed society's needs for goods and services. At that point, producers faced an acute need to push consumption to levels even higher than society's needs, in order to maintain the efficient use of their productive assets. We failed to see this, because it was indeed unprecedented in human history. Hyperconsumption became necessary for the welfare of the productive enterprises in society, and that remains the case today.

---

7. Ibid., pp. 162–163.

8. Durning, *How Much*, p. 118.

Clearly, it is the case in the global automobile industry. The worldwide capacity for production is about 45 million automobiles per year.[9] In the best years, the worldwide market can absorb only 35 million, even as it confronts a relentless campaign of advertising. And in spite of price cuts designed to look like anything but price cuts—rebates, low-interest financing—each model year ends with unsold autos clogging the sales lots. In recent years, it is not uncommon to see unsold models two years old.

Overcapacity, abundance, and hyperconsumption are epidemic in the American economy. The situations of red meat, energy, and paper have been described. Is there not also an excess of pomegranates, professional sports, hair dryers, and hockey pucks? For virtually every consumer good and service, we can produce more than the market can absorb. The consequent pressure to stimulate hyperconsumption is extreme—and so are the stimuli.

Excess capacity shadows a despicable flaw. Only in terms of aggregate consumption does our economy produce more than is needed. Millions of citizens are homeless, ill clothed, and badly educated. One sixth of our population is denied routine health care. Ten percent of American families, according to the U.S. Department of Agriculture, are malnourished: One household in ten "has limited or uncertain access to enough safe, nutritious food for an active and healthy life."[10]

A society that has solved the production problem and concurrently fails to distribute its abundance fairly and decently must be characterized in one of only two alternate ways: (1) It has retained collective control of its economic and political institutions but has a perverse agenda: Indifferent to the welfare of society at large, it favors instead a privileged few; or (2) It has lost control of its institutions to that privileged few who pursue their own interests at the expense of the larger community.

The American people do not have a perverse agenda. And our

---

9. Quoted in William Greider, *Who Will Tell the People: The Betrayal of American Democracy* (New York: Simon and Schuster, 1992), p. 399.

10. According to News Release no. f414.99, U.S. Department of Agriculture, a fact sheet derived from the report *Measuring Food Security in the United States* (FANRR-2), 1999.

self-destructive habit of hyperconsumption is not a conscious, collective choice. Our economic system—corporate capitalism—has turned with savage impact against the society it once served.

No conscious conspiracy is apparent among the "privileged few," but it is difficult to refute C. Wright Mills's case for the existence and operation of "the power elite," or the elitist view of politics expressed in Hellinger's and Judd's book *The Democratic Facade*.[11] The privileged elite of wealth, economic power, and political influence is an "open" elite. It is neither closed nor conspiratorial. Talent and skill in entertainment or sports are tickets to entry, and so are notable achievements in law and medicine, in politics, in scholarship, in public service both civil and military, and particularly in corporate management and finance.

It is facile but trite to rail against the managers of modern corporations as villains, as the corrupters of contemporary capitalism. They are instead caught in a *danse macabre*, taught in colleges of business administration and performed in boardrooms. The maximization of net revenue—or the current euphemism "shareholder value"—is so simple, so clean, so quantifiable, so venerable, and so quickly rationalized that the unfortunate social, environmental, and even economic consequences become invisible.[12]

Recent developments in the evolution of capitalism include the globalization of corporate business and the "downsizing" tactic. The General Agreement on Trade and Tariffs embodied in the World Trade Organization is an invitation carte blanche to exploit those biophysical environments and labor pools exhibiting the least protection anywhere in the world. Corrupted capitalism has

---

11. C. Wright Mills, *The Power Elite* (New York: Oxford University Press, 1959); and Daniel Hellinger and Dennis R. Judd, *The Democratic Facade* (Pacific Grove, CA: Brooks/Cole, 1991). We will inspect these works below.

12. The innovation of money, as we saw earlier, allowed the study of economics to be quantified. From economics it is an easy step to "management science" and the techniques of "optimizing." Alternately known as "operations research," "systems analysis," and "decision theory," management science includes the vital elements of mathematics, cardinal measurements, statistics, and quantitative modeling—there are no other elements. It utterly dominates the curricula in schools of both business administration and professional resource management. A folk homily explains the fatal shortcoming with felicity and great clarity: Money isn't everything.

become global, but the myopia of simple profit-maximization will eventually prove to be fatal.

Indonesian women working for pennies a day cannot afford to buy the expensive athletic shoes they assemble. Neither can the unemployed American workers they have displaced. When the Ford Motor Company exports jobs from Detroit to the *maquila-dores* of transborder Mexico, a similar result occurs. Production costs of shoes and automobiles drop remarkably, short-term net revenues and "shareholder value" rise remarkably as a consequence—but future markets for both products are systematically destroyed. In the interest of maxi mizing short-term profits, a viable future is foreclosed.

The Overdeveloped Political System: Predatory Politics

The national political system in the United States today sustains a federal government notable primarily for its dereliction. That government has become an engine of plunder, an institutional corollary, indeed a mechanism of the corruption of capitalism. It no longer pursues and protects the collective good. It is used as a tool for the systematic looting of what is in fact the common wealth, both in concrete terms of the resource values of the federal lands and in abstract terms of the financial resources and obligations of the American people.

In the last decades of the twentieth century we witnessed a deliberate and systematic redistribution of the nation's financial wealth from the poor and the middle class to the already wealthy. The scale was unprecedented in the history of the republic, and it began during the presidency of Ronald Reagan. There is no more tangible indicator of institutional overshoot.

The policies undertaken during the Reagan years and the consequences for the public at large are detailed in Kevin Phillips's book *The Politics of Rich and Poor: Wealth and the American Electorate in the Reagan Aftermath*. Neither President Reagan nor the Republican party, however, could claim exclusive credit for the policies. At least one predates the Reagan years slightly, and none has been undone by the Clinton administration: Predatory politics is an institutional difficulty, not the achievement of a single party.

In 1976 the top .5 percent of American families held 14.4 percent of the nation's wealth. President Carter, in the last attempt in the twentieth century to maintain progressivity in the tax code, suggested raising the capital gains tax rate and lowering individual tax rates. In 1978, a Democratic Congress rebuffed him: It cut capital gains taxation in half, lowered the corporate tax rate, and made permanent the temporary tax credit on investment. Then came Reagan's tax bill of 1981 that collapsed the number of tax brackets, trivializing the progressivity of the tax code. The law also cut individual tax rates by 25 percent—a benefit far more important to the wealthy than to the poor. Two years later that top .5 percent of American families held 26.9 percent of the nation's total wealth: They had nearly doubled their share.[13] Between 1978 and 1990, the tax burden on the richest 1 percent of the nation's people fell by 36 percent. On the middle class it rose 7 percent, and not factored into these inequities is the searing regressivity of the massive increases in Social Security taxes during the period.

Not only did the mortal rich benefit handsomely from the policy shifts, but so did the immortal: Corporate welfare blossomed and grew. The nation's corporations saw their income taxes cut almost exactly in half. Some, like General Electric, did even better. From 1981 through 1983, GE registered corporate profits of $6.5 billion, but received a tax rebate of $283 million. Prior to the Reagan tax cuts, GE's tax liability had run about $330 million per year: Afterward, it generated annual tax credits of $90 million—money the Treasury Department owed the company.[14]

Not only were today's poor and middle class forced to contribute their wealth to the wealthy, but so was the community to come, the unborn generations of Americans far into the distant future.

Ronald Reagan campaigned in the fall of 1979 explicitly and vigorously as a social and fiscal conservative, promising to do three things: cut taxes, increase defense spending, and balance the federal budget. He managed the first two with aplomb. But budget deficits in the hundreds of billions became commonplace, and the national debt exploded. In 1980, at the beginning of the Reagan presidency, the debt stood at about $1 trillion. In eight years it rose to more than $3 trillion.

---

13. Kevin Phillips, *The Politics of Rich and Poor: Wealth and the American Electorate in the Reagan Aftermath* (New York: Harper Collins, 1990), p. 241.

14. Greider, *Who Will Tell*, pp. 342–343.

If the continuing upward redistribution of the nation's existing wealth displays the breakdown of responsible governance, the obligating of future generations to pay for contemporary consumption displays predatory politics at its worst. Today both parties, measured not by their rhetoric but by their actions, continue the pattern with enthusiasm, chronically loading huge financial obligations onto the taxpayers of the future.[15]

The federal government incurred twice as much debt during the administration of Ronald Reagan as it had during the presidencies of all his predecessors combined. In those eight years, the United States was transformed from the world's primal creditor to its largest debtor nation, as foreign interests bought U.S. Treasuries by the billions. At the end of the Bush administration, the debt had risen another 25 percent, to $4 trillion. By the end of the Clinton years, despite the hypocritical braying in Washington about budget "surpluses," the debt had risen another 50 percent, to $6 trillion.[16] The predation is bipartisan.

The Reagan policies of relieving taxes for the rich and the corporate; slashing budgets for education, welfare, and health programs; deregulating industry after industry; increasing defense spending; and borrowing heavily to finance the deficits enriched the wealthy, burdened the middle class, and savaged the poor.

Could a single president do all this on his own initiative? Or had the political system been captured and turned to advantage by the nation's rich and powerful elites—the owners and managers of corporate enterprise and the Wall Street architects of the "financialization" of the nation's economy?[17] Had politics come

---

15. The budget "surpluses" that appeared as the century closed were hypocritical sleights-of-hand of accounting, described by the Concord Coalition as "gimmickry." See its Web site at http://www.concordcoalition.org.

16. The annual increases in the public debt of the Clinton administration for fiscal years 1993 through 1999 were as follows, in billions: $346.8, $281.3, $281.2, $250.8, $188.3, $113.0, $130.1. See the U.S. Treasury Web site, http://www.publicdebt.treas.gov.

17. The term *financialization* refers to the profound shift in emphasis, beginning perhaps in the 1970s and exploding in the 1980s, from seeking profit in the production of goods and services to making money through financial manipulations: leveraged buyouts, currency trading, forward contracts, futures, options, and the like. American industry, some commentators observed, came to be held hostage by American finance. Others, Kevin Phillips among them, described the situation as the "financialization" of the American economy.

to serve simply and singly this narrow band of wealth and influence, having abandoned the public weal? Had the pluralism of American democracy, engendered by the Constitution and developed over two centuries of institutional innovation, become predatory?

Only the tragically deluded will answer no.

Neither the Bush nor the Clinton administration altered the pattern. Between 1988 and 1998 the average annual income of the poorest fifth of American families rose $110, about 1 percent, to $12,990. For the richest fifth of families, it rose by $17,870, about 15 percent, to $137,480.[18] The rich grew richer by more than the total income of the poor. The predation is indeed bipartisan.

Our institutional history has guaranteed the maladies outlined here: Since constitutional days, the prosperity of the individual (initially organic individuals, subsequently corporate ones) has always taken precedence over the common good. The political institutions in particular were designed that way, deliberately and ingeniously.

Consider the public asset of *seignorage* that was given without hesitation to the banking industry early in the history of our nation.[19] When banks make loans, they do so by creating money literally out of thin air: They write up a new checking account for the borrower and credit it with a positive balance, or simply add to the balance in an existing account. They must maintain a "reserve account" with a Federal Reserve bank in cash amounting to 3 percent of their outstanding loans, but the other 97 percent is ethereal. Thus banks earn income—interest payments on loans—from assets they never bought, never owned, never even borrowed, but simply willed into being.

Suppose seignorage today reverted to the federal government. The reserve requirement for commercial banks, by definition, would become 100 percent. Banks could loan only the real money

---

18. "Income Gap Widens for U.S. Families," Associated Press story dated January 18, 2000, at http://dailynews.yahoo.com.

19. The value received from the creation of money is termed *seignorage,* and in earlier societies with different institutions it was always reserved to the "government," not infrequently a monarch.

in the accounts of their depositors.[20] Then the banks might choose to borrow up to, say, 97 percent of the amount of their deposits from a Federal Reserve Bank and loan that out, too. This time the Federal Bank would create the money by simply crediting the account of the borrowing bank—and charge interest for the loan. Now the billions and billions of dollars in seignorage would be earned instead by the federal government. If used for public expenditures, it could drastically reduce, perhaps eliminate, the need for taxation.

Just as we chose initially, however, to privatize the federal lands and subsequently to privatize the resource values, so we chose to privatize the public asset of seignorage. The later outrage of the savings and loan scandal represents overshoot and excess, certainly, but not malfunction.

An interest group making a claim in its own behalf is the essence of American political pluralism. In our fully developed, not yet overdeveloped political system, such claims were lodged against other interest groups, and in the tug and pull of political compromise, a greater public interest was served.

This argument was put forth by Charles Lindblom in his classic book *The Intelligence of Democracy*. On a foundation of "partisan mutual adjustment," American democracy rested on the same basis—enlightened self-interest—as Adam Smith's free-market system, and functioned just as effectively. Without prior planning or centralized orchestration, the bargaining among a plurality of interest groups would guarantee social optima in public affairs. Lindblom's model served well to explain the development of public policy in the twentieth century until overshoot took place.

Interest groups have a history, indeed a raison d'être, of making claims against one another. In that light, one might say that the groups prey on each other, that pluralism is predatory by nature.

The predation by interest groups to be concerned about is not the "transfers" they effect among themselves. That is a zero-sum

---

20. This discussion owes much to Herman E. Daly and John B. Cobb Jr., in *For the Common Good: Redirecting the Economy Toward Community, the Environment, and a Sustainable Future* (Boston: Beacon Press, 1994).

game, in which the transfer advances social equity in some fashion. But in the closing decades of the twentieth century, the great emergent defect of the U.S. Constitution was discovered. Because the Constitution guarantees the silence of the majority, the public at large is utterly defenseless against a willful attack on its wealth and well-being. To gain at the expense of another interest group is difficult, because the target interest will resist the attack with all its skill and resources. To gain at the expense of the public at large, on the other hand, is easier than pilfering the confections of infants: Resistance is constitutionally foreclosed. Once the facility of doing so was discovered, plundering the common assets quickly became epidemic as the twentieth century neared its end.

It is when interested minorities prey on society at large that pluralism is predatory in a fashion that truly makes a difference.

The most significant of such predators today are corporate enterprises, the embodiment of capitalism turned corrupt. Consider the corporations that now dominate health care: primarily HMOs, insurance companies, hospital chains, and pharmaceutical companies. No civil and humane society withholds basic health care from 16 percent of its citizens and sweats the rest of them to meet the extortionate costs, so candidate Clinton made that issue a pivot point of his first presidential campaign. He delivered a workable solution early in his administration, a moderate even timid package, and the threat to the incomes of the doctors, hospitals, insurance companies, pharmaceutical corporations, and HMOs was trifling. Even so, the health care lobby annihilated the proposal. It never even reached Congress. Then the industry succeeded in obliterating the issue of health care altogether: It was simply removed from the public agenda.

Since the savings and loan miscarriage, no other recent example of predatory politics can match this one. Health care reform has been rendered moot; the quarter-million dollar annual incomes of the nation's physicians (on average) will continue to grow, at a rate that outpaces inflation.[21] So will the equally disproportionate revenues of HMO, drug, insurance, and hospital corporations. The transfer of wealth, from those who can pay for

---

21. In 1994, the average annual income for all physicians was $250,310. See *Medical Economics*, September 11, 1995, p. 189.

health care at all, will continue to flow to the hugely wealthy, predatory professionals and executives in this industry. Forty-three million Americans will continue to have no access to health care at all, and for everyone else health care has displaced food as the largest single item in family budgets.[22]

As a matter of public policy, "the American health care system is at once the most expensive and the most inadequate system in the developed world."[23] That is a definitive dereliction of government.

Let us return momentarily to the level of concept, if only to gain respite from the disquieting details of empirical politics.

Economic overdevelopment has occurred when the entities of production transcend or escape their service to society, and become self-serving instead, to the absolute detriment of society. Similar language can be applied to politics. When the entities of representation—elected officials, career administrators, and corporate and other interest groups—transcend or escape their service to society, and become self-serving instead, to the absolute detriment of society, then political overdevelopment has occurred. This can be described in more troubling terms. If self governance by free people seeking the welfare of all is a good definition of democracy, overshoot has taken place when democracy is overridden, and the welfare of the few—that is to say elitism—becomes paramount.

The question of elitism has been addressed provocatively and well in the scholarly and popular literature. In his classic book *The Power Elite*, C. Wright Mills argued that corporate, political, and military hierarchies share common interests and cooperate to further them.[24] The top strata of the hierarchies constitute the power elite, and it sets the strategic course of national affairs. The middle strata are the administrators and managers who neither express the public will nor much affect the strategic decisions made above. The lower strata—the public at large—are undifferentiated mass.

---

22. See the *Kiplinger Washington Letter* of December 11, 1998, p.1.

23. Marcia Angell, M.D., editor, in an editorial in *The New England Journal of Medicine*, January 7, 1999.

24. Mills, *The Power Elite*.

Later, Thomas Dye and Harmon Zeigler took a more benign view in *The Irony of Democracy*.[25] Noting the common distrust for democratic principles—survey research reveals the popular suspicion of the Bill of Rights—the authors build a case for a magnanimous elitism. Only elites can advance and protect democracy—hence the irony. The tug and pull of interest groups, the leaderships of which constitute the American elites, will result in socially optimum policy outcomes. Dye and Zeigler echo, in many respects, Lindblom's *Intelligence of Democracy*.

Professors Daniel Hellinger and Dennis R. Judd do not. According to them, elites throughout U.S. history have orchestrated, precisely on the other hand, a "facade" of democracy—a shell game of democratic trappings and tinsel that hides today the real self-serving power structure of corporate wealth and political influence.[26] They support their argument throughout the book with empirical evidence. Their chapter "The Best Elections Money Can Buy," for example, describes with hard data the enormous impact of corporate wealth on today's elections.

A thoroughly researched and intelligent book by William Greider reinforces this argument, and it carries a disturbing title: *Who Will Tell the People: The Betrayal of American Democracy*.[27] Greider speaks of Washington as the "Grand Bazaar," in which governmental structures serve not the nation, but "clients" who seek either financial gain or policy advantage. The clients are overwhelmingly corporate and reciprocate with generous flows of campaign contributions for favors granted. The system is self serving, self regulating, and self perpetuating.

Greider also provides evidence for his compelling argument that our economic and political systems have overshot. He does not use that term, nor the words *corruption* and *predation*, but he makes a persuasive case that our institutions have undergone a profound deterioration in the past several decades.

Greider would be labeled a "liberal" by those who find the term distasteful, but Kevin Phillips, the astute political commen-

---

25. Thomas R. Dye and L. Harmon Zeigler, *The Irony of Democracy* (Belmont, CA: Duxbury Press, 1972).

26. Hellinger and Judd, *The Democratic Facade*.

27. Greider, *Who Will Tell*.

tator in Washington, is not known for frequent or distant wanderings to the left of center. He, too, is convinced that a transition in our institutions has taken place. Following his study of the redistribution of wealth in the Reagan years, Phillips produced in 1994 a broader analysis of the federal government: *Arrogant Capital: Washington, Wall Street, and the Frustration of American Politics*.[28] The self-service of the entrenched policy-making elite is documented, detailed, and explained in both historical and comparative contexts. Phillips argues that Washington has become isolated from the people of the country, elevated, distant, and arrogant, in much the way that Rome, Amsterdam, and London did as earlier great economic powers reached their zeniths. Without using that explicit terminology, here is what Phillips has to say about political overshoot:

> The last thirty years have produced a national-capital influence structure that represents multinational corporations who move jobs from Wisconsin to Taiwan, not the anonymous Americans who suffer, that protects the financial giants who run the bond markets and mutual funds, not the ordinary folk who are at their mercy, and that favors the professionals—the lawyers, lobbyists, accountants, stockbrokers, trade consultants, and communicators—who enjoy record incomes from the globalization and polarization that has brought Middle America two decades of decline in real manufacturing wages.[29]

Phillips's book displays the virtual capture of the political system by corporate capitalism, which uses a grotesquerie of constitutional politics to brutalize the American people and the American landscapes—and increasingly brutalizes people and landscapes on a global basis as well.

In the preceding section, the transition of service-capitalism into corruption was described. How did the benign politics of earlier times become counterproductive, now inflicting positive social damage? For the better part of a century—from the appearance of

---

28. Kevin Phillips, *Arrogant Capital: Washington, Wall Street, and the Frustration of American Politics* (Boston: Little, Brown, 1994).

29. Ibid., p. 177.

a workable pluralism of interest groups, say about 1870 or so, until thirty years ago (to adopt Phillips's chronology)—a sharp distinction could be made in political activities and institutions.

The political parties conducted the personnel management function of American politics, recruiting, campaigning, electing, and reelecting the dramatis personae of government. We might call this "electoral politics," and that to a very large extent is all the parties could accomplish. The parties had little influence on public policy, for a number of reasons detailed in earlier chapters. The constitutional exclusion of majoritarian governance was the primary one. Electoral politics, then, was the function of partisan politics.

The plurality of interest groups, on the other hand, had everything to do with public policy. In more respectable days the interest groups formulated policy: They addressed issues, proposed solutions, bargained, negotiated, and compromised among themselves, and took products with fine degrees of finish to Congress for confirmation or ratification by enactment into law. The laws were just and in the interest of the public at large: This is the process that Lindblom described as "the intelligence of democracy." We might call this "policy politics," and that to a large extent was all the interest groups chose to do. Certainly, they had their favorites among the political actors, but they were largely indifferent to partisan affiliations. There were Republicans the environmental groups could count on, and there were Democrats—and industry trade associations made similar extra-partisan alliances.

The activities of electoral politics took place before elections. The activities of policy politics took place afterward, and there were essentially no overlaps, no linkages, no commonalities. The two kinds of politics, and the two sets of organizations that pursued them, were almost entirely separated in time, space, objectives, motivation, financing, personnel, dynamics, loyalties, and tenures.

Still honoring Phillips's chronology, an institution emerged within the past thirty years to bridge the gulf between the two sorts of politics, to cement them together, and eventually to crystallize the self-perpetuating elite of arrogance, power, and influence in Washington today. It was the political action committee, or PAC.

Campaign law has long prohibited profit-earning corporations from making direct financial contributions to political campaigns. It was a vessel, not without occasional leaks, meant to contain the outright purchase of public officials, or at least the purchase of influence. The agglomeration of labor unions, the AFL-CIO, however, was not a profit-earning corporation, and its political action committee happily raised funds and contributed them, chronically to Democratic candidates. Not surprisingly, the Republicans complained, but they were also sensitive to the advantage of institutionalized PACs. Both parties agreed quickly to grant statutory recognition to PACs and the legitimacy of their campaign contributions.

General Electric cannot contribute to a campaign as the General Electric Corporation, but GE can contribute to a PAC. And any number of trade associations funded by GE can create a political action committee to contribute to campaigns freely and virtually without limit. (The statutory limits are laughably porous.) So can SIXPAC, representing the nation's brewers, and so can thousands of other PACs representing any industry, any environmental interest, any professional association, religion, coalition, foundation, or interest group of any stripe. The financial pipeline from political interests to political campaigns is now straight and direct, and all the valves are open.

With the advent of political action committees, American politics was systematically monetized, and the sharp distinction between electoral and policy politics disappeared. The ability to make campaign contributions to candidates of their choice propelled the practitioners of policy politics directly into the center of electoral politics, and few of the interest groups, corporate and otherwise, failed to seize the opportunity.

To say a campaign contribution does not constitute an obligation for reciprocal favors is to raise delusion to an art form. Table 1 correlates corporate PAC donations and their payoffs, and the returns on the investments are noteworthy.

All candidates for political office came quickly to have vested interests in the vested interests in Washington, but the advantage granted to incumbents was dizzying. PACs were far more likely to contribute to experienced legislators, known quantities, than to new and aspiring servants of the public.

To imply that the evolution of the PAC system was the single

Table 1. Program, Fiscal Year Benefits, Benefiting Corporations, and PAC Contributions, 1993–94 Election Cycle

Program	Fiscal Year Benefits	Benefiting Companies	Their PAC contributions '93–'94
Market promotion	$110 million	Sunkist Growers	$123,820
Export enhancement	ca. $238 million	Cargill, Continental Grain	$105,497
Advanced light water reactor	$40 million	General Electric, Westinghouse	$804,470
Export/Import Bank	$125 million	Hughes Aircraft	$248,000
Overseas Private Investment Corp.	$170 million	U.S. West, Inc.	$319,610
Salvage logging deficits	$19 million	Weyerhaeuser, Georgia Pacific	$58,982
Reduction in FDIC premiums	$4.4 billion (industry total)	Citicorp	$333,168 (Citicorp alone)
Foreign military financing	$1.9 billion	General Dynamics, Lockheed/Martin	$1,500,000
U.S. sugar program	$1.4 billion (industry total)	Flo-Sun, Inc.	$35,038
Alternative minimum tax reduction	$2.2 billion (program total)	Exxon, Amoco, Atlantic Richfield	$1,500,000

Source: Contained in a letter from Ralph Nader to Senate Majority Leader Robert Dole and House Speaker Newt Gingrich, December 28, 1995. A copy of the letter was included in a news release from Janet Shields, Coordinator, Corporate Welfare Project and Taxwatch, Center for the Study of Responsive Law, P.O. Box 19367, Washington, DC 20036.

cause of political overshoot is seriously to oversimplify. Many other factors came into play. In the benign days of 1950 politics, money was important to the conduct of political campaigns, but only in quantities that could be imagined. The parties could raise enough to buy lapel buttons, bumper stickers, posters, occasional display ads in the newspapers, bunting, and the railroad fares necessary for whistle-stop campaigning.

The Kennedy-Nixon TV debates in the 1960 presidential race are alleged with good reason to have changed that, to have ushered in the campaign of electronic mass media speaking directly to the nation at large, bypassing the parties. The importance of the TV imagery of the candidate became all important. "Character" displayed and "trust" engendered won elections, or their absence lost them, and imagery was the stock in trade of the commercial advertising industry. Candidates could sell their characters directly to the electorate in dozens of carefully crafted "spots" each day—and the historic functions of the political parties became less and less important. TV selling of "personality candidacies," the harshest critics would say, finally rendered irrelevant the American party system.

But it rendered critically important spectacular quantities of money. Television advertising of political candidates is terribly expensive, because the competition for air time is intense: A political campaign must outbid Anheuser-Busch selling conviviality, Proctor and Gamble selling self-confidence, Merrill Lynch selling CDs for neighborhood S&Ls, General Electric selling itself, Exxon apologizing for the oil spill, Ford Motors selling prestige, McDonald's selling self-indulgence and obesity, and Phillip Morris selling untimely death. The political campaign must compete with the awesome imperative of maintaining hyperconsumption.

The role of PACs was made opportune by the declining importance of the parties and the steeply increasing importance of money. But there were yet other elements in the emergence of counterproductive politics. After years of serious jousting among themselves for temporary advantage in administrative or regulatory matters, the array of interest groups discovered the potency of law for making claims against one another. No other form of social sanction carries equivalent force, and if you could render your opponents' behavior illegal, your advantage could be permanent.

An example from federal lands policy is that of the Wilderness Act of 1964. For years the wilderness interests applauded the administrative designations by the Forest Service of primitive, wild, and wilderness areas in the national forests, and stood ever ready to protest their invasion by loggers, miners, and dam builders. As the substantive on-the-ground activities of the commodity interests intensified, however, the wilderness people concluded that logging, mining, and dam building must be declared illegal in the designated wilderness landscapes. (Grazing eluded them; they were no match for the livestock industry.)

The wilderness lobby was anxious about administrative designation for another reason. If a wilderness area could be created by the stroke of a bureaucrat's pen, it could be just as easily undone. The declaration of wilderness in law was far more secure: Repealing laws is a difficult undertaking, and the prospect was bright that the wilderness system would never be diminished. The legislative dynamics of repealing a law, however, are identical to the dynamics of passing one, so the wilderness groups' reasoning could be applied in the other direction. If wilderness had to be established in law, the system could be expanded only with great difficulty, too. This reasoning appealed to the logging, mining, and irrigation lobbies, which thereupon supported with enthusiasm the passage of the Wilderness Act of 1964.[30]

The politics of passing that law exemplified the central argument of *The Intelligence of Democracy*. It was politics behaving in a socially responsible way, and the Wilderness Act can be said to serve the interests of the American people at large. The proxies granted the wilderness groups and the commodity groups were exercised with skill and integrity, and a point of agreement was found.

It was, however, a law. Both sides agreed that a statutory solution was superior to any alternative. Their well-intentioned commitment to law was adopted across the spectrum of public issues and their interest group representatives as the 1960s and 1970s unfolded.

A widespread and rising commitment to law in a city that manufactures it is likely to spur a substantial growth in the enterprise—and in the professional cadre of attorneys. In 1950, Phillips tells us, the District of Columbia bar listed not quite a thousand attorneys.[31] By 1975, there were 21,000, and in the late 1990s there were 61,000. No city or country on earth has more lawyers per capita of population than Washington, D.C., and the United States, respectively. The emphasis on law, lawyers, and litigation in

---

30. The commodity groups, it turns out, were mistaken. It proved so easy to pass wilderness legislation that the original 9 million acres in 1964 have now become 104.5 million, an eleven-fold increase. As that took place, however, commodity production from the federal lands exploded as well. The federal lands estate was large and rich.

31. Phillips, *Arrogant Capital*, p. 32.

the country today is without contemporary parallel and without historical precedent.

Employment prospects in Washington grew rapidly. The personal and committee staffing in Congress grew from 6,255 persons in 1960 to 10,739 in 1970, and to over 20,000 by the mid-1990s. "No other major nation's legislative branch employed a staff of even one quarter the size," according to Phillips.[32] And the interest groups were not far behind. The environmental issue became a sizable one in the late 1960s. Membership in national environmental lobbying organizations grew in step, and at least five new ones were created between 1967 and 1972. At the end of that year, total membership in twelve such interest groups amounted to 1,117,000. By 1979 that figure had grown to 1,576,000. And then, after Ronald Reagan appointed James Watt as secretary of the interior, aggregate membership stood at 1,994,000 in 1983. Six years later it had grown to 2,724,000, and by 1990 it had reached 3,103,000. The budget resources for the twelve organizations aggregated, in 1990, nearly $220 million, and most of them were headquartered in Washington.[33]

In the earlier, happier years of conservation lobbying, it was the hunters and fisherfolk, mountaineers, hikers, and birders who volunteered to staff the political barricades when necessary. Similar patterns obtained in the commodity groups: Loggers, millers, miners, and stock raisers took time off for politicking.

That was largely before the obsession with law took place. Afterward, the dedicated amateurs were clearly out of their element, and soon enough there was good use to be made of the $220 million environmental war chest.

> Organizations of amateurs such as these were fully capable of dealing with first-generation issues, but the second-generation issues were far more numerous, diverse, and complex, and their resolution often took years of sus-

---

32. Ibid.

33. Riley E. Dunlap and Angela G. Mertig, *American Environmentalism: The U.S. Environmental Movement, 1970–1990* (Philadelphia: Taylor and Francis, 1992), p. 13.

tained effort. Dealing with them required a high level of legal and scientific expertise. It was no accident, therefore, that the earlier amateurism was rapidly transformed into professionalism by the early 1970s, a professionalism whose hallmark was the sizable cadre of lobbyists, lawyers, and scientists employed full-time by the national environmental organizations.[34]

The commodity groups developed war chests, too, and they hired parallel staffs of professionals: Ph.D.s in the natural and managerial sciences, economists, accountants, engineers, and lawyers, lawyers, lawyers. There were 4,900 national trade associations in 1956. Twenty years later there were 12,500, and by 1990, 23,000. And they, like the environmental groups, began moving their headquarters to Washington. In 1971, 19 percent were so located; by 1990, 32 percent of them were.[35]

By 1992 the interest group population of Washington had grown to 14,000 organizations employing 90,000 people. No longer are any of them amateur volunteers. All are well educated, urbane, sophisticated, knowledgeable, and well paid, and on the Hill are the professional politicians, the elected legislators in Congress, who enjoy essentially permanent tenure. In pages to come we will call these people the "policy professionals," an altogether new and different kind of paternalistic aristocrat.

Kevin Phillips says this:

> There was also a bipartisan awareness, involving perhaps a hundred thousand people, that the city on the Potomac had become a golden honeypot for the politically involved, offering financial and career opportunities unavailable anywhere else. Washington was not simply a concentration of vested interests; in a sense, the nation's richest city had itself become a vested interest—a vocational entitlement—of the American political class.[36]

---

34. Ibid., p. 21.

35. Phillips, *Arrogant Capital*, p. 32.

36. Ibid., p. 37.

A popular periodical put it this way:

> The cost of operating the U.S. Congress plus its 38,696-person support staff has zoomed from $343 million in fiscal 1970 to an estimated $2.8 billion in 1992—an astounding 705% rise, more than double the 311% increase in defense spending over the same period.[37]

The enormous growth in the career professionalism of Washington politics was made necessary by the commitment to statutory resolutions of public issues. Law was everything.

Concomitantly, an institution virtually absent in the benign days of politics has blossomed since: the "Washington law firm." Such firms house the hired guns of counterproductive politics: the enormously competent, well-connected, highly paid upper-strata attorneys who lobby any position on any issue for any interested party able to pay. No sizable American corporation is unable to pay, and a client list of the Washington law firms reads like the membership of the U.S. Chamber of Commerce.

The Washington law firm is the mechanism, if a single one can be isolated, by which benign politics was transformed, and through which corporate capitalism turns public policy to its advantage. The most influential, most experienced, best connected lobbying talent is for sale, and corporate America has cornered it. It is not used to further the interests of the nation at large.

Greider's book describes the Washington law firms in detail. They are staffed by former members of the cabinet-level secretariats—and future members as well. Senators and congressmen, with their contacts on the Hill, find ready employment there, should they lose an election or leave Congress voluntarily for the higher incomes in lobbying.

The firms include high-level party officials—Robert Strauss, former chairman of the Democratic National Committee, is typical. Strauss's firm—Akin, Gump—represents Drexel Burnham, the firm that paid Michael Milken, in a single year, $550 million in brokerage fees; and also the Motion Picture Association of

---

37. Walter L. Updegrave and Carla A. Fried, "What Congress Really Costs You: $2.8 Billion a Year," *Money Magazine*, August 1, 1992.

America; McDonnell Douglas; and AT&T. In 1991, Strauss, or "Mr. Democrat," as he is called in the press, served as Republican George Bush's ambassador to Russia. It is not partisanship, but the welfare of corporate America, that is important in Washington. Ron Brown, of the firm Patton, Boggs, and Blow, chaired the Democratic National Committee, the party of American labor for generations. President Clinton appointed Brown to head the Commerce Department, the agency representing American business.

These firms channel much of the business community's contributions—through PACs set up by their own firms—into the campaign treasuries. The contributions are not paltry: A *Washington Post* writer estimated that 70 percent of the campaign contributions—for candidates in both parties—now come from corporate sources.[38] It seems that corporations have bought the political system, and turned it to prey on society at large.

Given this context of institutional overshoot, it is no surprise that federal land resource values are so quickly plundered. The public at large is defenseless to prevent it. Nor could anything of substance be achieved when remedies were sought locally to the difficulties professional equilibration had posed: Solutions were sought exclusively in the nation's capital.

Potomac Fever, Planning, and Pillage

The influence of large corporate interests in Washington— described and decried by Greider and Phillips—includes the dominant companies of the forest products industry, the mining industry, the livestock industry, the agribusiness industry, the energy industry, and the outdoor recreation industry. They work independently and they work cooperatively, through their trade associations and collateral PACs.

Standing ostensibly opposed to the "commodity interests" are the large national environmental groups: the Wilderness Society, the National Audubon Society, Greenpeace, Friends of the Earth, the National Wildlife Federation, Environmental Defense, the World Wildlife Fund, the Natural Resources Defense Council, and oth-

---

38. Cited in Greider, *Who Will Tell*, p. 259.

ers. That opposition was, at one time, far more than ostensible, but as we saw earlier in the chapter, the environmental groups became professionalized, permanent bureaucracies, and opened large, expensive, well-staffed offices in Washington.

The National Wildlife Federation built, owns, and rents out space in an office building that occupies half of an entire city block in downtown Washington. Less interested in managing real estate, other environmental groups lease office space, some like the Wilderness Society spending as much as $6 million per year. That is more than five times what the Louisiana-Pacific Corporation pays for its headquarters space in Portland, Oregon.[39]

To paraphrase Greider and Phillips, the environmental groups followed suit in betraying American democracy and turning Washington into an arrogant capital. By co-optation or choice they formed oblique but significant alliances with the rich and powerful interests in the city, and that meant the corporate interests.[40] Some of the alliances were formed with money. Others depended on the venerable corporate practice of interlocking directorates.

Greider describes the first process:

> Corporations, including the major polluters, have discovered . . . that they can buy into the environmental movement itself through tax-deductible contributions to the mainline organizations. Waste Management, Inc., the largest waste-disposal company and a company frequently fined for its environmental violations, has donated more than $1 million to various environmental groups in recent years. The company's generosity bought its CEO a seat on the board of the National Wildlife Federation. The National Audubon Society, which got $135,000 from

---

39. Information about the Wilderness Society is taken from Jeffrey St. Clair, "Whither the Wilderness Society?" *Wild Forest Review* (February 1994), p. 5.

40. Noticeably absent from the groups listed above is the Sierra Club, which stands apart. Like the others, it is a large and complex bureaucracy, and it maintains a lobbying presence in Washington. Unlike the others, it has an elaborate regional, state, and local network of grassroots subdivisions; it has a century-long history and a tangible ideological heritage; it maintains its headquarters in San Francisco not Washington; and it has taken a candid, bold, even a daring leadership role in opposing the economic, political, and global misfortunes wrought by corporate enterprise.

Waste Management, expected its corporate gifts to top $1 million in 1989, up from $150,000 a few years earlier. The Conservation Foundation received money from Chevron, Exxon, General Electric, Union Carbide, Weyerhaeuser, Waste Management, and a long list of other corporations during the year before its president, William Reilly, became EPA administrator [in the Bush Administration].[41]

Jeffrey St. Clair describes the second process:

The Wilderness Society's board is culled from the elite of corporate America and the nation's social registry of genteel heirs and heiresses. It includes Edward Ames (trustee of the Mary Flagler Cary Trust and heir to Henry Flagler's Standard Oil billions), Thomas Barron (an investment banker and venture capitalist . . .), John Bierworth (the former CEO of defense industry giant Grumman Corporation), David Bonderman (CEO of Continental Airlines), Ernest Day (Boise real estate tycoon [and brother of Supreme Court Justice Sandra Day O'Connor]), Caroline Getty (Getty Oil heiress), Christopher Elliman (a Rockefeller heir and director of Geraldine Dodge Foundation), Walter Minnick (CEO of timber giant TJ International), Gilman Ordway (rancher and heir to the . . . Minnesota Mining and Manufacturing fortune), Arthur Ortenburg (Wall Street player, foundation director, and Liz Claiborne's spouse).[42]

Pipelines to corporate largesse and executive talent have transformed the environmental organizations into large, complex, immortal, virtually corporate entities in their own right. The environmental groups in Washington today, the Big Greens, as they are sometimes labeled—without admiration, respect, or appreciation—are altogether a part of the politics of overshoot.[43]

---

41. Greider, *Who Will Tell*, p. 220.

42. Jeffrey St. Clair, "Whither the Wildnerness Society," *Wild Forest Review*, Vol. 2, No. 3 (February 1995), p. 4.

43. For a candid indictment see Mark Dowie, *Losing Ground: American Environmentalism at the Close of the Twentieth Century* (Cambridge, MA: MIT Press, 1996).

Potomac Fever

The disease of "Potomac fever" is well known among students of public affairs. It describes the affliction of policy profession-als in Washington of every stripe: The conviction that problems of public controversy and concern—in the case at hand, those of the federal lands—can best be resolved in the nation's capi-tal. Legislators and bureaucrats are sure of this. So are the Washington law firms, the agents for corporate interests. So are the Big Greens. What it means in practice is the continuous production of civil law. The manufacture of law is the basic industry of Washington, D.C., and when a controversy is sent there, or forcibly appropriated, its solution is guaranteed to be a statute.

Determining the volume of timber cutting on a particular national forest hardly needs to be defined in law, but the Alaska National Interest Lands Conservation Act of December 1980, did so. It specified that 4.5 billion board feet of timber would be cut each decade on the Tongass National Forest. The law also transferred $40 million each year directly from the Trea-sury to the U.S. Forest Service—wholly outside the normal appropriations process—to sell the timber and build the roads to reach it. That is the price the Big Greens paid for what they wanted: millions of acres of new wilderness designations in Alaska.

Unremarked in passing the law was a $13 million deficit between the costs incurred and the revenues received for the tim-ber in 1980—a direct subsidy to the Louisiana-Pacific Corpora-tion and the Alaska Lumber and Pulp Corporation.

These two corporations displayed levels of arrogance and ill will in southeast Alaska that challenged belief. They were indicted and fined for conspiracy in price fixing, they were indicted and fined for pollution violations, they ravaged their labor forces, they violated repeatedly the terms of their timber sale contracts. For eight years one particular assistant secretary of agriculture, over-seeing the Forest Service, never spoke out against them: John B. Crowell had come to the Reagan administration directly from the executive ranks of the Louisiana-Pacific Corporation. Eventually, the two corporations did what Champion International had done in Montana: They left behind a ravished landscape and devastated local economies; they wrote off or liquidated their mills and departed.[44]

The subsidy provided them in 1980, which some described as corporate welfare, continued until the first statutory fix was supplanted by another, the so-called Tongass Timber Reform Act of December 1990. That law repealed the 4.5 billion-board-foot directive, and the $40 million funding guarantee—but directed the agency to provide Louisiana-Pacific and Alaska Lumber and Pulp with enough timber to satisfy "local demand." In fact, very little was "reformed."

There is always some distance between de jure and de facto policy, and Greider describes how that distance is often widened: After a law is passed, corporate interests bargain with the policy professionals to see that it will be administered in favorable ways.[45] In this case, the rate of cutting on the Tongass continued unabated, the special funds were replaced by appropriations, and the subsidy scarcely wavered.[46]

No such bargaining is necessary when an industry simply dictates the language of the law. In 1995 a rider specifying an "Emergency Salvage Timber Sale Program" was attached to an unrelated bill.[47] A "salvage timber sale" was defined as follows: "a timber sale for which an important reason for entry includes the removal of disease- or insect-infested trees, dead, damaged, or down trees, or trees affected by fire or imminently susceptible to fire or insect attack."

Virtually any tree in the national forest system, the slightest acquaintance with forest ecology will confirm, is "imminently susceptible to fire or insect attack." Another feature of the rider directed the secretaries of agriculture and interior to award some

---

44. For a detailed history of this issue, see Kathie Durbin, *Tongass: Pulp Politics and the Fight for the Alaska Rain Forest* (Corvallis: Oregon State University Press, 1999).

45. Greider, *Who Will Tell*; chapter 5, "Hollow Laws."

46. See Paul W. Hirt, *A Conspiracy of Optimism: Management of the National Forests since World War Two* (Lincoln: University of Nebraska Press, 1994), p. 91.

47. The bill was Public Law 104-19, Emergency Supplemental Appropriations for Additional Disaster Assistance, for Anti-Terrorism Initiatives, for Assistance in the Recovery from the Tragedy that Occurred in Oklahoma City, and Recissions Act, 1995.

pending sales of healthy, green timber. This feature applied to the "lands covered by Option Nine"—thousands of acres of old-growth timber in the Pacific Northwest embroiled in the spotted owl controversy. (Option Nine will be explained later.)

The rider was hugely vulnerable to administrative appeals and litigation, but there would be neither. Administrative review of the salvage sale and Option 9 programs was expressly prohibited in the legislation, and legal recourse was severely limited. A more explicit betrayal of American democracy is difficult to find.

In both salvage and green-timber sales, the rider relaxed a number of environmental and other procedural requirements, and decreed that the law's provisions "shall be deemed to satisfy the requirements" of six specific statutes and "all other applicable Federal environmental and natural resource laws." The program came immediately to be described as "logging without laws."[48] It was to expire on December 31, 1996, but it committed 4.73 billion board feet of federal timber to the forest products corporations. That much timber would build 475,000 attractive homes.

The rider was attached by Senator Slade Gorton of Washington State, where the Weyerhaeuser and Louisiana-Pacific corporations stood to benefit immensely. In the 1993–94 election cycle, the Weyerhaeuser and Lousiana-Pacific corporations made PAC contributions of $58,982,[49] and between 1989 and 1994, Senator Gorton alone accepted a total of $74,954 from timber industry PACs.[50]

Only the particulars would differ—the names of the policy professionals and the corporate beneficiaries—if we looked at issues respecting other federal lands resources.

---

48. Disclosed in a press release from the Western Ancient Forest Campaign dated August 14, 1995, and forwarded over the Internet by Alan McGowen, amcgowen@hpos102.cup.hp.com, to multiple recipients of list ecol-econ@cfs.colorado.edu on August 15.

49. Disclosed in a news release from Janice Shields, coordinator, Corporate Welfare Project and Taxwatch, Center for the Study of Responsive Law, P.O. Box 19367, Washington, DC, 20036, jshields@essential.org, and submitted over the Internet by Brian P. Griner, griner+@pitt.edu, to ecolecon@csf.colorado.edu on January 1, 1996.

50. Disclosed in a press release from the Western Ancient Forest Campaign dated April 21, 1995, and forwarded over the Internet by Alan McGowen, amcgowen@hpos102.cup.hp.com, to multiple recipients of list ecol-econ@cfs.colorado.edu on April 22, 1995.

Planning and Pillage

The controversies on the Bitterroot and Monongahela national forests were not resolved at the local level. Nor were other controversies in other agencies.[51] Instead, they were transported up the parallel hierarchies in the federal agency, the Big Greens, and the industry associations. They were appropriated by the policy professionals in Washington, D.C., and soon there was a spate of legislative proposals.

Senator Jennings Randolph of West Virginia, where the Monongahela National Forest is located, introduced S. 2926 on February 4, 1976. The Randolph bill was constructed not by the policy professionals, however. It was fashioned by a citizen's committee under the senator's direction, whose members included several professors of forestry, a dedicated Forest Service retiree, an Izaak Walton League staffer, and an attorney who had been involved in the Monongahela controversy. It was almost exclusively an amateur effort. The foremost historian of the legislation said this: "What distinguished the origin of the Randolph bill was that it was developed by people who were, for the most part, not closely associated with the legislative process."[52]

The bill placed explicit limitations on clear-cutting and impacted directly and negatively the flow of public wealth to corporate hands. It never got out of committee.

The Randolph bill addressed the problem forthrightly; the citizen's committee proposed a tangible solution. In circumstances of betrayed democracy, however, the concrete resolution of a public problem is apparently to be avoided. It is the continual seeking of solutions, not their discovery, that sustains the policy professionals, but Randolph's amateurs seemed not to understand this. And nothing must stand, as their prescriptions did, in the way of service to wealth.

---

51. See R.W. Behan, "Political Dynamics of Wildlife Management: The Grand Canyon Burros," in *Transactions of the 43rd North American Wildlife and Natural Resource Conference*, 1978. This paper compared the burro situation to the Bitterroot controversy and found the political dynamics identical.

52. Dennis C. LeMaster, *Decade of Change: The Remaking of Forest Service Statutory Authority During the 1970s* (Westport, CT: Greenwood Press, 1984), p. 63.

Instead of prescriptions for substantive change, then, another approach was sought. Senator Hubert Humphrey turned to the policy professionals and on March 5, 1976, introduced a bill that simply sidestepped the original issue of timber-cutting techniques. The bill, S. 3091, called for a detailed and comprehensive ten-year management plan to be written for each national forest. Again the historian's description:

> The origin of the Humphrey bill, S. 3091, is typical of many bills that develop when there is a perceived problem. . . . Key people in the affected agency simply work with interested members of Congress and their staffs to devise a solution. Hence, such bills are written by people knowledgeable about the issue of concern and closely associated with the legislative process.[53]

The dedicated amateurs putting together the Randolph bill were doomed to failure: they were not closely associated with the process. The policy professionals proceeded, with a shared conviction: "The authors of S. 3091 believed that through proper land-management planning, which necessitated public participation, conflicts over the use and management of the national forests could be resolved or avoided."[54]

And they succeeded. S. 3091 became the National Forest Management Act.[55]

The policy professionals either ignored reality, or they had another agenda. In neither the Bitterroot nor the Monongahela controversy was the adequacy of planning even an ancillary issue. The localized complaints were starkly simple: Too many trees were being cut, in ways that damaged or obliterated other forest resource values. The issue was one of timber management tech-

---

53. Ibid.

54. Ibid., p. 60.

55. Other controversies in other agencies produced similar mandates for comprehensive planning. The technical aspects of planning for all the land management agencies are compiled in a competent volume by John B. Loomis, *Integrated Public Lands Management: Principles and Applications to National Forests, Parks, Wildlife Refuges, and BLM Lands* (New York: Columbia University Press, 1993).

nique; it had nothing to do with planning, and it certainly did not require the involvement of the U.S. Congress for its resolution.

The policy professionals in the arrogant capital thought otherwise, obviously, and it is difficult to escape a conclusion: They wanted not to solve a problem, in fact, but only to perpetuate a process.

The history of subsequent years has not been kind to Senator Humphrey's goals. While the agency was busy writing management plans, the crucial forest management decisions continued to be made in the federal budgeting process, and we have seen what those decisions were. They accommodated the plunder. For the best part of fifteen years after the planning law was passed, the national forests were dedicated to road building and logging and little else. And the other federal lands were treated in similar fashion: Public wealth continued to flow into corporate hands, while environmental values were sacrificed and the externalized social costs continued to mount. By design or default, the National Forest Management Act proved to be a diversionary smoke screen.

No one expected the planning effort to be inexpensive. When the first implementing regulations were completed in 1979, the Forest Service estimated that it would have to spend about $20 million per year to complete the first round of 154 plans by 1985.[56] According to the President's Private Sector Survey on Cost Control, appointed by President Reagan to study waste and inefficiency in the federal government, the Forest Service estimate was off by a factor precisely of ten.[57] The Grace Commission in 1983 found the planning costs were running about $200 million per year.

That figure made the cost of planning the largest single item in the Forest Service budget during the years the planning effort was underway. It would edge out, in FY 1988, such historic and richly endowed programs as road construction ($171.8 million) and timber sales administration and management ($185.6 million). It was nearly twice the combined annual expenditures for wildlife and fish habitat management, range management, and soil, water, and air management programs ($111.9 million).[58]

---

56. LeMaster, *Decade of Change*, p. 160.

57. President's Private Sector Survey on Cost Control, 1983. Report on the Department of Agriculture, pp. 232–248.

58. USDA Forest Service. 1989 Budget, Explanatory Notes for Committee on Appropriations. Washington, DC: USDA Forest Service.

The forest planning process did not "resolve or avoid" the conflicts in the national forests. Instead, it catapulted the Forest Service into a quagmire of adversarial legalisms, a predictable (and
predicted) consequence of planning under the mandate of law.[59]
By the spring of 1989, four years after the Forest Service expected
to have the plans finished, only 94 of approximately 150 had been
completed in draft form. Of those, 92 had been targeted by 332
formal appeals, and 5 of the plans had gone on to litigation.[60]

By the beginning of fiscal year 1992, the total of formal appeals
had risen to 1,453, and the chief of the Forest Service testified
that he was spending $150 million per year answering them and
defending the agency in various courtrooms of the nation.[61]

If the plans took ten years to complete at the Grace Commission figure of $200 million per year, the aggregate cost amounts
to $2 billion. To that must be added another half billion for three
years or so of appeals and litigation. What has $2.5 billion of pub-
lic expenditure bought?

Certainly not a resolution of the controversy over the management of federal forests, as Senator Humphrey and his colleagues
had hoped. A replication of the conflict occurred in the spotted
owl controversy in the Pacific Northwest, which led President
Clinton to convene a "Forest Summit" in 1992 in Portland, Oregon. That fostered a monstrous study by FEMAT, the Forest
Ecosystem Management Assessment Team appointed by the president and staffed by scores of academicians and policy professionals. That resulted in "Option Nine," the Clinton administration's proposal to resolve the controversy. And Option Nine was
followed by more acrimony, more lawsuits, and more laws, such
as an infamous provision for "logging without laws" in 1995,
detailed earlier.

The $2.5 billion did not buy planned, rational, balanced man-
agement of the national forests, either. Timber cutting rose from
$8^{3}/4$ billion board feet (bbf) in 1975 to well over 10 bbf in 1990,
driven up by the Reagan administration's and Senator Mark Hat-

59. See R.W. Behan, "RPA/NFMA: Time to Punt," *Journal of Forestry* 79:12,
    802–806.

60. The Wilderness Society. *Bi-weekly Update—The National Forest Action Center,*
    April 19, 1989, pp. 4–5.

61. See Resource Hotline (a newsletter published by the American Forestry
    Association), vol. 7, no. 18 (December 17, 1991).

field's direct manipulation of the appropriations process. Then it dropped back to $7^{1}/4$ bbf in 1993, driven down largely by lawsuits and restraining orders—and by an open rebellion by Forest Service field personnel.[62] The level of timber cutting is the most significant feature of national forest management, in both environmental and social vectors, and it was determined utterly independently of the forest plans. Those were simply irrelevant.

Certainly $2.5 billion has not bought sustainable land use or biophysically healthy landscapes for the federal forests. They lie ravished and overused. Neither the public at large nor its forested estate has benefited from the National Forest Management Act. The planners have, the attorneys have, the policy professionals in Washington have, but neither the forests nor the people.

Trifling compared to the savings and loan outrage, this miscarriage of politics is sufficiently troubling in its own right, and similar circumstances obtain in the other federal lands agencies. Those lands, too, are overused and freighted with bureaucratic planning, litigation, and acrimony; they too are attended by coteries of policy professionals happily fashioning yet more laws in Washington, D.C. And they too continue to be pillaged by corporate capitalism.

In the 1990s, however, there were signs of substantive change. The management professions' techniques of "sustaining the yield" of single resources were being displaced by a more comprehensive view of "ecosystem management." There were signs in the public at large of discontent with both the economic and the political systems. A new form of communication, wholly free of domination or control, ultimately democratic—the Internet—was alive with critiques of large corporations, large bureaucracies, and entrenched and professionalized lobbies in the nation's capital. A rich literature critical of megacorporations and arrogant, isolated governance was appearing. A third-party candidate gained nearly 20 percent of the vote in the 1992 presidential election, and *Time* magazine ran a series on corporate welfare.[63] If recognizing problems is the first step toward solution, the process was evidently underway.

---

62. Hirt, *A Conspiracy of Optimism,* passim.

63. A three-part series ran in vol. 152, nos. 20, 21, and 22, November 16, 23, and 30, 1998.

Chapter 6

Revoking the License

We have seen how the institutions of individual liberty were debased and transformed into corporate license, and how the tangible resource values of our common estate, the federal lands, were ravaged. It is time to think about revoking the license.

The pathologies in our economic and political systems must be confronted, and two intelligent agendas of reform will be summarized below. The renegade institution of the modern corporation must be recast, an intimidating but not insurmountable challenge. Here, too, intelligent voices offer promising patterns of revision. Meanwhile, other critics suggest community-based decision making for the federal lands, to counteract their current centrally driven and unsustainable pillage. We will see what neighbors and their guests might do in spite of the policy professionals.

In the short term, a "systems" view advocated long ago by Aldo Leopold and articulated by Black Elk will be essential in managing and restoring the federal lands. Longer term, the neighbors and guests will have to triumph over private profit and plunder, and reclaim those lands for a public service of great promise.

Revolution, Revision, and Recasting

In his book *Arrogant Capital: Washington, Wall Street, and the Frustration of American Politics,* Kevin Phillips argues persuasively the need for a revolutionizing of our national politics. "Serious revolutions," he writes, "are usually about politics, government, privilege, unresponsiveness, and anger. This is exactly what is simmering . . . in the United States of the 1990's."

He continues:

> Revolutions can be renewing without being violent. Even an election can be a revolution of sorts when it brings sweeping change in politics, ideology, and the nature of the ruling establishment. Not many elections qualify, but a few do. Thomas Jefferson and Andrew Jackson both saw their watershed presidential victories of 1800 and 1828 in that light, as political revolutions or electoral reincarnations of the spirit of the American Revolution.[1]

In the presidential campaign of 1992, candidate Bill Clinton promised a revolution in health care delivery. After twelve years of Republican presidents, the nation elected Democrat Clinton to the White House, and he enjoyed a partisan majority in the Congress. President Clinton, all but the truly mean spirited would agree, gave the issue of health care a sustained and intelligent effort. But nothing was achieved.

In 1994, there occurred what was called the "Republican revolution." Displaying Newt Gingrich's banner of "A Contract with America," the Republican party gained dominance in both houses of Congress, by comfortably large majorities. Term limits, a balanced budget, a constrained bureaucracy, a line-item veto for the president, and welfare and campaign-finance reform were promised. Speaker Gingrich, all but the mean spirited would agree, gave the issues sustained and intelligent effort. But almost nothing was achieved.[2]

---

1. Kevin Phillips, *Arrogant Capital: Washington, Wall Street, and the Frustration of American Politics* (Boston: Little, Brown, 1994), p. 183.

2. Welfare was "reformed" by slashing federal programs, and a further cut in capital gains taxation was enacted. Both the Congress and President Clinton were willing to expand the increasing disparity in the distribution of wealth, begun consciously in the Reagan administration.

In 1998 the Democrats once more made a dramatic surge in the off-year election, but they succeeded only in preventing the partisan removal of an impeached and dishonored president.

What sort of revolutions are these?

They are the insipid and hollow "revolutions" of institutional overshoot. In Phillips's words:

> We have seen that since the 1960's revolutionary elections have been stymied by the interlock between interest-group power and the political system. Presidents can only govern by accepting, placating, and bargaining with the interest-group structure. And the public knows that its own voice is heard with only limited effect.
>
> As a result, for any national political revolution of the Jeffersonian and Jacksonian sort to take place at the ballot box during the 1990's will require a new premise. No candidate can implement outsider changes through the current two-party system. . . . [The] emphasis of any bloodless political revolution must be on ways of displacing the outdated party system with the emerging technology of direct democracy.[3]

Whereupon, Phillips lists ten categories of proposals, paraphrased as follows:

1. decentralizing or dispersing power away from Washington;
2. modifying the U.S. Constitution's excessive separation of powers between the legislative and executive branches;
3. shifting U.S. representative government more toward direct democracy and opening up the outdated two-party system;
4. curbing the Washington role of lobbies, interest groups, and influence peddlers;
5. diminishing the excessive role of lawyers, legalism, and litigation;
6. remobilizing national, state, and local governments through updated boundaries and a new federal fiscal framework;
7. regulating speculative finance and the "financialization" of the economy by reducing the political influence of Wall Street;

---

3. Phillips, *Arrogant Capital*, p. 183.

8. confronting the power of multinational corporations and minimizing the effects of globalization on the average American;
9. reversing the trend toward greater concentration of wealth and making the tax system fairer and more productive; and
10. bringing national and international debt under control.

For each of these categories, Phillips provides detailed and thoughtful agendas that have much merit and warrant careful scrutiny, debate, and consideration.

A book by Herman E. Daly and John B. Cobb Jr. makes parallel suggestions about our economic system. The title tells a great deal: *For the Common Good: Redirecting the Economy Toward Community, the Environment, and a Sustainable Future*. Daly and Cobb share Kevin Phillips's concern about "financialization," but they see it on a global, not just a national scale:

> Twenty years ago the greatest power over the global economy may have been that of transnational corporations engaged in production. Today that power has shifted to institutions dealing with finance. Investment has come increasingly to mean the buying and selling of productive enterprises rather than their establishment or expansion.[4]

Daly and Cobb argue that the global financialization of production is at the root of many domestic institutional difficulties. The mobility of capital utterly destroys the "comparative advantage" rationale for international free trade, the presumption that all nations prosper. They do when investment capital stays at home. But capital in flight simply lands instead where labor, raw material, and environmental costs are least. Comparative advantages are enjoyed not by nations, whose labor pools, natural resources, and environments are savaged, but by transnational corporations and their managers, who grow richer by doing the savaging.

"Free trade" as we know it today encourages hyperconsumption among the wealthy, exaggerates the underconsumption suf-

---

4. Herman E. Daly and John B. Cobb, *For the Common Good: Redirecting the Economy Toward Community, the Environment, and a Sustainable Future*, 2nd edition (Boston: Beacon Press, 1994), p. 437.

fered by the unwealthy, and needlessly impacts the planet's bio-physical environment in the process.

In the orthodoxies of the discipline of economics, however, "comparative advantage" and "free trade" are quasi-religious articles of faith. In a truly ingenious preemptive coup, Daly and Cobb quote one of the most respected economists in history, John Maynard Keynes:

> I sympathize, therefore, with those who would minimize, rather than those who would maximize, economic entanglement between nations. Ideas, knowledge, art, hospitality, travel—these are the things which should of their nature be international. But let goods be homespun whenever it is reasonable and conveniently possible; and, above all, let finance be primarily national.[5]

Daly's and Cobb's book can be read as a global description of institutional overshoot, and their remedies are sophisticated, complex, intelligent, and several. Ultimately, they seek, as the title of their book suggests, a massive decentralization of production and economic decision making, to the community level.

The engine of overshoot in both economic and political arenas is the modern corporation. Reform here revolves around a fairly simple proposition: Since corporations are created by citizens through publicly granted charters, the continuity of their existence should remain a matter of the public will, too. Any corporation that benefits at the expense of the greater community—arguably more the rule today than the exception—should have its charter rescinded. Perhaps the most unequivocal case for such redress is made by an organization named POCLAD, the Program on Corporations, Law & Democracy.[6] It is by no means the only sustained criticism of the corporate role in human affairs; some of the critical literature has been cited in earlier chapters,

---

5. Ibid., p. 209.

6. POCLAD, a project of the Council on International and Public Affairs, is located at P.O. Box 246, South Yarmouth, MA 02664, and on the Web at www.poclad.org.

and a large and growing complex of organized resistance is widely accessible.[7]

Corporate charters will be revoked neither easily nor soon, given the corporate lock on our structures of governance, but popular discontent is visible and rising. It is scarcely newsworthy any longer when a community opposes the intrusion of a Wal-Mart, a Home Depot, or some other "big-box store." The clash between corporate interests and community interests is becoming increasingly conspicuous.

It seems particularly conspicuous in a global context, wrapped in the contentious issue of free trade and the World Trade Organization. For five years after its creation, the WTO enjoyed almost total obscurity, but at its "Ministerial" in Seattle, Washington, in December of 1999, a threshold was crossed. An essentially spontaneous convergence of 40,000–60,000 people from many countries, demonstrating peacefully and otherwise, put the socially dysfunctional corporation on the global agenda of public affairs. The event was saturated with media coverage; was this the initial event in the first popular revolution of worldwide scope? Never before had such an eclectic coalition of civic-society interests from such a broad base of cultures around the globe come together to recognize and showcase a common threat. Transnational corporatism and the WTO will no longer enjoy the luxury of obscurity.

The literature critical of corporate hegemony is robust and growing, but also appearing is an impressive body of positive and constructive thought about alternatives, about recasting the role of the corporation in human commerce. Paul Hawken, Amory Lovins, and Hunter Lovins propose nothing less than a redevelopment of the industrial revolution in their work *Natural Capitalism: Creating the Next Industrial Revolution.*[8] Carl Frankel has contributed *In Earth's Company: Business, Environment, and*

---

7. The World Wide Web displays dozens of organizations concerned about the issue of corporate dominance and, through hypertext links, offers access to hundreds, perhaps thousands of others. Corporate Watch provides a large listing of such links. Other notable groups are Public Citizen, the Alliance for Democracy, Common Cause, the International Forum on Globalization, and the Positive Futures Network.

8. Paul Hawken, Amory Lovins, and Hunter Lovins, *Natural Capitalism: Creating the Next Industrial Revolution* (Little, Brown, 1999).

the Challenge of Sustainability (Conscientious Commerce).[9] David Korten speaks of "healthy markets," describing and applauding them in *The Post Corporate World: Life After Capitalism.*[10] Herman Daly's book *Beyond Growth: The Economics of Sustainable Development* is encouraging.[11] *Natural Capital and Human Economic Survival* by Thomas Prugh appeared in May of 1999.[12] The general strategy suggested in this literature is to recapture human decency, dignity, and well-being as the primal focal points of human institutions, and to assure the sustainability of the biophysical environment, on which an equitable prosperity—and survival—depends.

It is not likely that Champion International or Louisiana-Pacific, or for that matter the World Trade Organization, will soon lose their charters, but new road maps are being drawn.

In Pursuit of the Promise

If there is a common tactical thread in the reformist literature, it is the theme of decentralization and the corollary empowerment of people in their communities. How might this play out in regard to the federal lands?

Neighbors and Guests

If localized federal land managers chose to do so, and if citizens in the affected communities did too, they could undertake jointly and independently an alternative style of handling the federal lands.

The style has been described elsewhere and rather pedantically as "constituency-based multiresource management," in speaking

---

9. Carl Franken, *In Earth's Company: Business, Environment, and the Challenge of Sustainability (Conscientious Commerce)* (Gabriola Island, BC: New Society Publishers, 1998).

10. David Korten, *The Post Corporate World: Life after Capitalism* (San Francisco: Berrett-Koehler Publishers; West Hartford, CT: Kumarian Press, 1999).

11. Herman Daly, *Beyond Growth: The Economics of Sustainable Development* (Boston: Beacon Press, 1997).

12. Thomas Prugh, ed., *Natural Capital and Human Economic Survival* (Chelsea, MI: Lewis Publishers, 1999).

largely to other pedants.[13] Comforting support for the notion is found in two far more readable books, one by Steven Lewis Yaffee, and the other by Daniel Kemmis.

The spotted owl—the focal point of Yaffee's book—is a marvelous creature, but it becomes a matter of nationwide interest only when *Time* magazine features it in a cover story. It does not constitute a nationwide *issue;* the welfare of the nation is not at stake in resolving the controversy about the owl. The case is no stronger for the preservation of old-growth Douglas fir forests. Douglas fir forests and the northern spotted owl are preeminently localized, at best regional, issues, not matters with prospective national impact. That was true also in the case of the intensive forest management in the Bitterroot National Forest in the 1970s. And it was true in the cases of French Pete, the G-O Road, the Monongahela episode, the Magruder Corridor, the Lincoln Back Country, and countless other classic controversies in the national forests. It was true in the cases of the Yellowstone elk, the Grand Canyon burros, the grizzly bear in Glacier National Park, even the Hetch-Hetchy reservoir a century ago. All these controversies about the public lands originated in tangible places, with real people seeing real values to be lost or gained.

Why, then, was so much of the time, talent, energy, and political resources of the nation's capital involved in the debate over the northern spotted owl? Why was a "Forest Summit" convened, which the president of the United States orchestrated and conducted, and which was attended by the vice president; the secretary of the interior; the secretary of agriculture; the heads of the Environmental Protection Agency, the Fish and Wildlife Service, and the Forest Service; and various other policy professionals by the score? And what was accomplished?

The Forest Summit produced a huge, detailed, year-long scientific study and a series of carefully wrought alternatives based

---

13. "Elsewhere" is a scholar's reference, with carefully crafted modesty, to his or her previously published work. For the case at hand, see R. W. Behan, "A Plea for Constituency-Based Management," in *American Forests* (July–August 1988), pp. 46–48; and R. W. Behan, "Multiresource Forest Management: A Paradigmatic Challenge to Professional Forestry," in *Journal of Forestry* 88, no. 4 (1990), pp. 12–18.

on it. Finally, "Option Nine" was adopted as the "Northwest Forest Plan" to guide the Forest Service and the BLM forest management practices. But a "salvage-sale rider" was enacted by Congress several years later, explicitly to continue the clear-cutting of the region's old-growth Douglas fir timber, while a coalition of environmental groups pulling in the opposite direction sued the agencies for violating the Northwest Forest Plan. In August of 1999, a federal judge ruled in favor of the groups and froze with an injunction nine unlawful timber sales in Washington, Oregon, and California. Why can't this issue be resolved?

Steven Lewis Yaffee illuminates the difficulties:

> American resource policymaking is fragmented and uncontrolled, yielding decisions that are slow to appear and often inadequate to deal with the magnitude of the underlying problems. Decisionmaking is generally reactive and crisis-oriented, based on information that is often inadequate. Agencies are not unbiased sources of technical advice, interest groups act adversarily and strategically in ways that conceal accurate information, and elected officials focus on short-term survival in ways that are often counterproductive to the broader public and future public's interests.[14]

Yaffee is describing the behavior of what Daniel Kemmis calls the "procedural republic." Kemmis describes a set of institutions designed deliberately to enable the objective, third-party, and strongly centralized settlement of disputes, in order to preempt resolutions of a democratic, participatory, and highly localized nature. He refers to the Constitution, to the Madisonian distrust of participatory democracy enshrined therein, and to the historic, conscious, and ingenious mechanisms employed to "keep citizens apart," in order to foster the welfare only of the "unencumbered self."[15] And Kemmis is well aware of the development of political

14. Steven Lewis Yaffee, *The Wisdom of the Spotted Owl: Policy Lessons for a New Century* (Washington, DC: Island Press, 1994), p. 185.

15. Daniel Kemmis, *Community and the Politics of Place* (Norman: University of Oklahoma Press, 1990). Kemmis notes that the origin of his terminology is an article by Michael J. Sandel, "The Procedural Republic and the Unencumbered Self," in *Political Theory* 12 (February 1984).

institutions—interest groups, PACs, permanent careers of governance—that has taken place over the past two hundred years;
those institutions have served only to exacerbate the Constitution's purposeful divisiveness.

Kemmis argues for a new and revolutionary approach, having
put his finger on a most sensitive spot: the increasingly painful
legacy of Thomas Jefferson's failure to carry the philosophical day
in Philadelphia two centuries ago.

As we saw in earlier chapters, the Founding Fathers doubted
Jefferson's faith in the citizens' capacities for civic virtue, in self-
government, in mass democracy. They built instead a government
detached and isolated, administered by the gentlemen described
in earlier chapters as paternalistic aristocrats.

The policy professionals of today are no less paternalistic and
scarcely less aristocratic than their predecessors. The procedural
republic is in their hands now, but overshoot is apparent: Perpetuating the procedures is now far more important than the decent
resolution of public issues.

Kemmis's thin, powerful, gracious volume is entitled *Community and the Politics of Place*. He makes the case for revolution, for
relocating, and decentralizing the tasks of public discourse, for
relying now, finally, on participatory democracy in the construction of public policy.

As the procedural republic developed over time, as organized
interest groups and corporations became players, the procedures,
laws, and policies multiplied, giving the players all the tools they
needed to thwart the actions or the intentions of any prospective
opponents. Compelling evidence supports Kemmis's claim that
the conduct of public affairs has reached the point where "anybody can wreck anything."

Kemmis credits that phrase to William Jankow, the former governor of South Dakota, who was speaking of the politics of water
development on the Missouri River. Kemmis also quotes John
Gardner making an identical observation:

> How many times have we seen a major American city
> struggling with devastating problems while every possible
> solution is blocked by one or another powerful union or
> commercial or political interest? Each has achieved veto
> power over a piece of any possible solution, and no one

has the power to solve the problem. Thus, in an oddly self-destructive conflict, the parts wage war against the whole. And the conflict will destroy us unless we get hold of it.[16]

An excellent description of the procedural republic overshooting is that the parts flourish at the expense of the whole. Kemmis posits instead a "politics of inhabitation," and it is revolutionary, indeed.

What the procedural republic fails to engender is a sense of community, because the Founding Fathers doubted the ability of citizens to articulate one and to describe its nature. But a politics of inhabitation, a politics of place can do that.

In a macroscopic view, the Douglas fir forest of the Northwest constitutes a habitation for people as well as owls. It is a place of real and concrete dimensions, features, properties. People who live and work there share a love for their place, their habitation. The resident loggers love the forest where they work and want to see their livelihoods maintained—and it is not difficult to cut trees and still maintain a forest. The resident defenders of the spotted owl also want to see the forest maintained. There is community, there is a common good, there is a tangible expression of a public interest. Why can't this community come together, to construct some way to maintain their habitation?

Because the procedural republic, designed to keep citizens apart, succeeds magnificently. The inhabitants are not trusted by the neo-aristocrats, the policy professionals in the nation's capital, who prefer to import localized disagreements to Washington, D.C. There they broker the interests of the "unencumbered selves" and provide a statutory fix.

Suppose instead that the federal land managers, say on the Olympic National Forest in 1985 or so, had invited their neighbors, the loggers and the advocates of the owl, to participate in designing a program of timber cutting—magnitude, location, timing, and techniques. Suppose they had sought a localized, negotiated settlement. Who is to say they couldn't have succeeded in maintaining the perpetuity of their habitation, in keeping the loggers at work and the owl healthy?

---

16. Ibid., p. 47.

The policy professionals in Washington, D.C., would say they couldn't: It was those professionals who claimed priority of decision responsibility and who sent down the ASQs, the hundreds of millions in appropriations to build roads, the monolithically centralized forest planning program specified in the National Forest Management Act, the Forest Summit, Option Nine, and finally "logging without laws." Note the locus of decision making: a distant, remote, federal government that owns the land and resources on which the neighbors' livelihoods and sense of well-being depend. This is reminiscent of imperialism.

Kemmis states his conviction that neighbors can indeed negotiate an agreement:

> It would be an insult to these people to assume that they are incapable of reaching some accommodation among themselves about how to inhabit their own place. Such accommodation would never be easy, and it would probably always be open to some redefinition. But if they were allowed to solve their problems (and manage their resources) themselves, they would soon discover that no one wants local sawmills closed and no one wants wildlife habitat annihilated. If encouraged to collaborate, they would learn to inhabit the place on the place's own terms better than any regulatory bureaucracy will ever accomplish. But this kind of collaborative citizenship is withheld from them by a combination of proceduralism and imperialism.[17]

The Constitution's successful mechanisms to "keep citizens apart," and two hundred years of subsequent institutional development, have essentially stripped American people of the true democratic status of their citizenship. The policy professionals have been handed—in later years they have usurped—the pursuit of public affairs.

President Clinton and his entourage toured to Portland, Oregon, to settle the spotted owl controversy, but they failed. They failed after the forest plans had failed to settle it, after "hearings" by the dozen had failed to settle it, after appeals and litigation had

---

17. Ibid., pp. 126–127.

failed to settle it, after dramatic, local demonstrations from both the loggers and the spotted owl defenders had failed to settle it. All the failures have one thing in common: They display the actions of citizens kept apart and orchestrated into conflict, as enemies, adversaries, litigants. The failures display, finally, the bankruptcy of the procedural republic's end-game—except for the resource corporations and the policy professionals, who continued to thrive.

Could the loggers and the spotted owl advocates, informed by the technical skills and ecological understanding of the resource professionals of the Forest Service, and encouraged by a district ranger, have negotiated a workable compromise? Let us turn again to Kemmis's insights:

> The actual practice of finding solutions that people can live with usually reaches beyond compromise to something more like neighborliness—to finding within shared space the possibilities for a shared inhabitation. Such neighborliness is inconceivable without the building of trust, of some sense of justice, or reliability or honesty. This practice of being neighbors draws together, therefore, the concepts of place, of inhabitation, and of the kinds of practices from which civic virtues evolve.
>
> Most people, most of the time, do not think about these features of the art of being good neighbors. What they do know is that neighborliness is a highly prized quality of life. Where it is present, it is always near the top of people's lists of why they like a place, and where it is absent, it is deeply lamented. This deep-seated attachment to the virtue of neighborliness is an important but largely ignored civic asset. It is in being good neighbors that people very often engage in those simple, homely practices which are the last, best hope for a revival of genuine public life. In valuing neighborliness, people value that upon which citizenship most essentially depends. It is our good fortune that this value persists.
>
> So it is that places may play a role in the revival of citizenship. Places have a way of claiming people. When they claim very diverse kinds of people, then those people must eventually learn to live with each other; they must learn to inhabit their place together, which they can only do through the development of certain practices of inhabita-

tion which both rely upon and nurture the old-fashioned
civic virtues of trust, honesty, justice, toleration, coopera-
tion, hope, and remembrance. It is through the nurturing
of such virtues (and in no other way) that we might begin
to reclaim that competency upon which democratic citizenship is dependent.[18]

Yes, the loggers and the spotted owl advocates could have
negotiated a way to keep the sawmills running without annihilat-
ing the owls. And certainly the Bitterroot controversy could have
been settled in similar fashion.

The reigning in of predatory politics can be accomplished by
initiating and building a politics of inhabitation, a politics of
neighbors face to face, of participatory democracy. Working on the
problems of the federal lands might be an excellent place to begin.

In the national forest context, that would mean the reconstitution of the district ranger as the focal point of the management
hierarchy. The ranger would need real decision-making authority—and if it is not freely granted by the higher levels of administration, the ranger should simply claim it. Doing so would endan-
ger a career, of course, but support mechanisms are available and
growing in strength. (The Association of Forest Service Employees for Environmental Ethics and various other organizations support whistle blowers.) No less risk would be run by the neighborhood member of the local chapter of the Audubon Society, or by
the logger. They all face hierarchies of their own, the upper strata
of which are policy professionals in Washington, D.C.

Given courageous neighbors, much could be accomplished. In
spite of contemporary institutions, they could push toward a politics of inhabitation as hard as they chose.

Courageous neighbors have two rudimentary but remarkable
examples to follow. The Applegate Partnership in Grant's Pass,
Oregon, and the Quincy Library Group[19] in northeastern California are localized coalitions of industry people, environmental
interests, county officials, and local land managers. In an exercise
of participatory democracy, they were successful in forging work-

---

18. Ibid., pp. 118–119.

19. So named because the meetings were held in the town library, on neutral
turf.

able agreements about the use and nurture of their habitations, but not without bitter opposition by the policy professionals in Washington, and not without having to play their game. The Quincy agreement was introduced as legislation by Senator Dianne Feinstein and Congressman Wally Herger, and eventually passed as the Quincy Library Forest Recovery Act on October 21, 1998. It was vigorously opposed by the Sierra Club and the National Audubon Society—which had to contradict directly and openly its local chapter in Quincy, one of the participants in the Library Group.

The Audubon Society headquarters in Washington complained that the bill would "set bad precedents for inconsistent and unreliable public participation in public resource management. . . ."[20] Michael McCloskey of the Sierra Club echoed the sentiment: "If Quincy can do it so can people around the country. There's a precedent being set here. So we don't have national forests anymore, but just forests run in local dictates."[21]

James Madison could scarcely have expressed any better the Big Greens' distaste for participatory democracy and their distrust of neighbors practicing a politics of inhabitation. Instead, a greater "national interest" must be discerned and protected—by the new breed of paternalistic aristocrats in Washington, D.C.

National environmental organizations, and not a few legislators and Washington bureaucrats, see an inherent bias toward commodity production evident in localized venues. The greater "national interest" would always suffer in cow towns, mining towns, and mill towns, in that view. But "cow towns" such as Bozeman, Montana; "mining towns" like Telluride, Colorado; and "sawmill towns" on the order of Flagstaff, Arizona, are grown up and sophisticated today; none is deficient in environmental advocacy.[22]

The Quincy episode was prototypical, and the process was not

---

20. This language was contained in the official position statement of the Audubon Society, mailed to each senator, dated September 17, 1997.

21. Quoted in a news story, "Cooptation or Constructive Engagement? Quincy Library Group's Effort to Bring Together Loggers and Environmentalists under Fire" by Patrick Mazza, in the *Cascadia Planet*, August 9, 1997.

22. An excellent description of how cosmopolitan the localized politics in federal lands communities has become is contained in Paul Culhane, *Public Lands Politics* (Baltimore: Johns Hopkins University Press, 1981).

flawless. When the Big Greens learn they can trust their local chapters, when the management agencies can relax the bureaucratic obsession with consistency and uniformity of policy, and when everyone involved can forgo the need for statutory resolutions of localized issues, a politics of inhabitation can flourish.

There remain two sizable problems in neighbors cooperating with neighbors to fashion negotiated solutions, and Kemmis addresses one of them forthrightly: "What is to be gained by trying to cooperate with a multinational corporation?"[23]

The rootlessness, the placelessness of the corporation makes it a strange "inhabitant" of anywhere. In spite of its proclamations otherwise, Champion International was never an "inhabitant" of Montana, and one can scarcely imagine a more despicable "neighbor."

Kemmis continues:

> Talk of revitalizing public life by encouraging greater reliance on civic virtue seems like the height of sentimentality, given the track record of many of these corporations. There is no easy or comprehensive answer to this problem. But unless we are willing to accept the accelerating pattern of blocked initiatives, [anybody can wreck anything] we seem to have little choice but to look for answers that are neither easy nor comprehensive.[24]

He suffers no naive illusions:

> This is not, of course, a new problem. Throughout American history, many of the most significant declines in the vitality of public life have been accompanied by a rise in the political influence of monied interests, and particularly of large corporations. To the extent that Jefferson was right in seeing the new Constitution as an overreaction to events like Shays' Rebellion, it was clearly the creditor class which was doing the reacting. Again in 1896, when republican principles under the populist banner surged to

---

23. Kemmis, *Community and the Politics of Place*, p. 129.

24. Ibid., p. 128.

a new height of influence, it was Mark Hanna's brilliant orchestration of corporate money which stemmed the tide, resulting in what Lawrence Goodwyn characterizes as both a lasting decline in democratic self-confidence and a (so far) permanent entrenchment of corporate political power.[25]

Some contemporary critics argue that corporate charters should be placed in direct, open, and serious jeopardy whenever they threaten the general welfare.[26] Kemmis might be sympathetic to something of this kind. "A healthy public life," he asserts, "would be one in which the public knows its own mind well enough and trusts its own will far enough that it would never allow itself to be controlled by its own creations."[27]

The second problem with a politics of inhabitation seems not apparent to Kemmis. He implies a residency requirement: If you want to play the game, he seems to say, you have to be a local.

But the federal lands, as the policy professionals are lightning-quick to point out—and did, in the Quincy case—are national assets. They don't belong to localized communities. The people of the Olympic Peninsula do not own the Olympic National Forest any more than the citizens of the Bitterroot Valley own the nearby national forest, or the citizens of Arizona own the Grand Canyon. That much is indisputable, but not the next assertion, also made quickly by the policy professionals: They must be managed in the national, not the local, interest, and that is best seen from Washington, D.C.

The national interest in any issue is essentially unknown. Because of the Constitution's divisiveness, it is also virtually unknowable. There is no mechanism by which the national interest can be determined, as we saw in chapter 2. A majority could

---

25. Ibid.

26. On September 10, 1998, a coalition of thirty environmental, human rights, and women's groups petitioned the California attorney general to revoke the charter of the Union Oil Company of California (Unocal). They referred to Unocal as a "dangerous scofflaw corporation." Violating no one's expectations, the attorney general dismissed the petition in a three-sentence letter, offering no explanation.

27. Kemmis, *Community and the Politics of Place*, p. 130.

articulate one, but the Constitution rendered the majority silent on purpose.

The residency requirement, if strictly applied, excludes the rest of the nation's stockholders in the federal estate, all of whom, ostensibly and in fairness, have an equal vote. Not all the stockholders, however, are aware of all the issues of concern, and of those who are aware, not all are sufficiently concerned to care about the outcome. And of those who do care, a great many are busy with other matters and are likely not to object to any resolution.

Suppose we could forestall these barriers of ignorance, apathy, and acquiescence, to encourage participation. Suppose we had sophisticated and economical systems of transportation and communication, and could provide any stockholder with quick, easy, and inexpensive information and access to any issue of federal lands management, anywhere in the nation. Suppose? Those capabilities are already in place.

Now suppose the neighbors issue an open, nationwide invitation to come and participate in resolving the issue at hand. Anyone from anywhere who responds will know and care about the Douglas fir–spotted owl issue. The residency requirement has been relaxed, and all the guests are consciously included as coequals. In doing all this we can recognize what could be called the issue's "constituency," and a politics of inhabitation is rationalized for the federal lands.

Empirically, we will always find that the constituency clusters closely to the geographic locale of the issue. So long as the clustering is by default and not by conscious exclusion, there can be no objection to "constituency-based management" of the federal lands.

Citizens living on the West Coast are vaguely aware of Acadia National Park in Maine, the Green Mountain National Forest in Vermont, and the Everglades in Florida. They rarely choose to learn more and don't often care much about the management issues in those places. Probably, they can tolerate any resolution of them.

Their disdain is not occasioned only by limited resources of time, energy, and the financial capacity to buy plane tickets, or by personal civic sloth. They are well aware of other stockholders, fellow citizens of the United States who also pay taxes, who live within or near Acadia, the Green Mountains, and the Everglades, and presume them to be intelligent, informed, capable people. They feel no need to travel to the East Coast to participate in the democratic resolution of federal lands issues, because they are quite willing to grant their proxies to the clustering citizens in those locations. They trust them to arrive at resolutions that accommodate and protect the co-equal interests in jointly owned assets. The westerners will claim the proxies of the easterners, too, when resolving issues in the West.

Proxy-swapping is ubiquitous, and it should be. And as the negotiated resolution of localized issues gets underway, the information streams available are anything but localized. A neighbor in the Audubon Society taps a national newsletter and brings an information base into the dialogue that transcends the locale. A neighbor who works in the sawmill is connected to a national network of information called the price system, the market for dimension lumber. By no means is constituency-based management the least bit isolated, insular, or parochial.

If we look at constituency-based management as a system operating nationwide, with proxies and information flowing freely, the management of the federal lands in the aggregate can easily claim to be in the national interest. The fixes are negotiated, not statutory; they are constructed on the ground where the problems are, not centralized in Washington; and the participants are people once more in possession of their democratic citizenship, not career professionals crafting policy for all to abide.

For the Near Term and First: Behold Black Elk, Listen to Leopold

Working out the handling of national forests, parks, wildlife refuges, and grazing districts at the localized level will have to be done with common views of the habitations. Black Elk's admonitions and Leopold's prescience—that land and people form an interacting unity—must be that common view.

Adopting a politics of place means that real people in their real habitations are paramount, not distant and abstract procedures. In their reality, habitations inescapably display the entire range of biological and social complexity. Part (but only a part) of the habitation of the Olympic Peninsula is characterized by large Douglas fir trees and spotted owls, as we have seen, and also by salmon streams and salmon berries and salmon—and bears, deer, bushes, flowers, grasses, cedar trees, mosses, lichens, slugs, and nematodes, and so on and on down the entire list of plant and animal species and physical characteristics that some people call an "ecosystem." It is easy to focus on an ecosystem when you're living (or a guest) in one. In subtle but powerful ways, the politics of place simply forces a systems view.

When management decisions are made far away, the reality of ecosystems disappears. To the Champion International managers in Stamford, Connecticut, their forests in Montana were not ecosystems at all but simply "assets." When ASQs were sent down from Washington, they had nothing to do with ecosystems, either, but only with the power politics of the budgetary process. When you're living (or a guest) in an ecosystem, you're likely to be sensitive to its complexity and its condition.

For the land management professionals, a systems view has been a long time arriving.

In 1949 Aldo Leopold described the two sorts of forestry we encountered in an earlier chapter. Type A forestry saw land as commodity, grew trees like cabbages, and viewed them as cellulose. Type B forestry saw land as a community and considered all the elements of the forest and the interacting relationships between the parts—an explicit systems view.

Leopold was acclaimed in principle and ignored in practice. Cabbage patch forestry continued to be taught and applied without another visible challenge for twenty years. Then the Bitterroot controversy erupted, followed soon thereafter by a similar issue on the Monongahela National Forest. Subsequent analyses made explicit critiques of single-resource forestry and posed a need for a systems view.

The Society of American Foresters undertook a curriculum development project focusing on systems forestry; a textbook was produced, and several forestry schools undertook major revisions in their curricula. The term "multiresource forestry" began to appear in the technical literature.[28]

---

28. In the early 1970s the Forestry School at Northern Arizona University implemented a fully integrated, team-taught curriculum in "multiresource management," something of a buzz phrase, and a proprietary term for Type B forestry. Dean Charles O. Minor and Professor William P. Thompson were the architects of the program.

Congress took notice of cabbage-patch forestry with the National Forest Management Act of 1976. Recall Senator Humphrey's words as he introduced the legislation: "The days are ended when the forest may be viewed only as trees and trees only as timber. The soil and water, the grasses and shrubs, the fish and wildlife, and the beauty that is the forest must become integral parts of the resource manager's thinking and actions." That is Leopold's Type B forestry precisely described, and the forest plans written under the legislation made good-faith attempts.

In spite of the forest plans, as we have seen, the agency continued cabbage-patch forestry with a vengeance during the Reagan-Bush years, as ASQs were set as high as Senator Hatfield could establish them, and budgets for everything else were slashed. Predatory politics would not easily be displaced.

Forest Service researcher Dr. Jerry Franklin was the first to discover and to publicize that Douglas fir did not need, for the purpose of securing regrowth, to be clear-cut. He developed a concept called the "new forestry," which sought to maintain not a yield, but the "biological legacy" of the old-growth forest. As a variation on Type B forestry, new forestry held great promise, but it was implemented at the scale of a pilot project, at best.

By 1992 timber cutting in the national forests of the Pacific Northwest was virtually paralyzed with litigation and restraining orders, a response to the political predation during the Reagan-Bush years. The old-growth capital of the Northwest was nearly gone anyway, but Forest Service Chief Dale Robertson announced on June 4, with ruffles and fanfare, the agency's intention to adopt "ecosystem management" and to reduce clear-cutting dramatically. Forty-three years after Aldo Leopold had articulated the notion, Type B forestry arrived, as declared policy for the national forestlands.[29]

Type B forestry, multiresource management, the new forestry, and "ecosystem management"—netting out the differences and the commonalities, we can probably call this an exer-

---

29. Secretary of the Interior Bruce Babbitt announced in February of 1993 a similar policy for the Interior agencies.

cise in synonyms, but they do describe a quantum jump. System forestry is clearly superior to the tradition of sustaining a yield of commercial timber, but it needs to accommodate a wider "system" than any of the four manifestations alone encompasses.

All of those manifestations are explicitly and appropriately based on the science of ecology. But ecology focuses exclusively on biophysical phenomena, on "natural" systems. In the garb of science, ecology maintains the rigid separation of man and nature discussed earlier. The concept of "ecosystem" does not systematically include humanity, and until we've redefined the term to do so, the romantic and misguided conclusion is frequently reached: The highest-quality ecosystem is the one that is uninhabited. That legacy of George Perkins Marsh is at best a meaningless guide to public policy or professional practice.

Part of the Olympic Peninsula habitation is characterized by a biophysical complex of plants and animals, and hydrologic and geologic features and processes. The rest of the habitation is characterized by a social complex of houses, streets, stores, schools, churches, libraries, mills and factories, dentists' offices, police and fire departments, telephone lines, water, power, and sewer systems, city councils, PTAs, Little League teams, Pony Clubs, and so on and on.

There is general agreement that we don't want to degrade the biophysical elements of habitations. We don't want soil erosion, species extinction, or water or air pollution. There is also general agreement that we don't want to degrade the social elements. We want our streets and houses to be nicely maintained, our schools to be well staffed for quality education, our utility systems to be reliable, our fire departments to be fully equipped and quick, and our people to have dignified livelihoods.

Can we envision a single "biosocial" system and seek to keep the whole thing in good condition? At the University of California at Berkeley in the 1960s an economist and a plant ecologist thought so. Professors Henry J. Vaux and Arnold Schultz posited such a single system and coined the term. A Ph.D. student, Thomas Bonnicksen, was intrigued, and relied on the concept in his dissertation research.

A brief exposition of the biosocial system is contained in a paper Bonnicksen later published in the *Journal of Forestry*.[30] He rejects as inadequate the "one-way adjustment models" that suggest either of two dynamics: 1) that the natural world imposes limits on the activities of humankind, or 2) that people everywhere have so impacted the environment that "nature" no longer exists. Both rely on a rigid separation of man from nature. In the biosocial system, however, humanity and its biophysical environment exist in a state of constant and mutual adjustment. The two subsets of the biosocial system are interactive, interadaptive, interdependent, and inseparable.

The biosocial construct appears to be a scholarly restatement of Leopold's community, and a revisitation of Black Elk. Compare it to another description of the Native American view:

> When Indians referred to other animal species as "people"—just a different sort of person from man—they were not being quaint. *Nature was a community of such "people"*—people for whom man had a great deal of genuine regard and with whom he had a contractual relationship to protect one another's interests and fulfill mutual needs. Man and Nature, in short, were joined by compact . . . a compact predicated on *mutual esteem*. [Emphasis in the original.][31]

A final concept of a unified system is provided by James Lovelock and his Gaia hypothesis: that the earth is a single, living, self-

---

30. Thomas M. Bonnicksen, "Managing Biosocial Systems: A Framework to Organize Society-Environmental Relationships," *Journal of Forestry* (October 1991), pp. 10–15.

31. Calvin Martin, *Keepers of the Game: Indian Animal Relationships and the Fur Trade* (Berkeley and Los Angeles: University of California Press, 1978), p. 186. The quote is reproduced in J. Baird Callicott, "Traditional American Indian and Western European Attitudes toward Nature: An Overview," *Environmental Ethics* 4, no. 4 (Winter 1982). Callicott's depiction of the Native American views is no different in essentials, but nevertheless he and Martin were engaged in a lively debate. Martin thought that the relationship of Indians to their environment was "contractual." Callicott insisted it was instead *ethical*. The matter can be left for them to resolve, and interested readers at least have the citation.

regulating organism.[32] It seems to have maintained a remarkably constant body temperature over the stately accumulation of eons, even surviving the ultimate in pollution: the onset and convulsive shift to an oxidizing from a reducing atmosphere.

Gaia, Mother Earth, a unified biosocial system, Leopold's land ethic—again, netting out the distinctions and commonalities, we encounter convergent bodies of thought. However expressed and organized, the totality must be incorporated into the localized management of all the federal lands. To address the welfare of only one subset—either the biophysical or the social—is to guarantee damaging the other, and hence to compromise the whole.

In the Long Term and Finally: The Triumph of Promise over Plunder

Economists make intelligent distinctions between private and public goods and services, distinctions of particular relevance to the federal lands and their future.

Private goods and services are bought and sold in markets. They can be exchanged that way because they are divisible into discrete units, like grapefruit and the performance of a concert, say. Since they appear as discrete units, they can be granted or withheld, according to the behavior of a prospective buyer: Private goods are granted to those able and willing to pay the price for them and are withheld from those who are not.

Public goods and services cannot be divided into discrete units. And that means they cannot be granted to some and withheld from others. And that means markets for public goods and services cannot exist.

These are tricky definitions. Consider that concert again. The concert is not in fact divisible: Everyone in the concert hall hears it and presumably enjoys it. What is divisible is access to the private auditorium where the concert is performed, and that is restricted or rationed by the sale and purchase of tickets. Move the concert to a city park, where access cannot be denied, and

---

32. J. E. Lovelock, *Gaia: A New Look at Life on Earth* (New York, Oxford University Press, 1979 and 1987). Reprinted with a new preface, twice in 1988.

it becomes a public service. So is a sunset. It cannot be divided, and no one can be excluded from its enjoyment by any reasonable means. If the sunset occurs, any and all are free to enjoy it.

In their respective ranges, raccoons, songbirds, deer, and other forms of wildlife on the federal lands are frequently the source of much visual and auditory pleasure, and so provide public services. They do meet the divisibility criterion, but if they are there to be seen and heard, then everyone is free to see them and hear them, and no markets exist to exchange the associated sensory delights.

Consider, however, what happens with the purchase of a hunting license and the slaying of a deer. The hunter has purchased the right to exclude all others from enjoying any deer he happens to shoot, and with the gunshot a public service has been transformed into a private good.

This vignette displays a feature that has escaped our attention in defining resources as functions of perceived utility. We have not so far remarked the obvious: that in any given substance a number of coincident and differing utilities might be perceived. Clearly, the perception of utility in watching can be coincident with the perception of utility in shooting. A given "substance" can generate public service and constitute a private good simultaneously.

If one citizen should happen to shoot the deer that another citizen is happily watching, there is likely to be great civil if localized conflict. Is one perception of utility superior to the other? Should one take precedence?

The great debates over the use of the federal lands revolve around these questions. There are no definitive and exclusive answers, but public services as a general proposition should be favored over private goods, most would agree, when there is reason to constrain either in situations of simultaneous utilities.

Simultaneous perceptions are characteristic of many federal lands resources, and the conflicts are apparent. Timber, coal seams, and range forage all provide examples of simultaneous perceptions, similar to the deer vignette: A tree is board feet but also beautiful; coal seams are energy resources but also provide geologic integrity to underground aquifers; range forage is the point of departure for hamburgers but also wildlife habitat and watershed protection. And in every case the "hunter" is present—converting and diminishing the public services by transforming them into private goods.

Resources are indeed dynamic; value perceptions arise, and resources "become." On a grand scale, we are witnessing exactly that social process on the federal lands.

Public, stated concerns over diminished visual beauty, loss of biodiversity, species extinction, air and water quality degradation, and other environmental impacts are compelling evidence of resources becoming. The resources that are becoming are the ones providing public services. They must take precedence over those that provide private goods.

The time has come to begin a process of imposing constraints.

For the better part of two centuries, the federal lands, as we have seen, have been dedicated to the production of private goods. Furthermore, the production of private goods contributes significantly to the hyperconsumption of energy, paper, and red meat. To withhold or limit the resources that contribute to such hyperconsumption will elevate the general physical welfare of society at large, by definition. If in doing that we free resources to provide other goods and services of positive benefit to society, the case is stronger still for a new regimen of federal lands use and management.

We should begin shifting the productive capacity of the federal lands away from the output of private goods and tilt it heavily toward public services. That is to say, we should wind down grazing, logging, mining, and water development—commodity production, to use a different term. We should begin vigorously to enhance and expand the production of public values instead.

This suggestion will not be endorsed with enthusiasm across the spectrum of the public lands community. Some at the "environmental" end may find it attractive. Others will not. Certainly, the subsidized resource corporations will be disappointed, and so will the "wise use" and "property rights" people. But there is also a deeper and diffuse source of concern.

Loose on the national scene today—and the international as well—is an ideological agenda described as "neo-liberalism." The liberalism that is "neo" is not the twentieth century version of progressive thinking and politics, but the nineteenth century espousal of "liberty"—of laissez-faire. It appeared in the Reagan years as "free-market environmentalism," to rationalize privatizing the federal lands. Idealizing an Adam Smith market as the sole source of trustworthy social evaluations, and stylizing federal managers exclusively as bureaucratic empire builders, the neo-liberal solution to any environmental problem was and remains unerringly a market solution.[33] Neo-liberalism fails utterly to acknowledge the existence of the mega-corporation in the marketplace—or as the driving force in politics—and so, with an innocent face and wondering eyes, it raises the question "Since the federal lands are producing private goods, why should not the lands be privatized?"[34]

The answer to that is compelling: Those private goods may be enriching private, large, and corporate producers, but they are detracting significantly from the well-being of American people. A different question, therefore, is far more relevant: Since the federal lands are public lands, why should they not produce public services?

The public services generated by the federal lands are already many and substantial: scenic beauty, carbon sinking, open space, biodiversity, watershed quality, wildlife habitat, gene pool maintenance, recreational opportunities, historic and archaeologic preservation, and a baseline for biophysical research come quickly to mind. Sunsets, certainly. And magnificent locales in which public-spirited musicians might perform.

There will be other public values perceived in the future, and

33. Typical of the genre was John Baden and Richard Stroup, eds., *Bureaucracy vs. Environment: The Environmental Costs of Bureaucratic Governance* (Ann Arbor: University of Michigan Press, 1981). For a critique of free-market environmentalism in that time, see R.W. Behan, "The Polemics and Politics of Federal Land Management," in Phillip O. Foss, ed., *Federal Lands Policy* (Westport, CT: Greenwood Press, 1987).

34. Though privatizing the federal lands is no longer a visible policy issue, the more zealous proponents still take pleasure in preaching to their neo-liberal choirs. A recent performance, charming in its childlike simplicity, presented the following argument: The federal land management agencies *lose money* and incur ecological damage. Particularly notorious is the National Park Service. The appropriation for the agency in 1996 was $1.316 billion. Revenues from entrance fees and concessionaire royalties were $0.078 billion. Therefore, the Park Service lost $1.238 billion, and the bison herd in Yellowstone Park is overgrazing its range. Therefore, the national parks should be sold to private interests. See Terry L. Anderson, Vernon L. Smith, and Emily Simmons, "How and Why to Privatize the Federal Lands," in *Policy Analysis*, no. 363 (November 9, 1999). Washington, DC: the Cato Institute.

maintaining the federal lands' capacity to generate them is a value in itself. The future values will be limited only by our imagination and our capacity to regenerate a public life.

A "public life"? The term is Daniel Kemmis's, and it refers to the behavior of good neighbors evincing a concern for each other, for their community, and for their habitation. To regenerate a public life we must become good neighbors once more.

Some in the wise-use movement are real people, and they are neighbors. They use the federal lands to earn their livelihoods, operating a family ranch or an independent logging operation. These neighbors need to know they can cut timber or graze livestock on the federal lands until they agree freely to do otherwise. There can be no power solutions imposed on them. Good neighbors don't do that. Good neighbors care enough to be patient.

Others in the wise-use movement are corporate users of the federal lands, and they can scarcely be neighbors because their existence is independent of place. It is not wholesome livelihood but petty profit that drives them, and neighbors needn't be patient with that. A power solution may be the only solution in those cases.

If we want to be good neighbors and if we want to achieve on the federal lands a transition in emphasis from private goods to public services, we cannot rely on the procedural republic.

Business-as-usual predatory politics tried to do so, however. Late in 1999, late in a presidency besmirched in history, William Clinton sought to "protect" with executive branch prerogatives 40 million acres of unroaded national forest land by prohibiting development. Whether to counter history's image of his impeachment, or to further the presidential ambitions of his vice president was immaterial. The Big Greens in Washington, D.C., applauded. Their counterparts in the capital who represent the resource corporations cried, "Foul!" and the fight was on. As usual. To occupy their daily routines, the policy professionals had yet another "issue" to "resolve."

We must achieve a transition to public services instead by Kemmis's "politics of inhabitation," and making the process work will be every bit as important as the result. We will need to be good neighbors and work toward the transition with respect and patience.

There will need to be a nationwide agreement that the transition is desirable. Achieving that will be difficult, discontinuous, and contentious, and it should be. In a healthy participatory democracy, quantum shifts in public policy should never be easy. Some will see the transition as necessary. Some will come to see it as inevitable. Others will need time, time, lots of time.

To initiate a politics of inhabitation regarding the federal lands, a critical early step is to publicize more widely their existence and their potential. There are many good reasons for a citizen to be apathetic or acquiescent about any particular public issue, but both are precluded by ignorance.

Publicizing the existence of the federal lands estate, and the many substantive questions of its use, is easy, inexpensive, and expanding. The Center for the Rocky Mountain West, for example, publishes every morning on the Internet a clipping service of stories in the region's newspapers about the federal lands (and much else). It is called Headwaters,[35] and a similar service, Tidepool,[36] covers the lands, forests, waters, and people of the northwest coast of the United States and Canada. It is sponsored by an organization called Ecotrust.

If all or even most Americans were fully aware of their coequal share in 673 million acres, they would indeed know they were part of a hugely fortunate community. Six hundred seventy-three million acres of uncultivated, temperate-zone landscape, much of it contiguous and all of it subject to common mandate is a rare and astonishing public asset. It should qualify as the largest village green in human history.

We look at a village green, however, not as a prospective source of private wealth, but as part of our habitation, and we enjoy its public services. Shouldn't we, can't we come to see the federal lands as a similar part of our national habitation?

Every citizen occupies the national habitation—immigrant Americans from everywhere, Native Americans, everybody. Asserting that, we go to work on becoming good neighbors.

Confronting our experience of living in the national habitation, however, we face a history of genocidal conquest, of living as

---

35. Headwaters can be found at www.headwatersnews.org.

36. Tidepool is located at www.tidepool.org.

predators and prey, not a history of living as neighbors. Most of us will have to join with Barry Lopez as he says:

> This violent corruption needn't define us. We can say yes, this happened, and we are ashamed. We repudiate the greed. We recognize and condemn the evil. And we see how the harm has been perpetuated. But . . . we intend to mean something else in the world.[37]

Then, if we mean those words, any and all existing treaties with Native American tribes will be honored, without exception, to the letter, immediately. Honoring them would be neighborly. But neighbors aren't bound only by contracts.

A group called the Intertribal Bison Cooperative is composed of forty-six tribes in sixteen states. It seeks to bring back the bison and the native plants on which bison depend, and to restore in the process the spiritual and cultural values the bison represented. The group has suggested that 2.9 million acres of national grasslands, administered by the U.S. Forest Service in Wyoming, Nebraska, and South Dakota, might be returned to the tribes for those purposes.[38] Let us do that. It would be neighborly, and the public services generated for everyone to enjoy would be novel and huge.

After the contracts are honored and the neighborly requests fulfilled, we might adopt far more widely a respectful, even a spiritual regard for the unity of life and habitat. Aldo Leopold asks this of immigrant Americans; Native Americans need not be reminded. Then we can learn to reinhabit our land with a better view of "habitation."

Shifting the emphasis on the federal lands from private goods to public values has to be worked out by neighbors and their guests in strongly localized dialogues, not by phony presidential

---

37. Barry Lopez, *The Rediscovery of North America* (New York: Vintage Books, 1992), p. 11.

38. See John Stromnes, "Tribal Alternative: Give Us the Grasslands," the *Daily Missoulian*, Missoula, Montana, September 22, 1999. See also, "Buffalo Nations, Buffalo Peoples," in Winona LaDuke, *All Our Relations: Native Struggles for Land and Life* (Cambridge, MA: South End Press, 1999).

pandering and certainly not by statute. The details, specifics, and scheduling are the critical elements, and these can be determined only by real people debating real alternatives for tangible, visible segments of the federal lands.

The public value of re-creating an Indian-bison economy on 3 million acres of national grasslands will be disputed by those who hold grazing leases on them now. But there are large forces at work that will bear on the localized dialogues, forces more chronic than acute, more diffuse than localized. A rising appreciation for low-fat nourishment is evident today, and it may someday doom the franchised hamburger as a consumer staple. How would that impact the 'appeal of a grazing lease? The New Road Map Foundation proposes "voluntary simplicity" as an alternative to the high-income, high-consumption, high-stress lifestyle.[39] A Web site called Adbusters[40] lampoons the persuasion industry and its products, and in 1999 was conducting a petition campaign to rescind the corporate charter of the Philip Morris corporation. A world wide repugnance for the World Trade Organization and all it represents is being orchestrated by the International Forum on Globalization, which once took out a full-page ad in the *New York Times* to tell its story.[41] The Positive Futures Network promotes social equity and sustainable living.[42] There are large and growing countermeasures to our institutional difficulties that will at least condition the politics of inhabitation. Given time, such countermeasures may define the enterprise.

Thomas Jefferson wrote, in a letter to James Madison on January 30, 1787, "I hold it that a little rebellion, now and then, is a good thing, and as necessary to the political world as storms in the physical." We must learn to rebel if the politics of inhabitation is to succeed. Such a politics calls aggressively for courage among neighbors and guests to fashion resolutions of the tangible, on-the-ground issues of the federal lands, and then to insist on their adoption.

The aggregate status and the destiny of the federal lands are

---

39. The New Road Map Foundation's Web site is at www.newroadmap.org.

40. Adbusters is located at www.adbusters.org.

41. To visit the International Forum on Globalization, go to www.ifg.org.

42. The Positive Futures Network can be found at www.futurenet.org.

national issues, decided now by corrupted capitalism and predatory politics. A politics of inhabitation is rebellious and revolutionary, and it can transform us into a nation of neighbors. How else can civil decency, a public life, and true democracy survive?

Pursuing a politics of inhabitation to seek not private goods but public values from the federal lands will show these lands to be a true res publica. The lands can counteract, finally, the intentional divisiveness of the Constitution: They can become the public thing that forges a true national community, preeminently built on a sense of place. That is the promise of these lands.

Index